Living on Island Time in the Caribbean

MELINDA BLANCHARD *and*
ROBERT BLANCHARD

THREE RIVERS PRESS
NEW YORK

Published by Three Rivers Press, New York, New York. Member of the Crown
Publishing Group, a division of Random House, Inc.
www.randomhouse.com

Three Rivers Press is a registered trademark and the Three Rivers Press
colophon is a trademark of Random House.

Originally published in hardcover by Clarkson Potter in 2000.

Printed in the United States of America

Design by Caitlin Daniels Israel

Library of Congress Cataloging-in-Publication Data
Blanchard, Melinda
    A trip to the beach / by Melinda Blanchard and Robert Blanchard.
    1. Anguilla—Description and travel. 2. Anguilla—Social life and customs.
3. Blanchard, Melinda—Homes and haunts—Anguilla. 4. Blanchard,
Robert—Homes and haunts—Anguilla. 5. Restaurants—Anguilla. I. Blanchard, Robert. II. Title.
F2033 .B53 2000
972.973—dc21   00-029466

ISBN 0-609-80748-x

10 9 8 7 6 5

First Paperback Edition

This book is dedicated with all our love to Jesse

Anguilla

PRICKLY PEAR CAYS

DOG ISLAND

SANDY ISLAND

Sandy Ground

Long Bay

South Hil

Long Bay Village

Meads Bay

Barnes Bay

WEST
END

Rendezvous
Bay

Maunday's Bay

ST. M

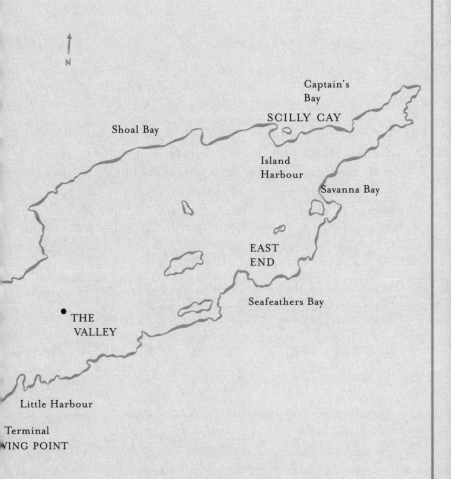

N

Captain's
Bay

SCILLY CAY

Shoal Bay

Island
Harbour

Savanna Bay

EAST
END

Seafeathers Bay

THE
VALLEY

Little Harbour

Terminal
VING POINT

Anguilla Channel

Author's Note

The following is a true story, and although some names have been changed, the characters are real. Conversations are written as accurately as we can remember them and are not intended to be exact quotations. In the course of our lives together we have had eight businesses, ranging from retail stores and food manufacturing to mail-order catalogs and restaurants. The sequence of events in this book took place over a span of ten years and two restaurants in Anguilla. We have taken the liberty of condensing the time frame so as to capture the spirit of life in Anguilla and give the reader a feeling of the different seasons on the island.

Acknowledgments

The people of Anguilla hold a very special place deep in our hearts. With enormous gratitude, we thank you all for changing our lives and letting us become a part of yours. Special thanks to Lowell Hodge, Clinton Davis, Miguel Leverett, Garrilin Nisbett, Renford "Bug" Gumbs, Ozzie Rey, Alwyn Richardson, Huegel Hughes, and Winston "Shabby" Davis. Thanks also to Joshua Gumbs, Evelyn Gumbs, Jeremiah Gumbs, Bennie Connor, Claude Richardson, Eustace Guishard, the crew of *De Tree*, and the Government of Anguilla. To all the concierges and taxi drivers who have sent us business over the years, please accept our heartfelt appreciation. We offer our sincere apologies to our Anguillian friends who are not mentioned; you are very important to us as well, but there just wasn't room for everyone.

We are deeply grateful to our agent and dear friend, Michael Carlisle, for helping us from concept to completion. Without Michael, this book would not have existed, and we would have missed one of the most wonderful experiences of our lives. Special thanks to our editor, Annetta Hanna, whose support, understanding, and vision kept us on track throughout. Her magical ability to make rewriting painless, and in fact enjoyable, made this project a pleasure. Many thanks to everyone at Clarkson Potter for their boundless enthusiasm: Lauren Shakely, Vanessa Hughes, Margot Schupf, Marysarah Quinn, Barbara Marks, Leigh Ann Ambrosi, Caitlin Daniels, Debbie Koenig, Maha Khalil, Jennifer

Stallone, Andrea Rosen, and everyone else behind the scenes who made the process of publishing a sheer delight.

Our great thanks to the many friends whose readings and input were invaluable: Betsy Siebeck, Libby and Peter Robbie, Pat Merrill, Susan Harris, Sally Peterson, Nina Freedman, Michael Rosenbaum, Jane and Jim Harmon, Joan Kron, Richard and Melinda Stucker, Hilary and Ethel Lipsitz, Maggie Orem, and of course, Jesse.

We are grateful to Michael and Judy Steinhardt, Milt and Carolyn Frye, Edgar Bronfman Sr., Dave Cioffi, Penny McConnel, and Susan Pierres for their support. Many thanks also to Joel Chusid at American Eagle for always finding Jesse a seat at Christmastime, Leon and Nigel Roydon for years of advice on doing business in Anguilla, Sheila and Sherm Haskins and the staff at Tropical Shipping for efficiently delivering boatloads of supplies from Miami, Rachel Klayman and David Edelstein for helping us find our voice, Marvin Shanken at *Wine Spectator* magazine, and all of our loyal customers who have dined with us over the years.

Part One

Chapter 1

FROM THE AIR ANGUILLA LOOKED narrow, flat, and scrubby, but that was only part of the picture. In my mind, I saw the real Anguilla: sea grape and crimson flamboyant trees, women steadying pails of water on their heads, sand that might have been poured from a sack of sugar, the cool terra-cotta floors of the Hotel Malliouhana. The sunshine alone was enough to make me smile. Stepping off the plane, I felt the breeze from the east, scented by the hibiscus that grew alongside the terminal. Those cool currents made the sun seem unthreatening. Poor Bob, with his fair complexion, would be pink in a matter of minutes.

In Anguilla it is customary to greet everyone with a courtly "Good morning" or "Good afternoon." As we approached the young woman at the immigration counter, we were greedy enough to hope for more. We'd seen her many times on our visits to the island. We wanted to be recognized, to be told that we were different from mere tourists—connected.

"Good afternoon," the young woman said, smiling. "Welcome back." Anguilla had begun to cast its spell.

As our taxi made its way westward—slowing for potholes, speed bumps, people, goats—I counted the ways I loved this little island. Unlike its neighbors, Anguilla (rhymes with *vanilla* and pronounced *Ann-gwilla*) had no casinos, no duty-free shopping, and no cruise ships. Visitors here looked for less, not more. They tended to arrive one or two at a time and not in packs. Their intentions were simple: to walk on the beach, go snorkeling, read a good book, take a dip in the water. They'd found a place where handmade signs beckoned them to Easy Corner Villas, Sandy Hill, and Blowing Point. Drawn to this tiny British outpost only sixteen miles long, they appreciated the rhythm, the balmy pace. Little schoolgirls in handmade uniforms skipped along the road, holding hands.

The idyllic life on Anguilla isn't an illusion manufactured for tourists. The island's standard of living is higher than its neighbors'. No gambling means no gambling problems. Limited work permits for outsiders ensures plenty of jobs for locals. This is a country with no taxes, where a dollar earned is an actual dollar. There is no unemployment, and eighty-five-degree temperatures with sunshine almost every day. Life is good.

There are several world-class hotels on the island, all criminally luxurious. Over the years we had alternated between them, savoring their brands of exquisite tranquillity. One, Cap Juluca, boasts villas with Moroccan-style domes, and bathrooms so vast that they have their own gardens. Another, Malliouhana, was created—and is lovingly cared for—by a retired English gentleman whose lifelong dream had been to preside over such a hideaway. Here life is serene, with white stucco arches, ceiling fans that seem to lull away one's cares, and a breathtaking view of the clear turquoise water from the top of a cliff.

Our taxi driver, Mac Pemberton, had driven us around the island many times, but that day was different. He had called us in Vermont with urgent news. We had spoken about opening a beach bar in Anguilla, and he had promised to help find us a spot. Now he had scheduled a meeting for us to meet Bennie, the landlord of an abandoned restaurant.

It wasn't a notion from the blue. Many years earlier, when Jesse was five, Bob and I had taken him to Barbados, where we'd spent a wonderful morning hunting conch shells and building an enormous sand castle complete with moat. By the time we finished we were ravenous, but there were no restaurants in sight. So we set off down the beach. We were all three healthy and brown with sun; even Bob had gotten past the sunburn stage. Jesse danced in and out of the surf, laughing at nothing and everything. I felt preposterously lucky. A good meal would complete the experience.

After about a mile we spotted a picnic table. A short distance away was a man leaning back in a beach chair, his feet propped up on a giant cooler, his head buried in a thick, tattered paperback. Above him was a small thatched roof with a blackboard sign.

HAMBURGERS—$10.00
LOBSTER—$25.00
BEER AND SODA—$4.00

It was like finding a lemonade stand in the middle of the desert. We stood in front of the man and smiled expectantly, but he must have been intent on finishing his page, because it took him a minute to acknowledge us. When he was ready, he slowly swung his feet off the cooler and looked up.

"Hungry?"

Jesse was the first to respond. "Starving. What do you have?"

With his head, the man gestured at the menu on the blackboard. He seemed eager to get back to his book, which I saw now was *Moby-Dick*. After a hasty conference, we ordered three burgers, two Cokes, and a beer. We handed him a wad of bills and in return received our drinks, three raw hamburger patties, and a long pair of tongs. Then he motioned toward a fifty-five-gallon oil drum that had been cut in half lengthwise with a torch, propped up on several lengths of steel pipe, and filled with hot coals. We realized we were about to cook our own lunch.

"We just paid forty-two dollars for a lunch that must have cost that guy five bucks," said Bob, standing over the grill. "And we have to cook it ourselves." His grumbling was mixed with admiration.

One bite was all it took to change our mood. "This is the best hamburger I've ever had," Jesse declared. We all agreed.

I marveled at the ingenuity of the setup. A secluded spot, sand like flour, customers arriving in bathing suits. The guy barely lifted a finger, cleared at least $35, and gave us a lunch we'd remember forever—an experience that seemed to me to rival the best white-tablecloth meals we had eaten in Paris. The man reading *Moby-Dick* had sold us a frame of mind.

When Mac called, he insisted we had little time to waste. We caught only bits and pieces of his excited conversation—"restaurant closed," "great location," "bank repossession," "get down here immediately." It was far from a sure thing, but if we could work it out, it would mean moving to Anguilla. We had already decided to start again from scratch, and this could be our chance. No more snowstorms. No more speed dial.

We drove right to the site before checking into the hotel. Mac parked his van in front of a deserted shack, and we followed him over vines and scrubby bushes covered with prickles. It took only a minute before we found ourselves on the familiar beach at Meads Bay. To the right was Carimar Beach Club, and Malliouhana, on the cliff, was practically next door. To the left was nothing but white sandy beach for almost a mile, then several small hotels bordered by dunes covered with sea grape. The sun was high in the sky and reflected off the water like a string of sparkling diamonds. It was a picture postcard spot. I could envision a tiny restaurant here.

Minutes later we were on our Malliouhana balcony, only twenty-four hours after Mac's call, watching pelicans dive for fish.

My shoulders had already softened, and I felt an urgent need to make a list of things we might do just in case the beach bar didn't work out. There were still many obstacles to overcome. Taking over a repossessed restaurant in a third-world country seemed like a long shot. I seized a sheet of the hotel's embossed stationery and summarized our position.

"We have *some* money," I said. "Granted, not as much as we should after selling Blanchard & Blanchard."

At the mention of Blanchard & Blanchard, Bob stood and walked to the suite's minibar, and my mind drifted back to the events leading up to the sale.

There had been as many friends warning us not to start Blanchard & Blanchard as there were regarding our decision to move to a Caribbean island. I could still hear them. "Start a specialty food company in your house in Vermont? Make what? Salad dressings, fudge sauce, mustards? Why? Do you know how to do that?" We were asked all kinds of questions regarding our sanity. The fact that we had only $4,000 to begin with came up often.

We chose to ignore their advice, and in almost no time we had over a thousand accounts across the country. We had built a large factory where endless rows of bottles were whisked along stainless-steel conveyor belts and huge machines filled, capped, labeled, and prepared them for sale.

Our lives would have been different if one of our largest accounts hadn't suddenly defaulted and if we hadn't been forced to make a hasty deal to keep from bouncing all our checks. We brought in two New York investors who saved the day.

As the popularity of our products spread, we began doing business with supermarkets and were, in turn, thrown out of our prestigious accounts, like Bloomingdale's and Macy's. Selling to supermarkets is like dating Darth Vader. It's a world of deal making, discounts, and payoffs. We found ourselves in the back rooms of places like Piggly Wiggly, haggling over pennies with fleshy men in gold chains and pinky rings. And as the business grew, our share mysteriously became smaller and smaller.

"Relax," said our partners. "You have a smaller piece of a bigger pie."

Sitting at our dining room table on the night we finally yielded to pressure to sell our shares for a fraction of their worth, Bob shook his head. "I'll never think of pie the same way again," he said sadly. "And I've always loved pie."

"We need to focus," I said impatiently. "I can't relax and pretend we're on vacation when we have no income and a sketchy plan."

"We've only been here an hour," said Bob. "Give me at least another minute before I have to decide what to do with the rest of my life."

Bob joined me at the round table on the balcony, carrying a half bottle of merlot. "End of relaxation," he announced. He poured a little wine into his glass and savored its bouquet.

"We have a good plan," he insisted. "This is going to work out. We're moving to Anguilla."

"Well," I said skeptically, "I'd feel better if we had some alternatives. Can we just look at our options? The only thing I'm absolutely sure of is whatever we do, it's just you and me. No partners."

"No partners," said Bob, raising his glass in a toast. He sniffed and sipped. "I don't even care about making a lot of money anymore. I just want a small business without all the stress. Just you and me sounds good."

"If this doesn't work out," I said, "the only other thing we've talked about is building an inn in Vermont and living happily ever after as gracious hosts."

"The retirement fantasy of every investment banker," said Bob.

I asked if he had other suggestions.

"No, it's a great fantasy," he said. "And we'd do it better than a banker. We'd create the perfect Vermont experience. The rooms would be rustic, so you know you're in the country, but they'd have every luxury you could want. Great food, walking paths through the woods, apple orchards, a pond . . ."

"Sounds like a Vermont version of Malliouhana."

"Yes, it does," he said wistfully. "This is a pretty good model."

The more he talked, the more heady he got. Sheep grazing in the field. A horse barn. "We could make maple syrup and let the guests gather sap from the trees," he said. "Then they'd carry it in buckets to the sugar house—a small one, maybe with a woodshed on one end. They could help boil it down to syrup, then put it in a bottle and stick on a handwritten label that says MAPLE SYRUP BY ETHEL SMITH."

"Bob," I said gently, trying to summon him back to earth, "I don't want to say it's impossible, but do you think we have enough money for a project on that scale? We couldn't afford the land, let alone the inn or the—"

"Sugar house."

"It's a very sweet idea. Maybe someday . . ."

Bob nodded. He was still worried about our future, but an element of playfulness had crept into his voice; the juices were flowing. He gazed steadily at the tiny boats off the shore.

"If the restaurant doesn't work out," he declared suddenly, "we'll make Caribbean sauces, sell them to tourists. There are plenty of tourists," he said. "Tourists want sauce. It could be a Caribbean version of Blanchard & Blanchard."

We both stared apprehensively at the pelicans, wondering how many jars of mango salsa we would have to sell to cruise ships to afford Jesse's tuition. He was in an expensive college and on the ski team—the world's highest-priced extracurricular activity. Bob drained his glass.

"It doesn't matter what we do," he concluded. "Let's just find a way to do it here."

"We have to call Joshua," Bob said. "He'll have some good advice."

Joshua Gumbs. Our first taxi driver in Anguilla years before. The man who'd regaled us with stories about the island in his rumbling baritone, taught us the local patois, and invited us to Sunday dinner with his family—a rare privilege for outsiders. It was unthinkable to consider moving to Anguilla without consulting Joshua.

He couldn't have been much more than sixty, but he and his wife had ten children and a slew of grandchildren. Joshua had worn many hats—fisherman, taxi driver, landlord—and now supplied most of the island, including luxury hotels, with paper and cleaning supplies shipped by container from Miami. Joshua tended to preach, which could occasionally be trying, but most of what he said was indispensable. With no formal education, he was an entrepreneur as canny as any venture capitalist we'd ever met. And far nicer to spend time with.

He pulled up fifteen minutes later, his battered blue Chevy station wagon chugging serenely past the long double rows of royal palms and under the gracious white portico that greets Malliouhana guests. After we'd exchanged long hugs, we climbed into the back of his car and headed for his house on Rey Hill, near town. The ride was a jumble of talk. His son Lincoln was working at the airport, Bernice was a concierge at Malliouhana, and Griffith was now a policeman. Vernal was about to become a father. Evelyn, his wife, was still plagued by arthritis. I handed him a neck brace and a tube of cream that I'd brought her from an American doctor.

"Daughter, you and we is one," he boomed gratefully, setting the items down on the seat next to him.

The fact that we had sold most of our interest in Blanchard & Blanchard came up repeatedly in conversations with Joshua and provoked a thundering tirade. How, he demanded, could we sell what we'd created with our own hands? He had worked for almost fifty years to build his businesses, fishing during the hard times to feed his family. The sea had been good to Joshua Gumbs, and his businesses had flourished. To sell any one of them would be an *offense*. You might as well build your own house and then burn it to the ground! Bob and I looked at each other meekly; I squeezed his hand.

"You'd feel differently if you knew the people we did business with," said Bob, who proceeded to paint a dramatic portrait of Blanchard & Blanchard as we knew it.

"Gangsters!" Joshua swore. He began to lecture us again, this time on the subject of lying down with dogs.

Relief came as we pulled into the agreeable chaos of his front yard. Their house never changed. Two scrawny island mutts slept tied in the shade of a rusted car on blocks. A few feet away was Joshua's fishing boat, out of the water for repairs. Bundles of fish-pot sticks that had been brought in from St. Kitts were neatly stacked and ready for assembly. A garden plot of half-withered pigeon peas in desperate need of rain lined the side of the house, and the garage was filled to the ceiling with enough paper towels and canned goods for an entire militia.

Evelyn embraced us on the porch, two salt-and-pepper braids pinned on top of her head. She was hunched over with arthritis, but that never seemed to affect her mood. No time for it. She led us into the living room, where we settled into comfortable velvet-covered chairs. As usual, the television was tuned to CNN, and a newscaster spoke of the day's events in business: everything we wanted to escape.

"What would you think of us moving to Anguilla?" asked Bob with no preamble.

Joshua grinned. "You loves Anguilla, don't you?"

Evelyn chimed in, "Yes, they loves Anguilla." They sounded like proud parents.

"Yes, we love Anguilla," Bob returned obediently. It was our ritual, a call-and-response that affirmed our faith in the island. "We love it so much, we think we should never leave."

That went beyond our usual exchange, and Joshua grew serious. "What would you do?" he asked. "I don't think the government would let you fish. They saves that for the locals. See it?" He paused. "Unless you wants to fish with me."

Fishing had been such a part of Joshua's life—it was what held all the other, disparate activities together—that it must have seemed the most natural thing in the world to suggest to someone seeking a new livelihood.

Bob remembered the day a year earlier when he and Joshua had gone "fishing"—which turned out to mean hauling up fish pots by hand. Bob recalled Joshua bellowing out to his son in his deep voice, "Vernal, come up to the pot. Come up to the pot."

Vernal, perhaps fifteen at the time, had navigated the outboard motors with precise skill, maneuvering the open boat alongside each buoy so Joshua could reach out with his hooked stick, grab the rope, and pull it in. Then Joshua and Bob would haul up the rope hand over hand, each pulling in turn, until the huge wire fish pot surfaced and could be dragged up into the boat. Bob balanced it on the gunwale as Joshua unlatched one side, dumping the wriggling contents onto the boat's deck. Lobsters, parrot fish, grunts, and pufferfish came pouring out, and once a bright green moray eel slithered around the boat.

"Whatever goes in there, I catches," Joshua had proclaimed as he killed the eel with a sharpened stick. Bob had gained Joshua's respect by not complaining, but by the end of that day his hands were raw and he could barely stagger up the stairs to our hotel room.

But the more we talked, the more obvious it became that Joshua was too old to go back to fishing full time. We told him about Mac's call and Bennie the landlord and our beach bar idea. Joshua frowned.

"The government in Anguilla is not interested in allowing for-eigners to open any new restaurants," he said. "They wants to save that for Anguillians, see it?"

We saw it; Joshua explained that the island only has nine thou-sand residents, with that many more living abroad. There are thousands living in Slough, England, and a large contingent in New Jersey, many of whom would love to come home if they could earn a living here. When Joshua saw our faces fall, he took pity. Exceptions were always possible, he said, but his tone wasn't encouraging. I was glad we had the backup plan for making Carib-bean sauces.

He studied us for a moment. "Bennie Connor," he said almost to himself. "I'll call Bennie and tells him you good people and that he should rent to you. He can help you with the government too."

Joshua turned his back to make the call, so Evelyn ushered Bob and me into the kitchen and gave us spoonfuls of a delicious fish stew that was simmering on the stove. We tried to listen to Joshua's conversation but could hear only snatches—enough to know he was telling our story, but not enough to get the drift. When he rejoined us in the kitchen, he told us simply that Bennie Connor was a decent man and was ready for our meeting the next day. We wanted to pepper him with questions, but we didn't want to make him uncomfortable. The island was wary of outsiders, and we realized we were lucky to be getting a personalized introduction to Bennie.

That evening we sat outside, gazing at the stars in the dark quiet and wondering whether we really had the nerve to move to a small island in the Caribbean. A lone yacht anchored at sea was the only object in sight. Were we being hasty? Overreacting to the idea of escaping to a new life? How would we fit in to this tiny West Indian community, where all the inhabitants were of African descent? We spent a nervous night.

Breakfast was served on our balcony, surrounded by pink bougainvillea in bloom: *pain au chocolat,* muffins, croissants, and assorted jams, along with tall silver pots of coffee and a pitcher of steamed milk. Tiny yellow birds snatched single grains from our sugar bowl, flitting happily as if thanking us for their breakfast. There were crispy, apple-smoked slabs of bacon. Conversation was scarce. In between bites Bob called for another order of bacon. "A next one?" the woman from room service asked. "I send it right up." I had never felt so hungry in my life.

It was on our way to Bennie's that we realized we had no idea what kind of rent we'd be expected to pay. Five hundred a month? A thousand? The first number seemed high for a run-down little shack, but the location, we had to admit, was too spectacular to warrant less. It depended on what kind of negotiator Bennie was. We could always start at five hundred and work our way to the higher number if it turned out there was a market for grilled burgers and piña coladas.

"Maybe we should have called a lawyer," I said.

"No," said Bob. "No lawyers. I've had enough of lawyers." The appeal of doing business on a tropical island was the informality. Other people's lawyers had tortured us for months at Blanchard & Blanchard, and our own hadn't saved us from financial piracy. Bob thought Bennie sounded like the type who would be game for a handshake agreement. I said I thought so too.

The young man at Bennie's Grocery said that Bennie was upstairs. He walked outside and yelled toward the balcony over his head, "Dada, some people here for you!"

Bennie's office was one flight above Bennie's Grocery. It was also Bennie's living room. It was also, we soon realized, Bennie's theater: Welcome to the Bennie show. Stout but moving quickly for an Anguillian, Bennie gestured grandly toward the couch, where a hulk of a man was staring down at his bare feet: cousin James, the owner of the building and the land.

"Good morning, James," said Bob, and James said, "Yeah." His focus remained on his feet.

"James doesn't talk much," said Bennie. "I do the negotiating for him."

He swept his arm toward another couch and we sat. "I understand you would like to rent the property on Meads Bay and open a restaurant."

"That's right," I said, suddenly feeling as if I were Bennie's pupil. He remained standing, pacing, swiveling from Bob and me to James and then back. Bennie clearly relished the role of negotiator.

"We like the location," I continued, vastly understating the case. "But the building would have to be bigger, and we'd also need to do some landscaping."

"James," said Bennie, turning to his cousin. "Is it permissible to enlarge the building and to do some—" There was a long pause, whether for dramatic effect or translation I wasn't sure. "—planting?"

James stared at his feet and said nothing. Fifteen seconds passed, and he gave a small nod. We took this as a yes.

"Okay," said Bennie, who had turned his back to us. "You may add on to the building. You may plant. But you must go to Lands and Surveys and obtain a copy of the site plan that shows the property's boundaries, whereupon we can legally address setback requirements."

Bob asked whether Bennie was a lawyer.

"Not really," said Bennie with a laugh. "But I study law in my spare time." He turned to me. "If you would care to take notes, I'll dictate the terms of the lease and you can have the document typed."

Bennie disappeared into the next room, leaving us with James, who stared out the window as if he wished he were somewhere else. It occurred to me that he probably wasn't being rude, that he was just extraordinarily shy. Bob and I met each other's eyes but didn't speak. From a nearby room we heard drawers opening and closing vigorously, papers being crumpled and tossed aside, and something that sounded like dozens of ball bearings rolling on a tile floor.

Bennie re-entered with a legal pad and pen, handed them to me, and began to pace. His short legs stretched as he marched dramatically across the room, twirled, and reversed direction, dictating along the way.

"This lease is made—" He stopped himself in midsentence. In conversation Bennie was a tenor, but for purposes of dictation he became a baritone. He turned to James and his voice rose an octave. "When would you like the lease to begin?"

James said nothing. He stared at his feet.

Bob cleared his throat and said, "We'd like to have it start when we open."

Bennie scratched his head and continued to pace. "In that case," he said, "I would recommend that the term of the lease commence now, and perhaps James will grant a grace period on the rent until you begin to do business." He looked at James expectantly. No response.

"James, how does that sound with you?" Bennie prompted. He seemed mildly annoyed.

Bob tried to help. "James," he began, "what we're saying is, the lease would start on, say, June first. That's in a week. But the rent wouldn't start until we open."

His eyes focused somewhere over our heads, James finally spoke. "When you gonna open?"

Bob and I looked at each other. The conversation had suddenly gotten very serious. We hadn't even made the absolute decision to move to Anguilla, yet here we were negotiating a lease. Things were happening too quickly, I thought. But in retrospect, maybe that made the decision easier.

"It will probably take us three months to do the construction," said Bob, calculating out loud. "And we'd have to get building materials before we even start. Then we'd need equipment and dishes and . . . All the hotels are closed in September, so I guess . . ."

He glanced at me; I gave him a reassuring nod.

"We'd shoot for an opening in October."

Bob looked at me. I looked at Bennie. The three of us looked at James. After thirty seconds or so, James again shrugged and gave a little nod.

Bennie smiled. "That sounds good to James," he said.

Resuming dictation, his voice dropped an octave and he strode the length of the room, as if pacing off the distance. "This lease is made between James Maxwell, fisherman of Blowing Point, parenthesis, hereinafter called the lessor, which expression shall, where the context so admits, including persons deriving title under or through him, close parenthesis, and . . ." He instructed me to fill in our names and address.

We didn't have an address, said Bob. Not yet.

"We'll just leave that blank for now," Bennie continued. "But you will need a local address to make the lease a legal document. You should find a house as soon as possible." He looked up, smiled. "I may have something for you, but we'll get to that later."

I could see that Bennie was delighted at the prospect of brokering another deal.

He went on to cover the term of the lease (five years with an option for five more), insurance, utilities, maintenance, improvements—all of which, it became clear, would be paid for by the lessee, that is, us. He used words such as *covenant* and *hereinafter.* The idea of a handshake seemed far away.

Then he came to the clause about rent.

Bennie gave James a significant look. James raised his head so that his gaze just skimmed the tops of our heads, then locked eyes with Bennie. This time there was no hesitation.

"Five thousand a month."

My heart dropped through the floor. We thought it was outrageous. We *knew* it was outrageous. Bob gave me a look I recognized from the time he'd had the wind knocked out of him on a ski slope. He opened his mouth, but nothing came out.

"We were thinking more like a thousand," I said.

Amazingly, it was Bennie who chimed in next. "Five thousand's pretty steep, James," he said.

James glared at Bennie, then returned to examining his feet. The silence that followed was the longest so far. I was sure that everyone in the room could hear my heart pounding. Then James mumbled, "Three thousand U.S. dollars for five years, then five thousand."

Bennie bowed graciously, as if to say, "I have just saved you two thousand dollars a month." *I* was wondering whether he'd *cost* us two thousand. Then he grandly swept his arm from James to us, which I took to mean that the ball was in our court.

Bob asked for a minute to talk things over, and Bennie said, "Come, James." He and his cousin stepped out onto the balcony, leaving us alone.

"There goes the beach bar idea" was the first thing Bob said. "We can't pay that kind of rent selling rum drinks and burgers. We'd have to make it a serious restaurant. Waiters, a wine list, fancy desserts . . ."

"That's not what we had in mind," I said.

Bob shrugged. "Do you want to move to Anguilla?" he asked.

Over the years we'd often made sweeping last-minute changes, and they had mainly worked out well. Mainly. But Anguilla was a world apart. And a barefoot beach bar was a world apart from a fine dining establishment. It was out of the question.

"Let's do it," I said. "Let's live happily ever after in paradise."

So that was it. We agreed to the rent, we thanked Bennie for his help, and we got our handshake. Bennie smiled graciously and said to call him the instant the lease was typed.

"Nice to meet you, James," said Bob.

"Cool," said James, and lumbered out the door.

Back at the hotel, after calls to Mac and Joshua, who were waiting to hear how our meeting went, we celebrated with fish soup, crayfish-and-bacon salad, and crème caramel. Then we walked down the beach to our site, only minutes from Malliouhana. The momentousness of this decision hit us; what would it be like to live permanently on a tiny Caribbean island, thousands of miles away from friends, family, and all that was familiar? We tried to imagine a world without bagels, shopping, movies, bookstores, and snowstorms as we walked around our crumbling $3,000-a-month shack. We would come back in the morning to take measurements, said Bob, and then start on the drawings when we got the site plans from Lands and Surveys. With Bob's love of building, he was clearly in his element.

We took pictures, wanting always to remember that day. The sea grape leaves that bordered the beach were spectacular. But the building was in a state of extreme disrepair. Could it even be salvaged? It didn't matter. This close to one of the world's most breathtaking beaches, we'd make do. We batted around names for our restaurant until the day's events and our big lunch finally hit us. It was time, we agreed, for a nap.

On the way to dinner we discussed the fact that eating wouldn't be so straightforward anymore—it would fall into the category of research. What, we wondered, was our competition? What did our restaurant need to do to fit in—or stand out? What kind of ingredients were the island's chefs using, and where did they come from? And what did people feel like eating after a hard day of swimming, lugging around hardcover best-sellers, and sunbathing? We had to eat everywhere in Anguilla. We had to do *serious* research.

Pimms, the restaurant at Cap Juluca, is built on a rocky point where the waves lap against the side of the dining room. Spotlights fell on the water, which was clear enough to see silvery fish as they shot along the bottom. The waiters tossed rolls into the sea and the fish leapt up and devoured them as if performing for the crowd. "We can't top that," I said.

"You can forget about the dog-and-pony show," said Bob. "I'm not even sure you'll see the water from our dining room."

No question, Pimms—with its fabulous Moroccan arches and fabrics that billowed from the ceiling—was exotic. "Our place should give you a stronger sense of being in the islands," I said. I reminded Bob of Reid's and Raffle's in Barbados, two of our favorite restaurants, neither on the beach. "The trick," I ventured, "is to have incredible gardens visible from every table. Palm trees, bougainvillea, allamanda, maybe even lime trees. The building should echo the old Caribbean cottages with happy, colorful shutters and a peaked, shingled roof—it should radiate charm."

The idea set Bob off. As we waited for our table he talked of plants and lights and even a couple of gentle fountains—the sound of water would be transporting. "People are on the beach all day," he said. "At night they might prefer to relax in a tropical garden. It could be a nice change."

We waylaid a passing waiter and nabbed a menu from him. Every dish was seriously French—the same as at Malliouhana. "It's not that I don't love French food, but how much salmon mousse and foie gras can you eat?" I murmured.

"And trying to fit into a bathing suit the next day," said Bob. "Only the French can pull that off."

Farther up the island were restaurants with simpler fare—chicken and ribs and plastic tables. But in West End, near the hotels, the field was wide open for something more contemporary. We would have no cream sauces. Lots of tropical ingredients. Pineapple and citrus bases instead of heavy reductions and beurre blanc and meat stocks. Nothing would be sautéed in butter; almost everything would be grilled.

Bob studied the wine list. "Heavy, heavy French," he said. "It's a great list, but I'd mix in some California and Australian bottles."

"It's still quite formal," I concluded. "People come to this island to relax. I don't want our dining room to be hushed and uncomfortable. Guests need to feel more like they're at our house for dinner. Elegant but friendly."

Having shown sufficient lack of awe for our most formidable competitors, we sat down to an excellent meal. My quibbles were philosophical. The gazpacho was creamy and luxurious, whereas my ideal gazpacho is peasant food—chunky, full of crisp cucumbers and shallots and plum tomatoes and red bell peppers with a zip of lemon. Maybe a sprig or two of fresh dill. Homemade croutons on top. All right, not *exactly* peasant food, but rough-and-ready and exploding with flavors. I pulled out my notebook and made a few jottings. Bob's appetizer of lobster in puff pastry was made with locally caught lobster and my roasted rack of lamb had a crust of mustard and bread crumbs—heaven. This was serious competition.

As we ate, ideas bubbled up and I made a list. I wanted spices, varied textures, intensity of flavor. "What do you think of dumplings filled with local lobster?" I asked Bob. I was on a tear. "We need nicer glasses than these. Thinner stems and thinner rims. Crisp white linens and candles instead of oil lamps. Real silver instead of stainless."

"You're bankrupting us already," said Bob as he drained the last of his Châteauneuf-du-Pape.

We were still savoring that meal as we set out the next morning in search of a house to rent. None of the real-estate brokers could help us; they specialized in vacation properties for thousands of dollars a week. Bob and I decided to comb the island in search of FOR RENT signs. This did not seem unreasonable. The island of Anguilla, whose name means "eel" in Spanish, is only sixteen miles long with one main road running the entire length—thirty-five square miles of wiggly coast, scrubby desert, and rocky points that poke thrillingly out into the sea. We knew that even for the little we could afford to pay, we could find a stunning location.

We began at the very western tip of the island and explored every little dusty road we came to. We eased the jeep between two white pillars where a small sign discreetly marked the entrance to Covecastles. The eight contemporary buildings sat on a dune and had steps leading through the sea grape and down to the water in a private cove. Their smooth, curved rooflines were snow white against the blue sky.

"What a location," I said. "Let's see if we can rent one."

"Oh, no," the woman inside the office said. "These are not long-term rentals. Covecastles is a private condominium complex and the units are booked through the season. Besides, they rent for twelve hundred dollars per night. You wouldn't want to pay that kind of rent, would you?"

"No," said Bob. "That's a little high. Are there really that many people who can pay that much for a room per night?"

"Our guests are looking for a quiet hideaway. We get a lot of celebrities who don't want to be recognized; it's almost like renting a private home."

"Do you think they might go out if there was a good restaurant nearby?" I asked.

"They might," she said. "But these people travel all over the world and are accustomed to the very finest dining. It would have to be up to the highest standard for them to leave the property."

"Thanks for your help," Bob said. "Have a good day."

We got back in the car wondering if we were out of our league. No, we decided, but running this restaurant would certainly be a challenge.

Driving on the left took some getting used to, and pulling out onto the main road sometimes called for a sudden swerve to correct our position. Anguillian traffic circles, called roundabouts, were a challenge. The signs said GIVE WAY, which we were more than willing to do—if we only knew which way to give. Stopping seemed a sensible choice but induced a chorus of horns tooting for us to move along. A lot of the side roads went only a few hundred feet before dead-ending at yet another deserted beach, and most of the houses were on the main road, facing inland—as if turning their backs on paradise. By the end of the day we'd found six possibilities; only one was anywhere near the water.

In front of Bennie's Grocery, Bennie stood talking to his son, who sat in the car with the motor running. When he saw us, he patted the roof, signaling that the young man was free to go, and asked if we'd had the lease typed. We said we'd spent the day looking for a place to live, and queried him on the house he'd mentioned.

"The one I own needs some work," Bennie said. "Let's see what you found."

We spread our map on the hood of the jeep, and Bennie studied intently the places we'd marked.

Bob pointed to the one with a view of the water. "This would be our first choice," he said, "even though it's a drive from the restaurant."

Bennie shook his head. "That one's not owned by an Anguillian."

"Does that matter?" I asked.

"When you get your work permits—which I can help you with, by the way—there is a stipulation that requires you rent from an Anguillian. It's one of the ways we protect our economy."

We were happy to rent from an Anguillian, said Bob, but it was *essential* to our well-being that we have a view of the water.

"All the beachfront land is set aside for resort development," Bennie explained. "If we were to sell beachfront land to foreigners for private homes, we would have nothing left to provide jobs and income."

Bob and I stared at each other, dismayed, realizing this made perfect sense for Anguilla.

"Besides," said Bennie, "building on the beach is risky when we get a bad storm. Most locals prefer to be on higher ground— preferably facing the road to keep track of the neighborhood activity." He laughed. We didn't.

Bennie tapped on the map at an intersection in the west end. "Here's a house that's ready to move in to," he said. "Malroy Jefferson owns it. He lives in England but he's from Anguilla, so you can rent from him. His brother, Bertroyd, is a bellman at Malliouhana."

We knew Bertroyd, who agreed to meet us at his brother's house. It was instantly apparent that life as an Anguilla resident would not resemble life as a guest at Malliouhana or Cap Juluca. The hotels were lush with gardens. The house did not have a single plant or tree—or, for that matter, a single blade of grass, just rocks and dirt surrounding a white concrete box. Bertroyd's brother had tried to replicate parts of his English home, but something had been lost in the translation. There was a bidet in the bathroom, along with a cast-iron tub with gobs of dried cement oozing out the edges. More problematic, the entire house had been covered in various shades of beige and green wallpaper. The moist Caribbean climate is not conducive to wallpaper, which in this case had come unglued; strips were hanging down in all directions like half-peeled bananas. "We could tape it back to the walls," said Bob, always looking for the bright side.

Otherwise Bob and I stayed mum as Bertroyd guided us from room to room, past the toilet with the broken-off flush handle and the shower plugged with cobwebs. Hoping to let in some fresh air— the house was as hot as a pizza oven—Bob turned the rusted cranks on the louvered windows, but they just went round and round, refusing to catch. The kitchen cabinets were scattered with mouse droppings, and the refrigerator was smaller than the one we'd given Jesse for his room at college. "If the fridge a problem," said Bertroyd, "I think Malroy would get a bigger one. Everything else just need to be cleaned."

The rent, said Bertroyd, was eight hundred dollars a month. It was while I was processing this figure—which seemed exorbitant—that I noticed the Shell station across the road.

We drove back to the hotel in silence. The cons of moving to Anguilla were suddenly smothering the pros. What *were* the pros, anyway? We would trade our beautiful house in Vermont on its private, ten-acre hilltop for a rectangular concrete bunker on the main road with a view of a gas station. Opening a little beach bar with just the two of us was one thing—there wasn't much to lose. But now we were going to sink all our money into building a fancy restaurant. We'd need waiters and sous chefs and dishwashers and . . .

What the hell had we been thinking?

"Oh, God!" I said out loud, and started to sob.

Bob pulled off the road, shut off the engine, and put his arm around me. "We can keep looking for a better house."

"It's not just that!" I wailed. "You have no idea how much it's going to cost to build this restaurant, and even less of an idea how to run it."

"I'll take some measurements tomorrow," said Bob, patiently, "and we'll work on a design for the building. We'll get the best prices on materials."

"You always think you can build everything for less than it actually costs! You're such a goddamned . . . *optimist!*" The word came out like a curse. It certainly shut Bob up.

"I don't want to do this," I went on, glaring at Bob through tears. "Eight hundred dollars a month for an ugly house on the main road with no view, and three thousand dollars for that stupid little shack. We don't have the money." I knew I was losing it, but I didn't care. "We know nothing about living in a country with goats and lizards thousands of miles from anywhere. I just want to go home," I said, then exhaled and resumed crying.

Bob was quiet for a moment. "We'll leave tomorrow," he said. He started the jeep and headed for the hotel.

At Malliouhana I ran upstairs, hoping no one would see that I'd been crying, and Bob informed the front desk that we'd be checking out in the morning. He asked them to call the airline and get us on the flight to Boston. In the room, I broke down completely. I changed into a long T-shirt, climbed into bed, and pulled the sheets over my head.

My face mashed against the pillow, I heard the big door open and close, then Bob's voice telling me we'd been booked on a 2:05 flight the next afternoon. I heard the door leading to the balcony open, and the light behind my eyelids turned red—it was the setting sun. "How about dinner?" said Bob.

"I'm not hungry."

I had stopped crying, but my stomach hurt. An odd sense of guilt had swept over me. I felt as if I'd betrayed someone—but who? Mac? Bennie and James? They'd see us as impulsive foreigners who'd come into their lives and made empty promises, but they were businessmen—they'd survive. Joshua? Would he ever call me "daughter" again? Maybe it was Anguilla itself that I'd betrayed—my favorite place on earth, my refuge. Or had I betrayed myself?

"You could just have a salad," said Bob.

"Go down without me."

Bob sat on the bed and put his hand on my shoulder. "Let's go back to Vermont," he said softly. "We'll get jobs like normal people."

I raised the covers and looked into his eyes, which were bluer than I'd ever seen them. Those eyes could always do it. "Okay," I said, "you've hypnotized me. Let's have one last great meal before we leave."

The Restaurant at Malliouhana was presided over by Jacques, the quintessential maître d', and overseen by the great Michel Rostang, who'd fly in from Paris periodically to tweak the menu. We sat at our usual table, which overlooked the rocky cliff and the turquoise water below. The spotlights on the rocks attracted three-foot-long gar fish, whose glowing eyes seemed to meet ours as they drifted lazily past. Bob ordered a bottle of '85 Château Palmer, and as we waited for the salad of haricots verts and marinated scallops and roasted whole chicken from Bresse for two, I began to feel better. Who wouldn't? By the time the chocolate soufflé arrived, we were brainstorming about business possibilities back home.

I fell asleep dreaming of Vermont. I wondered, however, as I drifted in and out of sleep, why barefoot James was grilling burgers back in our barn.

At five A.M. my eyes snapped open. I crept onto the balcony to watch the day come in. The dark sea pounded on the rocks below as the sky turned from black to dusky blue and the stars disappeared. My favorite time; while the world slept, I could bring order to even my unruliest thoughts. I stretched out on the lounge chair and sucked in the strong scent of the sea. Five minutes later I unlocked the heavy mahogany door to our room, trying not to wake Bob, and slipped into the open hallway.

The only way to the beach at Malliouhana is via a long and winding staircase that looks as if it has been chiseled into the cliff. This time of day it bends almost literally from the darkness of the previous night into the blue and red of the dawn.

With each step I felt as if I was coming out of a cloud. I rounded the last curve of the stairs and saw the white beach below, and it seemed suddenly vital to reach its safety. The instant my bare feet landed in the cool, wet sand, I knew I was home. A wave broke around my legs and then receded, eroding the sand under my feet and causing me to sink farther down, as if the beach were claiming me. I was overcome with a sense of belonging.

When I woke Bob, breathing hard from my climb back up the stairs, I told him I wanted to live in Anguilla and open the greatest restaurant in the Caribbean.

"You're a nut case," he said, and gave me a big hug.

Signing a lease in Anguilla is a casual affair—at least for James. "Meet me at the shop in Long Bay," he said. And there the three of us signed the life-changing document on the hood of a jeep in a dusty parking lot. James had a Heineken in his hand and was barefoot, and Bob and I marveled at the absence of lawyers and witnesses.

Later we went for a drive, talking of names for the restaurant. Could we somehow combine our names and Jesse's? Bomeljes? Jessmelbo? Meljebob?

"Why don't we just call it Blanchard's?" Bob said.

"Perfect," I said. "That covers the whole family."

We rounded a corner and came to a small harbor, where a half-dozen wooden fishing boats were anchored, bobbing like brightly colored toys. The boats bore names such as *Falcon*, *Rumrunner*, and—our favorite—*It's a Business*.

We watched as one made its way to shore, its captain deftly maneuvering around the coral reef that protected the bay. His younger helper, bare feet planted firmly apart, kept his balance by holding a rope tied to the bow. He looked as if he were water-skiing on the deck.

We walked down to the water to see what they had caught. The captain passed a large, bright yellow plastic tub over the side to his assistant, who now stood waist deep in the water alongside the boat, which was called *Blue Runner*. The tub was crawling with lobsters. It was clearly too heavy for the young man, who struggled to keep it from sinking as he towed it out of the water toward the beach.

Bob kicked off his sandals, waded out next to the boat, and grabbed a handle. "Thanks," said the young man.

"I Thomas Rogers," said the captain when he got back to shore. "That Glenroy. He my youngest. You come to buy lobsters?"

"We were just passing by," Bob told him. "But we are starting a restaurant on Meads Bay. Would you be able to supply us with lobsters when we open?"

While they talked, I settled myself on the beach and burrowed my toes into the cooler sand under the surface. The sun was directly overhead, and its magical warmth penetrated my muscles as I adjusted to island time. I felt unaccountably happy.

Thomas didn't notice several giant lobsters that had escaped from the tub and were scrambling down the beach, looking disjointed and prehistoric. Bravely deciding to retrieve the runaways, I tried to corner them using my shoes as a blockade. Since Caribbean lobsters have no claws, I thought they'd be easy to catch. I grabbed one around the middle. Its tail snapped against my hand so hard that I yelped and flung the creature into the air. By that time Thomas and Bob were enjoying the show, and I wasn't sure what to do next. Saving me from further embarrassment, Thomas ambled over, lifted the feisty lobster by the antennae, and returned it and the other escapees to the tub.

Glenroy appeared from behind the sea grape, driving his father's truck onto the beach, and pulled up to the pile of buckets, gas cans, and other paraphernalia they'd unloaded from the boat. He and Bob stowed the lobsters and equipment onto the back of the truck while Thomas went back out, tied the boat to a buoy in the bay, climbed into a dinghy, and paddled for shore.

"Thomas gave me his number," said Bob as we drove back toward Malliouhana. "He said he can catch as many lobsters as we need. And his cousin catches snapper." He stopped, victorious. "Our first vendor on the island!"

Grilled lobster with a honey glaze . . . crispy crusted snapper with curried rice . . . I could almost see the menu.

Chapter 2

We had trouble paying attention in Anguilla. Unencumbered by walls, our blue beach umbrella created a delightfully distracting office. We forced ourselves to concentrate—to work in a spot where the rest of the world comes to play. We sketched floor plans, our toes wriggling deeper into the sand as each new idea struck. Fat lizards puttered around us, their tails creating intricate patterns in the sand. They snatched tiny bugs with the tips of their long, long tongues—we were hypnotized. *Concentrate,* we told ourselves, *concentrate.* We moved paper cutouts of tables and chairs around on the plans until we were satisfied we had a workable layout.

The existing restaurant was a disaster—the nautical theme reminded me of a poor imitation of "Pirates of the Caribbean" at Disney World. The bar was a termite-infested boat that crumbled when touched. Telephone poles draped with ropes and fishing nets held up the roof; lobster buoys, rusty anchors, and brass propellers rounded out the seaside memorabilia. The bathrooms were worse—hardly more than outhouses with a subway-corner scent. (I refused to go in.) A few pieces of equipment could be salvaged from the kitchen: a grill, a ten-burner range, and a small walk-in cooler. Serious scrubbing, we hoped, would revive them.

The plans took a week. Frequent dips in the sea to cool off easily turned into an hour of lazy floating. We walked the crescent mile and back again several times a day—the wide, soft beach rarely had footprints other than ours. Solitude, I learned, can be its own distraction. My mind was constantly tricked by the sun into thinking I was on vacation. *Concentrate,* we reminded ourselves, *concentrate.* Despite the diversions, we managed to compile a list of building materials that filled an entire legal pad. Bob detailed every piece of wood, how many pounds of nails and screws, the number of shingles needed for the roof, and how many gallons of paint to finish it off. I added a Cuisinart, KitchenAid mixer, pots and pans, furniture, linens, glasses, dishes, silverware, candles, and on and on and on.

"Where do we find it all?" I asked Bob.

"I think that lumberyard we keep passing is a good place to start," he said.

We pulled up in front of Anguilla Trading next to a tiny white Daihatsu pickup. Barely more than a toy, this adorable little truck seemed to be the vehicle of choice on the island. They were everywhere—hauling boxes, concrete blocks, even people.

This one was earning its keep. It was loaded with fifty or sixty pieces of lumber protruding up over the cab and dangling precariously out over the tailgate, almost touching the road. The miniature wheelbarrow-sized tires were squooshed down by the weight, and we admired the ingenuity of the loading job before going into the store.

From the outside, Anguilla Trading looked like it had a large selection, with toilets in a rainbow of colors displayed prominently in the window, tempting the passing motorist. Water pumps, rusty shovels, pickaxes, and five-gallon pails of paint adorned the entrance.

Inside, we were in the dark. Not total blackness, but the lights were off and the store appeared closed. I knew from childhood visits to Deer Isle, Maine, that generating electricity on an island is expensive. Understanding this conservative approach made me feel a tiny thread of connection to life in Anguilla; I respected the darkness. The amount of hardware heaped on the shelves (and floor) took us completely by surprise. The inventory was staggering. Anguilla Trading is the Caribbean version of Home Depot. Bob rummaged through nails, which were in worn wooden bins like in the old general stores in Vermont, while I wandered around the corner and found myself in the gift department. Dishes, glasses, and toys sat alongside alarm clocks decorated with eagles and hearts, and an extensive collection of mop buckets overflowed into the Christmas ornament display. The store rambled on forever through rooms with couches, appliances, tools, and paint. I knew we'd be good customers.

"Are you getting bitten in here?" I asked Bob, back by the nails. I balanced on one foot, scratching my ankle with the other.

"Yeah, I think they're sand flies," he said. "There's so much here, but I can't find what I need. Most of these nails are for concrete. Let's go out and look at the lumber." I followed him out the back door and down some rickety steps. Squinting to adjust to the bright light outside, we roamed around piles of cement blocks, rolls of rusty wire, and stacks of crooked lumber. I knew what Bob's reaction to the lumber would be. He is not only a good builder but a fussy one. Bob eyed the two-by-fours dubiously, picked up a few, sighted down the length of each, and discarded them in disgust.

"These things look like Twizzlers," he muttered. "I couldn't build a pigpen out of this stuff." It was apparent that the preferred material for construction in Anguilla was concrete, not wood.

Bob disappeared into another building, and I sat down on the pile of two-by-fours, tilting my face up to the sun—even in a lumberyard, it felt warm and reassuring. Across the channel, St. Martin's emerald mountains were circled in mist, and for a moment time was suspended. *This is not vacation,* I reminded myself for the billionth time.

"Mel, I found the plywood," I heard over the roar of a muffler-free dump truck. It was backing up directly toward me in a gray cloud of exhaust.

"Coming," I yelled back, knowing he probably couldn't hear me over the din of the truck. Jumping over muddy puddles and climbing over mounds of crushed stone, I made my way toward the ramshackle building where Bob had located the plywood.

"Here it is." He beamed as if he had unearthed a diamond mine. He was ecstatic to locate something on his list. Plywood has never really made me jump up and down, but Bob's excitement was contagious, and I admired the stack of splintery wood with equal enthusiasm.

Crossing the soggy yard, the dump truck splashed past us, splattering our legs with mud. We climbed back into the main building and stood for a minute while our eyes adjusted again from the bright sunshine.

"Good afternoon," said a good-looking gentleman from behind where we were standing. "Can I help you find something?"

"Good afternoon," we replied in unison.

Bob said we were looking for the plywood price, and the man was curious about who we were. Once we introduced ourselves, we learned we were speaking with Walton Fleming, an Anguillian entrepreneur who was taking good advantage of the island's growth. Walton owned not only this huge retail emporium, but also the Anguilla Great House Hotel. Unlike the more luxurious properties on the island, the Great House oozed Caribbean charm. Colorful little cottages trimmed with painted shutters and surrounded by palm trees lined the beach. Visitors who chose to stay with Walton were transported to a more low-key Caribbean. A week at the Anguilla Great House could make even the most high-powered executives relax. Life there was as simple as it gets.

Walton asked the young lady behind the sales counter to help us with prices, and she sifted through a giant black notebook searching for the information. I told Bob I'd meet him in the car; the sand flies had rediscovered my ankles, and I was anxious to get outside.

"Okay," he said absently, not wanting to turn his attention away from the sales clerk. "Do you keep the drill bits out back?" he asked, pointing to a plastic case that had clearly held drill bits at one time.

"Bits finish," she answered, and resumed her slow, patient search.

"But since the case is still here, you'll be getting in more bits, right?"

She stopped thumbing through the notebook and stared blankly at Bob. "I ain' know," she said with a shrug, and went back to her task. Like everyone in Anguilla, she was in no hurry. It was this same leisurely pace that had lured us to the island, yet it still took adjustment. Bob forced himself to let the woman look for the price at her own speed without interfering.

Outside, there was that sunshine again; I soaked it up like a sponge. Settled into the open jeep, I watched palm fronds overhead rustle in the breeze and puffy white clouds drift past the roof of the building.

I was better at relaxing when I was a kid. Long, lazy summers of doing nothing—riding a bike through Central Park, eating blue Popsicles, and not really having to be anywhere at any certain time. One of the most enviable Anguillian traits is the innocent ability to relax. No one can take it as easy as an Anguillian. *Limin'* is the term for serious relaxation here. It comes from sitting under a lime tree and doing nothing. I was limin' in my jeep, but I needed more practice. It was difficult to reach this superior level of leisure after a lifetime of goals, deadlines, expectations, and business plans. Not that Anguillians don't work hard and have goals. Quite the opposite; they are just not frantic about it. And there's always tomorrow. The word *stress* is not in their dictionary.

We've seen locals sprawled for hours on end. Be it on a concrete cistern, a porch, or even on a step in front of a shop, they stretch out as comfortably as if surrounded by down pillows and watch the world go by. They might doze on and off, but basically they just lie there, limin'.

As I soaked in the sunshine my instinct was to find my notebook and add "practice limin'" to a list, but I knew that was contradictory. I did, however, promise myself to remove the word *stress* from my vocabulary.

"How much was the plywood?" I asked Bob, emerging from my daydream.

"It doesn't matter. That whole pile was sold, and they had no idea when they would get more in. I didn't bother to ask the price of a twisted two-by-four. They told me to try Albert Lake in The Valley."

We drove slowly toward town, easing over speed bumps, dodging livestock along the way. We rounded a bend, and stopped in front of us was the little truck from Anguilla Trading. Bob jammed on the brakes just short of the dangling lumber. The load had apparently been too much for the miniature tires, and the driver was changing a flat right smack in the middle of the road.

We were becoming used to this island custom of stopping regardless of cars behind. People lean out the window to chat with passersby about whatever the topic of the day might be. Often cars block one lane while their drivers browse in nearby bakeries or shops. The part of this habit I find most extraordinary is that even if there is ample room to pull off the pavement, it is more acceptable to stop squarely in the road.

On this day there was plenty of room to ease the baby truck off the road and into a church parking lot. The driver chose instead to remain in the flow of traffic. We backed up a little and went around him.

The ride to town is only seven miles but took half an hour. I amused myself by reading signs along the way. "Lighthouse Chinese Bar and Restaurant," I read aloud.

"I wonder if it's real Chinese food," Bob said as he turned down the street toward the sign. "Let's go by and we can check it out." We slowed as we passed, spotting a Chinese family eating in the yard—a sure sign of authenticity—and agreed to give it a try sometime.

At the end of the street a cliff plummeted at least 150 feet straight to the sea, surrounding the quiet harbor below on three sides. We pulled over for a better look. The color blue must have been created right in this bay. The water looked as though it had been tinted by something artificial, something unreal. It was the bluest of blues, with patchy shadows of coral composing a canvas worthy of hanging in the Metropolitan Museum of Art. A long pier stretched out from shore, and we watched as bananas were unloaded from a cargo boat.

"I had forgotten about this view," Bob said. "We came here with Joshua and took pictures the first time we ever came to Anguilla. I love looking out at little Sandy Island with that miniature tuft of palm trees. It reminds me of Robinson Crusoe." He put his arm around me, and we contemplated the sailboats below; their masts rocked ever so slightly in the waves.

"I can't believe we live here," I said. "We can see this view every day."

We stood mesmerized by the serenity until Bob broke the silence. "Let's go find some lumber," he said, and we jumped back in the jeep.

More signs: HIGHWAY BAR, HIGHWAY PLAYSKOOL, HIGHWAY TYRE, HIGHWAY GYM. The term *highway* had been redefined. In my old world, highways were straight, boring thoroughfares rushing people from one place to another. This highway was much more my speed. At 30 mph I could see the sights: a roadside stand with coconuts for sale, a woman peddling pomegranates on a table in her yard, an old man getting a haircut on his front porch.

"Excuse me, do you sell lumber?" Bob asked the woman at the checkout in Albert's Department Store.

"See lumber there." She pointed to a chain-link fence across the road.

Following her directions, we walked past Lake's Home Decor, which connected to Lake's Gas Station. This was Albert Lake's corner, all right. In back of the gas station, we found Albert Lake's Lumberyard, similar in character to Anguilla Trading. We wandered into a large, dark warehouse and were greeted by an eager young man with a surprising Spanish accent. "Chew nee some help?" he asked.

"Do you have two-by-fours?" Bob began.

"Finish," he answered.

"How about half-inch plywood?"

"Finish."

"Sixteen-penny nails?" Bob continued.

"Finish."

Bob looked at me with dismay, and I could tell he was losing patience.

"Two-by-eights?" he tried again.

"Finish." The young man didn't seem to mind this line of questioning at all.

"Where are you from?" I asked, anxious to change the subject.

"I fron Santo Domingo," he told us, "but my fadda fron here. Why you ain' go south fo' dis stuff?"

"Go south to where?" Bob asked.

"St. Martin."

"I guess we'll have to *go south*," Bob said, emphasizing his new vocabulary. "Thanks."

We left the Albert Lake empire and drove past the high school, where hundreds of teenagers were getting out for lunch. They poured through an open gate in the yard, clogging the sidewalk and overflowing into the street. The girls were all dressed in bright green pleated skirts and tan blouses, and the boys wore light brown pants with tan short-sleeve shirts. Just past the school, at a four-way intersection, a slight fender-bender had occurred. Traffic had stopped as the two drivers stood in the road shouting in disagreement. In the middle of the intersection, a hand-painted sign propped up on a neat mound of tires read TRAFFIC EXPERIMENT— apparently the experiment had failed. We turned around and drove back past the school.

"Melinda." My name was being called from the sea of school uniforms, and I spotted an arm waving frantically in the air. The girl pushed through the crowd, yelling, "Melinda," and we recognized Marina, one of Joshua's grandchildren. She ran up to the car, smiling from ear to ear. "A lift, please," she said, and hopped in the backseat. We drove her home to Joshua's for lunch and found Evelyn on the front porch with two-year-olds Amalia and Kim-Misha running circles around her, tugging at her apron.

"Them's bad lil' childrens," Evelyn said lovingly, and shooed them into the house. Marina skipped inside, dropping her book bag on the front steps.

"You sure have a houseful," I said to Evelyn from the open jeep.

"I's gettin' too old for all these childrens." Evelyn shook her head, but we knew raising this next generation was what kept her going. We backed out of the yard, waving goodbye, and went to look for lunch.

Our lumber search was discouraging, but that did not hamper our appetites. Our stomachs were empty, and we needed to regroup. Patricia and Rosalind from the front desk at Malliouhana had recommended a local place called Hill Street Snack Bar, which we had noticed on the way into town. Although tempted by the Chinese food, we decided to save that for a special occasion and give Hill Street a try.

It was packed. We had discovered a local hot spot.

"Sit anywhere," a large, smiling woman said from behind the bar. "Everything on the menu is right here." She pointed to a blackboard hanging next to her.

We sat at a painted plywood table and considered our options, glancing at the wrestling on a TV over the bar. The menu was simple:

CONCH
GOAT
PORK CHOP
CHICKEN
OXTAIL
$16.00 E.C.

"Bob, sixteen dollars E.C.—that's only six dollars U.S.," I said. "That's a great deal."

"How much could they charge for oxtail?" Bob said.

We ordered one conch and one chicken, a Coke, and a Carib beer. We sat with our drinks and listened to the chatter around us. A group of five women in Cable & Wireless uniforms were laughing at the next table. Three men in blue coveralls with PUBLIC WORKS across the back were seated at the bar, engrossed in the wrestling match, and behind Bob, a table of four businessmen in suits discussed politics.

"So this is the power lunch scene in Anguilla," Bob remarked with a smile. A giggly young girl brought our lunch, and we stared at the enormous mounds of food, each plate heaped with enough rice and peas for an army. Giant pink conch shells had intrigued me on beaches for years, and I was curious to taste the meat. Bite-sized pieces had been simmered in a spicy curry sauce with plenty of onions, celery, and tomatoes, and I was surprised to find it so soft and tender. I remembered reading somewhere that conch was tough and chewy, and wondered if there was a trick I should know about. The rice absorbed the extra sauce, and the fried plantains on the side gave my mouth a sweet break from the spice. The chicken was fall-off-the-bone tender, stewed in a Creole-style tomato sauce with onions and green peppers. We devoured everything.

The woman from behind the bar came to ask if everything was okay. There is something comforting about large Anguillian women. At home, a woman of this size would be considered over-weight. Not in Anguilla. Generous weight is a sign of contented-ness, happiness, even success; a thin person, on the other hand, probably works too hard, worries too much, and doesn't eat enough. Here, a large woman has prospered and raised many chil-dren, and my need for mothering attracts me to them like a mag-net. This woman was no exception.

I responded quickly. "It was great. We're so happy to find you. I would love to know how you made the conch so tender."

"Pound it with a mallet," she said. "That's all you do." I wanted the complete recipe but figured it could wait until another time.

"We're opening a restaurant down on Meads Bay. I'm Bob and this is Melinda."

"I'm Cora Lee, and that's my daughter, Sweenda," she said, pointing proudly to the young girl who had brought our food and was now flirting with the table of businessmen. "My husband, Raimy, does the cooking. Where are you going to get your restau-rant equipment?"

"We don't know yet," I replied. "I think we're going to St. Mar-tin tomorrow."

"There's a place over there called PDG in Cole Bay," Cora Lee said. "They have quite a bit, but I think they're too expensive and they don't sell used equipment. I'm looking for a used restaurant stove—maybe six or eight burners. If you bring in a container from Miami, I would like to get a stove up there. I could give you the money before you go."

"Miami? Is that what people do?" I asked.

"It's really where everything comes from. There and Puerto Rico," Cora Lee said.

Digesting that new bit of information, Bob offered, "We'd be happy to help you find a stove. We'll let you know what we end up doing. Thanks for your help."

"And a great lunch," I added.

On the way back to the hotel, we met the little truck *still* inching along with its giant load. It hadn't made much progress.

"This guy's really making a day out of his lumber purchase," Bob said.

"Island time," I said.

At the front desk, we thanked Patricia and Rosalind profusely for sending us to Cora Lee's. Agatha was at the desk too and joined the discussion, now centered around planning a trip to St. Martin the next day. Her skirt was tight and short, exposing gorgeous legs that stretched to the sky. She reserved a rental car and gave us directions to Cole Bay and Phillipsburg, which, she explained, were on the Dutch side of the island.

Since our lumber search had been in vain, we opted for an afternoon enjoying the hotel. Once settled in our concrete bunker of a house, the luxury of Malliouhana, its pool, its food, and its service would be a memory. We changed into bathing suits and stretched out on lounge chairs next to the waterfall that pours over rocks from one pool and into another.

I studied the deep green lawns and swaying palm trees, wondering how much water it must take to keep everything so healthy on an island with so little rainfall. Splashes of red, purple, and orange bougainvillea cascaded over a white semicircular wall surrounding one side of the pool area. A terra-cotta path meandered past the wall and disappeared toward the villas scattered along the cliff. Next to my chair, a pink oleander bloomed happily, exploding with flowers in the relentless sunshine.

Where do they get all these plants? I wondered. *They must have their own nursery, and probably an army of gardeners too.* I let the sun work its magic while the sound of the water lulled me to sleep.

The next morning we were at the ferry terminal at seven-forty-five to make the eight o'clock boat. After paying our $2 departure tax, we sat down in the plastic chairs and waited. We watched the clock on the wall as eight o'clock came and went.

Island time lesson, number one: Anguilla schedules are about as dependable as the weather in New England. Bob asked the woman collecting the tax what time we would leave.

"Eight o'clock boat broke," she said. "Nex' boat, eight-thirty."

By eight-thirty, the ferry terminal was jammed with people. A few tourists were going over to explore St. Martin for the day, but mostly we were surrounded by locals chattering a mile a minute. I tried to understand some of the conversations around me, but when Anguillians talk amongst themselves, the English language takes on a new rhythm and sound. Every now and then I caught a recognizable word or phrase, but it took more concentration than I was willing to give it. Instead I sat patiently, surrounded by people who might as well have been speaking Swahili. *Living in Anguilla is going to be an experience,* I thought.

At eight-forty-five two full boatloads of people piled onto one boat. We stood in the aisle and tried to keep our balance as the miserable ferry churned its way across the channel. Women were holding children in their laps, most of them blissfully content as the boat ride rocked them to sleep. Several older women looked frightened and grasped the seat backs in front of them for security.

Tabitha, a ferry in the loosest sense, was a steel cargo boat fitted with rows of old airplane seats. The cabin was totally enclosed and the windows and doors were shut. I immediately felt claustrophobic, but outside there was no place to sit or even stand. I was trapped. The engines were so loud, neither of us could hear a word the other was saying, and the vibration of the floor and the smell of diesel fuel made the trip very unpleasant. The decorating job, however, kept us smiling. Blinking Christmas lights were strung all over the ceiling, and a VCR hung from the wall, entertaining the passengers with an old Eddie Murphy movie. The sound was completely inaudible over the roar of the engines. The most curious element, though, were the plaid curtains. Someone had gone to a great deal of trouble to create a certain ambience by covering the windows. To me, the best part of a boat ride is the view. Clearly, the locals saw the trip to St. Martin as no more than a taxi ride and had little interest whatsoever in the spectacular scenery behind the curtains.

The trip took thirty minutes, and by the time we stepped onto the pier in Marigot, I felt seasick and had a splitting headache. I sat down on a bench to recover while Bob went to locate the car rental agency. The car was a gem. Its front bumper was missing, the windshield was cracked, the passenger side was dented and smashed, and the door handle was gone.

"Great car," I said as Bob opened my door from the inside. "Was this Hertz or Avis?"

Bob smiled. "The contract just says Car Rental Agency."

We crept along through the one-lane streets past patisseries and bistros. We passed *la poste,* where lines of people stood holding baguettes they'd purchased earlier, and blocks of duty-free shops selling perfume, cameras, and jewelry.

It looked more like the French Riviera than the Caribbean— tall, skinny blond women hurried along the sidewalks in tight little dresses revealing as much of their tanned bodies as possible. Sleek-looking men in gauzy shirts and blue jeans also bustled past, many with a cell phone glued to one ear. Not at all like Anguilla. Instead of St. Martin, we could have landed in St. Tropez.

We plodded out of Marigot's traffic and were abruptly propelled onto St. Martin's version of the autobahn: a three-mile stretch of relatively straight country road with one lane traveling in each direction. At seventy miles an hour our mangled Toyota developed a severe wobble, warning us we had reached top speed. Bob felt as though he were in the Indianapolis 500 as other cars passed us in a wild race to some imaginary finish line. As drivers overtook us from behind they would flash their lights and blow their horns, and if they saw just a little bit of open road, they'd fly by as if we weren't moving.

"How can this island be so different?" I asked. "We're only seven miles from Anguilla, and look at this place. The traffic is worse than the New Jersey Turnpike."

"Thank God they all want to stay over here," Bob answered. His white knuckles gripped the steering wheel as we sailed past the sign welcoming us to the Dutch side of the island. Coming down the hill into town, the traffic slowed to a snail's pace, and a line of cars disappeared from sight. We parked illegally alongside the road with hundreds of others and walked the rest of the way.

Unlike Anguilla, St. Martin has no duty on purchases, making it a popular stop for cruise ships. On this particular day Bob and I counted five giant ships anchored in the harbor. A frenzied mob of sunburned shoppers had been shuttled ashore and turned loose. Hordes of tourists equipped with cameras pushed and shoved their way through the grimy streets, determined to find the best price on everything from T-shirts and Cuban cigars to Rolex watches. We fought our way through the crowd, in search of restaurant supplies and building materials.

We bought plastic dishes, an inexpensive set of pots and pans, some glasses, and cheap silverware, allowing us to set up house-keeping until our things arrived from Vermont. I bought an ice cream machine for $19.95, thinking it would be fun to start test-ing ice cream and sorbet recipes for the restaurant. Our search for building materials, however, was hopeless. After four frustrat-ing stops at overpriced and understocked lumberyards, Miami felt closer and closer.

The high point of St. Martin was lunch. Though the Dutch may be excellent merchants, there was no doubt in our minds that the French side was the place to eat. We drove back over the hill, then raced down the autobahn and back to Marigot.

Walking along the narrow streets, we wandered into a marina filled with sailboats and powerboats. Their gangplanks rested on the dock, affording their owners easy access to the dozens of restaurants and shops along the water. Menus were posted on easels, and we moved from one to the next, pausing at a small café called Tropicana. All twelve of its little cloth-covered tables were full, but the charming maître d' assured us that his best table in front was about to become vacant; if we could wait five minutes, he would get it ready. Just being around this tanned, gorgeous young Frenchman made us feel exotic and foreign. We turned and leaned on the railing to watch the boats. Our stomachs growled.

A bronzed boy with shoulder-length straw-colored hair climbed down from the pier into a rubber dinghy. No more than twelve or thirteen years old, he untied his little boat, started the engine, and sped out of the marina. As we watched, I thought how different Jesse's life of ski racing would have been had he grown up by the sea instead of in the mountains.

"I wonder if that boy goes to school or just lives on a boat," I contemplated out loud.

"Madame, monsieur, s'il vous plaît," we heard from behind, and gratefully settled in at the promised front table.

We shared a salad of well-chilled baby greens topped with warm, slightly melted rounds of goat cheese; the contrast of temperatures elevated the word *salad* to a new level. The sun glistened on the white sailboats and the heat blazed on the sidewalk just beyond our table, but we remained cool under our little awning. As we mopped up the last crumbles of cheese and drizzles of vinaigrette, our host presented us each with a daily special. The roast chicken was an entire half a bird, brown, crispy, and smothered with shallots sautéed in red wine. A huge bowl of *pommes frites* was placed in the center of the table, and to this day, I believe Tropicana makes the best in the universe. Deep golden brown and slightly crispy on the outside, they have a center of velvety potato that tastes as earthy as the ground from which they were dug. They were perfect.

"I feel like we're living in heaven," I replied. "Let's come for lunch once a week."

"I hope we find some restaurant equipment at PDG," Bob said, remembering we weren't on vacation. "We also need to buy a bed so we can move out of the hotel." We shared a *tarte tatin* piping hot from the oven for dessert, the apples rich with fragrance, their perfume almost ethereal. Ready for a nap, we reluctantly went in search of PDG.

The directions were a little sketchy. We had a map of St. Martin, but Cole Bay is a maze of roads that wind their way between warehouses and auto dealerships, around boatyards and little houses. Agatha and Rosalind had tried to tell us how to find PDG, but Anguillians have their own terminology for direction. The word *above* means east and *below* means west. So our directions read something like this: "Drive below till you reach an upstairs building with motorcycles. Turn and go up to the bakery. Go above at the bakery, then below where the old tamarind tree was. PDG right there."

We found the motorcycle building (a Harley-Davidson dealership with two stories—hence, an upstairs building) and turned to the right. That was easy because there was no left, but finding the bakery and a tree that was no longer there proved hopeless. Around and around, all roads led back to the motorcycles. Eventually we turned down a new street and triumphantly spotted PDG boldly marked on the side of a warehouse.

Jon, the owner and a transplant from Holland, was knowledgeable about outfitting a kitchen, but his inventory was too casual for what we had in mind. We examined his dinnerware selection, looking at sturdy dishes like those you might see in a diner and thick-rimmed wineglasses not at all suitable for the Lafite Rothschild Bob intended to serve. We looked at plastic ash-trays, blenders, bus tubs, and poultry shears. Most of the things we liked were in catalogs and needed to be special-ordered from the States.

"You want to check the flights to Miami or should I?" Bob said back in the car.

"I think that's a good idea," I said. "It's risky to order every-thing from catalogs."

We had spotted a furniture store called La Casa near the Harley-Davidson dealership and on the way back stopped to look at beds. I hated to spend the $1,000 on a mattress and box spring with no brand name, but we needed to check out of the hotel.

"How can we get it to Anguilla?" I asked the stout saleswoman.

"No problem," she said. "We'll deliver it to the *Lady Odessa*."

"What's the *Lady Odessa*?" Bob asked, curious.

"It's the freight boat that go to Anguilla. We deliver things to it all the time. It come over to Marigot every morning and waits at the dock until 'round two o'clock. Anything you need from St. Martin can be delivered to them. You does pay the cap'n once he reach Anguilla—it probably twenty-five or thirty dollars for a bed."

"Is that the boat I've seen loaded with goats and cases of Heineken at the ferry dock?" Bob asked.

"That's the one," she said.

We thanked her and drove back to Marigot, not looking for-ward to another ferry ride.

The trip back was nothing like *Tabitha*. We sat outside on the top deck of the *Deluxe*, and the glorious day caressed us from all around. Transported from St. Martin's lush, green mountains back to our own island paradise, we watched three Anguillian fishing boats race each other on either side of our ferry. The small, open boats were flying over the sea, each maneuvering from the top of one wave to the top of the next in an exhilarating splash of blue. The wind tore through our hair, and salt spray occasionally blew over the boat, sprinkling us and forming rainbows against the backdrop of St. Martin. As we approached Anguilla I could see the pristine white domes of Cap Juluca, the long white stretch of Rendezvous Bay, and the three West Indian cottage–style peaks of the ferry terminal. A thick grove of palm trees lined the beach to the right, and the water looked more green than blue as we neared the shore. I took in the beauty of the harbor and wondered why more people didn't live here. Why would anyone choose to live surrounded by concrete and traffic rather than fishing boats, water, and palm trees?

Back at the hotel, our island advisors were all behind the front desk. We reported the day's events and Bernice, Joshua's daughter, confirmed Miami as our next course of action.

"Dada brings in containers from there all the time," she said. "Why you don't go call and ask him how to do it?"

While Bob made notes of Joshua's instructions, I sat on the balcony and summarized our position. We were thousands of miles from home, investing our life savings into reconstructing a building on someone else's land. We had not yet been granted our license and work permits from the government, and money would be tight. We were being impulsive, and I knew it. But Anguilla's allure was so seductive, we would do whatever it took to make it work.

Bob joined me on the balcony and recapped Joshua's conversation. "They load everything in Miami into tractor-trailer bodies, called containers, and stack them on a boat. We have to call Sheila Haskins, the Tropical Shipping agent, to make the arrangements. He also gave me prices on freight, and it's not inexpensive; a twenty-foot container from Miami to Anguilla is twenty-seven hundred dollars, and a forty-footer is forty-two hundred dollars."

"Okay." I took a deep breath. "I'll go to Vermont, pack up our things, and call the movers. Then I'll go to Miami, buy everything we need, and ship it down. You can stay here and keep pushing for our work permits and alien land-holding license."

"You can't do all that yourself," Bob said.

But I was determined. "Look, if we both go, I think everything here will stop. Out of sight, out of mind. Bennie means well, but he's a busy guy, and if somebody doesn't stay on top of this, I've got a feeling it won't go any further."

"You think you can buy the lumber?" Bob was giving in a little.

"I'll just take your list into Home Depot—they'll price it all and deliver it. It's easy. Besides, they do have phones in Miami, you know. Also, what if you need to measure something else on the building or make a change to the plans? Wouldn't it be better if you were here?" I knew that would cinch it.

"Okay," Bob conceded. "But if you can't do it alone, I'll come up to help."

"We'll save on plane fare this way," I added. "Also, if I get everything in Vermont shipped quickly, maybe you can unpack and organize the house before I get back."

We stood on the balcony, holding on to each other, staring out at the sea for a very long time.

At the airport the next morning, I was bluntly reminded of my status here by a small sign:

DEPARTURE TAX
BELONGERS: $10.00 E.C.
NON-BELONGERS: $25.00 E.C.

I said goodbye to Bob after reviewing the lists a final time, and caught one last glimpse of him waving as the plane lumbered onto the runway. I stared out the window as we took off, picking out Joshua's house and then the sleepy harbor at Sandy Ground. Spotting the restaurant, I mashed my head against the window trying to see it for as long as possible. The color of the water looked like a painter's palette—blues and greens mingled with white where the waves broke over the reefs or hit the shore. When Anguilla disappeared from view, I pulled out a pad and pen and made a list of things to do in Vermont.

I packed our house in record time. After three eighteen-hour days, a forty-foot tractor-trailer loaded with everything we owned pulled out of our yard, destined to become a container in Miami. I stood for a minute in our empty living room and looked out at the view. Our spring green fields rolled away from the house to the edge of the woods. Across the valley, the historic white clock tower at Dartmouth College was nestled in the hills. In the distance, Mt. Ascutney rose majestically over the Connecticut River. I listed the house with a broker, said goodbye to several neighbors, and drove down our hill for the last time, trying not to look back.

With a generous bag of Chinese food, I drove to Betsy and Gary's house for a farewell feast. Over the years Betsy had become my food ally. Together we had baked pies, canned peaches, and put every restaurant within a hundred miles through its paces.

They were in rare form. Over a dinner of ginger chicken with string beans and soft-shell crab with black bean sauce, Gary bitched about taxes and Betsy, perpetually stuck in the sixties with her long black hair, rumpled sweatshirt, and fuzzy clogs, rolled her eyes. I was going to miss them. I caught myself staring out the window of their old farmhouse at the herd of Black Angus cattle and realized it was the end of an era.

"I may ask you to ship me one of those cows if I can't find a source for beef down there," I said to Gary.

"No problem," he said through a mouthful of noodles. "I'll deliver it."

We parted tearfully, and I drove to my friend Pat's house to spend the night. It was almost midnight by the time I pulled into the yard, and Pat was waiting up for me. I had so much to tell her about Anguilla, but I was falling asleep. We would talk in the morning.

"Can you believe I'm doing this?" I said the next day as we drove south to Logan Airport.

"No, but you do a lot of things I can't believe."

"I hope you can visit soon. It really is beautiful. Our house is a little odd, but there is an extra bedroom. I can't wait to show you the beaches. They're pure white powder, and there's never anyone on them. The ocean is the most amazing shade of turquoise, and the water is so warm, it's like swimming in a bathtub. There's this one beach that not too many people know about called Captain's Bay—it's way up at the eastern tip of the island, far away from any of the hotels. You drive on this bumpy dirt road, which is really more like a goat path, and when you get there, it's totally deserted—no houses, not a building in sight. Only this perfect beach. The waves are a little rougher, and on either side are these craggy rocks that look like craters on the moon. They go right down to the water. The waves crash against the rocks and roll up onto the beach, and you feel like you're a million miles from anywhere."

We drove in silence for a while, and I remembered Bob was getting the bed that afternoon from St. Martin. I pictured him unloading it from the funny green freight boat, the *Lady Odessa*. I wondered how many goats were napping on my bed.

Chapter 3

THE LADY ODESSA WAS TIED UP alongside
the dock in Blowing Point, and Bob spotted the
bed leaning against a sizeable wall of Heineken boxes
that had apparently been unloaded from the boat. Mac was
standing among a group of taxi drivers who congregate, while
waiting for a fare, in the shade of a loblolly tree just outside the
ferry terminal.

"You goin' south?" Mac asked.

"No, I'm here to get that bed." Bob pointed toward the dock.
"Do I have to pay duty on a bed?"

Several of the taxi drivers chuckled, and one said, "You gotta
pay duty on everything in Anguilla."

"Customs is right there," Mac said. "Go see those boys.
They'll take your money."

"Bed has to go in the warehouse," said the customs officer.

"But I need to sleep on it tonight," Bob explained. "I've
checked out of my hotel. I thought I could just pay the duty and
get the bed."

"No, man," the officer said sternly. "You gotta put the bed
in the warehouse and do an entry. It'll take two or three days to
process the paperwork."

"Look." Bob was trying to remain calm. "If I don't get the
bed now, I'll have to sleep on the floor."

"Give the man he bed," said a voice from behind. It was Bennie, and after several minutes of playful arguing and idle threats, he convinced the customs officer to release the bed to Bob.

"Nex' time it go in the warehouse," said the officer as he completed the necessary forms, rubber-stamping every page. Then he told Bob that the duty was $537.64.

"That's over half the cost of the bed," Bob said, shocked at the amount.

"No, man. That E.C. dollars. You wanna pay in U.S., it two hundred dollars."

Two hundred dollars was certainly better than $537.64, but it still seemed like a lot. Bob was nonetheless grateful for something to sleep on.

The late-afternoon sun reflected off the tin roof of the terminal, and Bob squinted as he walked down onto the dock toward the *Lady Odessa*. The boat's light green hull was nearly camouflaged by the aquamarine water, and it looked like something you might come across in the South China Sea or cruising up the Amazon. Its wooden bow scooped up high to a point, and a boxy cabin covered the rear of the boat. From under the deck, soggy cases of raw chicken parts were being passed up to a man who tossed them to another on the pier, where they were stacked in a dripping pile.

Bob tried to shake the word *salmonella* from his mind. The cartons of chicken sat defrosting in the sun, surrounded by a growing puddle of water, and were marked KEEP FROZEN.

He waited for someone to stop tossing chicken, but they ignored him. "I'm looking for the captain," Bob said finally. "I'm here to pick up that bed."

"Cap'n down in the hole." The man stacking the chicken pointed to an opening in the deck. "Jus' wait till he finish countin' the chicken."

So Bob sat down on the Heineken boxes and waited. *Island time,* he told himself. He looked at the ferryboats anchored in the harbor and tried to picture the dugout canoes used by the Arawak Indians who had lived here before the island became a British colony. He envisioned the boatloads of slaves brought in by the English settlers.

The *Lady Odessa* rose and fell with the waves, softly thudding against the rubber tires that cushioned it from the pier. As it rocked, the bowline creaked like a squeaky floorboard, tightening, falling slack, then tightening again. It was clear how Blowing Point got its name. The soft trade winds from the east funneled down the channel between St. Martin and Anguilla and blew steadily over the small protrusion of land. One of the ferryboats roared into the quiet harbor, leaving a frothy white trail behind. The *Lady Odessa* rocked wildly in the wake, and Bob watched as the waves calmed and turned into gentle ripples against the shore.

Observing a stream of passengers pour out of the ferry, Bob felt very much a part of Anguilla. Tourists would come and go, but he and I would stay. We were no longer visitors here, but locals. *I wonder where we'll go on vacation,* he thought.

A snorkeler swam past the boat and in toward shore, his air tube bobbing above the waves. Once in shallow water, he stood up, holding his bag proudly for Bob to see.

"Lobsters," he said as Bob got up to take a closer look.

"How'd you catch them?"

"Caught 'em with my lasso." He held up a stick about four feet long with a piece of wire tied in a loop at one end. "I dives down an' looks under the rocks where the lobsters live. Then I take my lasso like this." He held his stick out as if to touch an imaginary lobster. "I slip the noose over his head and then . . . gotcha." He yanked the stick back, demonstrating how it was done, and handed it to Bob for closer examination.

Bob admired the tool, paying particular attention to the wire at the end.

"How many lobsters do you have in there?" he asked.

"About twenty-five or so, and I shot this snapper with my spear gun." The lobsters snapped their tails violently, making the bag shake. "Whatcha' doin' down here on the freight dock?"

"I'm trying to pick up a bed I bought in St. Martin. I can't seem to find out how much to pay the captain. He's busy unloading chicken."

"Lemme see if I can help." The man tossed his bag of lobsters onto the pier and pulled himself up out of the water. He was wearing a black wet suit and was built like Arnold Schwarzenegger, his narrow waist expanding upward into a huge chest and massive shoulders. His biceps were bigger than Bob's legs, and his thighs bulged with muscle, presumably from a life of swimming around the bottom of the sea.

He walked toward the *Lady Odessa,* leaving a wet trail behind him, and Bob followed, feeling very small.

"Yo, Rupert," he yelled to the man unloading the chicken. "The man come for he bed. Stop now. How much it tis?"

"Fifty dollar," came a reply from below as another case of chicken was handed up.

"Fifty too mucha money, man," he said, jumping down onto the deck of the *Lady Odessa* and kneeling next to the opening to negotiate the freight bill. "The man say twenty-five."

"Forty. Nuttin' less," the captain answered.

"Come." The snorkeler motioned for Bob to come aboard. "Pay the cap'n. Leff we go with the bed."

Bob pulled out two twenties, offering them to the captain.

"No, man," Bob's new friend said. "Forty E.C."

Bob sheepishly put the money back in his wallet and pulled out two E.C. twenties (about $15 U.S.). He wondered how to determine if someone was quoting U.S. dollars or Eastern Caribbean dollars, and would be sure to ask in the future.

"Thanks a lot," Bob said as the two went for the mattress and box spring. "My name's Bob."

"I Shabby," he replied, offering a strong, wet handshake.

Shabby picked up the box spring as if it were a feather, balanced it on his head, and carried it to the roof of the rented jeep. Bob dragged the mattress along behind, but before he got too far, Shabby returned, lifted it to his head, and carried it off effortlessly.

They tied the bed onto the roof, and Bob offered to give Shabby a ride home.

"You wanna learn how to dive for lobsters?" Shabby asked with a killer white smile.

"I'd love to," said Bob.

"Meet me here tomorrow afternoon at one o'clock. I got extra snorkeling gear at home, and I'll make you a lasso tonight." Bob dropped Shabby at his house and drove away, anxious to tell me he was going to a tropical rodeo the next day to lasso lobsters.

The following afternoon Shabby was sitting in the shade of the taxi driver tree with the usual group, and he sprang up as Bob approached. The two walked down to the beach where Shabby had put the snorkeling gear.

"Leff we go," Shabby said, and disappeared under the waves, towing the nylon lobster bag by one foot and carrying his spear gun and lasso stick. Bob followed, armed with his new lasso, awed by the silent, colorful world he had just entered. On the way into deeper water, the sandy bottom gradually gave way to outcroppings of coral. Shabby motioned repeatedly for Bob to resurface so he could identify the innumerable kinds of fish. A bright blue and yellow angelfish, a luminous yellow grunt with blue stripes, red hind, needlefish, grouper, parrot fish, and oldwife. A large stingray drifted over Bob's head, and schools of fish scooted away in unison, darting in and out of the strange and exotic-looking coral. Patches of sea grass danced in the currents, and Shabby swam gracefully through it, gliding along the bottom like a big black fish. He was clearly at home under water and seemed able to hold his breath forever as he peered under every crevice in the reef. He would slip his lasso over a lobster, snap it out in a flurry of sand and bubbles, and add it to his bag.

A decent swimmer and a respectable athlete, Bob tried to keep up. Actually, the hardest part was keeping *down.* The incredible buoyancy of the salt water made him feel as though he had on a life jacket. He'd fight his way down toward Shabby but often would bounce back to the surface like a submerged beach ball.

After two hours Shabby had filled the lobster bag and Bob had caught one. He was exhausted, and as he stumbled out of the water back by the ferry dock his arms and legs felt like lead. Even the air felt heavy. He collapsed on the beach, wishing he'd put more lotion on the backs of his legs, which were beet red with sunburn.

"You got lobster for dinner tonight," Shabby said, holding up Bob's catch.

"I'm not sure I have the energy to cook it." Bob struggled to his feet.

On the way back Bob told Shabby about the restaurant.

"My brothers and me, we does construction work if you need help," Shabby offered.

"We definitely need help," Bob replied.

"Jus' leave me know and we be down there when you ready."

The next morning, Cable & Wireless, a British version of AT&T, came to the house to hook up our phone. Anguilla, Bob learned from the installers, has only had telephones since 1971. They had obviously come a long way. Before leaving, they reviewed the available services: call waiting, call forwarding, three-way conference calling, speed dialing, ring back when free, calling name delivery, automatic busy callback, and instant recall. As soon as they drove away, Bob left a message at my hotel saying we might have to attend night school to learn how to run the phones.

My first day in Miami was a fiasco. I wasted five hours in traffic, witnessed a shooting, saw three accidents on I-95, and was rear-ended in a parking lot. Cranes and jackhammers made it impossible to maneuver the city streets, and that night I moved to Boca Raton. It was more civilized, and I quickly learned my way around.

My schedule became routine. I arrived at Home Depot by six-thirty each morning, and after spending several hours with the men in orange aprons, I zoomed up and down the highway, systematically checking off everything on my list: a day designing menu covers, three days working with a plant broker who gave me a crash course in tropical gardening, almost a week scrounging through acres of restaurant equipment (which included the search for Cora Lee's stove), and repeated visits to Crate & Barrel and Williams-Sonoma.

Dining chairs were the biggest challenge. Finding fifty chairs in stock was difficult. Most required a special order, which would take twelve weeks, but I needed them immediately; on a tight budget, this appeared impossible. I covered every inch of South Florida and finally lucked out with forty-eight chairs someone had ordered and never picked up. They were a very tropical-looking white rattan, sturdy enough to take abuse, and best of all, 30 percent off.

Each night around eight I'd call Bob, who always had changes to make to the list, and then go to the local bookstore until midnight for study time. I spent hundreds of dollars on cookbooks for menu ideas.

Days turned into weeks, and at long last our permits were approved. Bob left a message on my voice mail at the hotel saying we were officially licensed aliens. Our furniture from Vermont had passed through Miami and was on its way to Anguilla. There was no turning back now.

Shabby and his three brothers began demolition with Bob. They arrived daily with sledgehammers and crowbars, gutting the bathrooms and ripping out walls. The old boat that had previously been the bar was removed easily, thanks to the termites and Shabby's bulk and strength. One kick with his size-fourteen shoe, and it was reduced to a pile of sawdust and rotten boards.

Clinton, the youngest of the brothers, had music in his blood—everything from reggae to gospel. He couldn't stop humming and singing, and his body had a way of swiveling as if made of rubber. Always eager to jump into any task, he would pay close attention to Bob's instructions and then dance his way through the project.

At four o'clock each day Clinton prepared his dilapidated minibus for the drive home. He inspected all four bald tires, adding air to at least one with a bicycle pump. His thirsty radiator usually needed some water, and a gentle push started the engine, since the battery often wouldn't. The little bus appeared to be an extension of Clinton and was blessed with a similar sense of rhythm as it danced and wobbled down the road.

Our furniture arrived, and Bob spent several days unpacking boxes, trying to make the house comfortable. He was knee deep in Styrofoam peanuts when he heard a man in our yard yelling repeatedly, "Inside. Inside."

Bob opened the front door to investigate. The man stood grinning and barefoot, his bare belly hanging prominently over his tattered plaid shorts.

"Good afternoon. I Rigby. I lives next door," he said, pointing to a house under construction. Bob would have been surprised to hear that someone lived there had Joshua not explained why so many houses are unfinished in Anguilla.

Locals rarely borrowed money to build their homes. They usually did all the work themselves with the help of brothers, uncles, and cousins, and the project went only as fast as spare money became available. Trickle-down economics was truly visible here. Tourists spent money, and it flowed directly to Anguillian homes.

"Hi, Rigby. I'm Bob. My wife and I just moved in."

"I done made some fish *suup*." He pointed again toward his house where several men were doing the Anguilla sprawl on his porch.

Taking this as a dinner invitation, Bob followed Rigby over his gravelly yard, strewn with debris in various stages of decomposition. Pieces of plywood, half buried by rocks and sand, lay rotting beneath weeds and an entanglement of vines. The jagged terrain was no threat to Rigby's leathery feet; he walked nonchalantly over the rubble.

As the two men approached the porch Rigby bent down, picked up a rock, and threw it at a goat standing on the makeshift table next to the Coleman stove used for cooking. The rock missed the goat but connected with a battered aluminum pot, which fell off the table and clattered across the concrete floor. The startled goat jumped off the table and sauntered around the back of the house to lie down in the shade.

If built from stone instead of cement blocks, Rigby's house could easily have passed for a Roman ruin. Most of the structure had no roof, except the one room where Rigby lived. The rest was nothing but columns holding up blue sky. A rusty cement mixer sat in the middle of the future living room. Next to it, bags of cement were kept dry under a graying piece of plywood covered with overgrown weeds and sea-bean vines. Shovels, trowels, and buckets lay on the floor where they had been dropped at the end of the last building effort—always handy whenever Rigby again became inspired.

"Your house is coming right along," Bob said.

Rigby grunted. One of the other men lounging on the porch opened his eyes and said, "He ain' done much after he woman leave."

"Wife done went back Nevis," Rigby muttered. "Took all the furniture with she. Kids too."

"Sorry," Bob said, wondering where all the furniture had been in a house with no roof.

"Local fish *suup,*" Rigby said, proudly presenting Bob with a brimming bowl of clear liquid containing a large fish head. Bob stared at his bowl, and a fish eye stared back. Rigby continued ladling soup into various containers, making sure everyone got a head.

Bob sat down on an overturned plastic pail, trying to avoid eye contact with his soup. The man next to Bob sat on the edge of the porch, legs dangling over the side, slurping from the bowl and chewing on his fish head. He intermittently threw the fish bones into Rigby's yard, where several chickens had appeared and were joining the feast. They clucked and scratched at the ground, picking up bones and other tidbits as they were discarded from the porch.

Bob continued to stare at his soup until another of Rigby's guests spoke up. "Rigby, the man need a spoon." Rigby stopped drinking his soup and, with a fish head in one hand, passed Bob a large cooking spoon with the other. Bob was embarrassed by the special treatment.

He knew he had to eat the soup or risk offending his new neighbor. Raising the foot-long spoon to his lips, he held his breath and sipped the broth. It was surprisingly good—garlicky and a little spicy. But he didn't know what to do with the head. *There's no way I can eat that thing,* Bob thought as he continued to sip from the serving spoon.

Several of the men were helping themselves to seconds, and one came over to Bob with a full ladle, pouring it generously into his bowl.

"Thanks," Bob said.

"You ain' like the fish head?" he asked.

"I just haven't gotten to it yet." Bob pulled out a piece of white meat from behind the gills and popped it into his mouth. It wasn't bad except for the bones. He chewed, trying to separate bones from meat and tossed them off the edge of the porch like the rest of the men.

Rigby disappeared, emerging a minute later with a half-gallon jug of Mt. Gay in one hand and a stack of paper cups in the other, and began filling the cups with rum.

"Not too much for me, Rigby," Bob said, again hoping not to offend anyone.

"I take he other half," the man next to Bob spoke up.

All but one very large man had finished eating, and Bob watched as he struggled to his feet and helped himself to more. He stood at the soup pot searching with the ladle for fish heads, finally giving up and filling his bowl with more broth. After plunking down in his place and polishing off the soup, he turned to Rigby and said, "Rigby, I still hungry. What for dessert?"

"Ain' got no dessert," Rigby replied. "Drink yo' rum."

"I have some dessert," Bob offered, remembering the coconut sorbet he had made the day before. He was going to surprise me by testing several recipes in our new ice cream maker. He hopped off the porch, causing the chickens to scatter, and made his way across the piles of junk and into our yard. He removed the tub of sorbet from the freezer, spooned it into the glasses we had bought on St. Martin, and pulled a loose shelf out of a kitchen cupboard to use as a tray.

"Ice cream?" the hungry man asked Bob. "I loves ice cream."

"Got any spoons?" Bob inquired, realizing he should have brought those too.

"No man, jess the one you was usin'," Rigby answered, taking a long swig of Mt. Gay.

"I'll get some," Bob said, and he ran to the house, hoping to return before the sorbet reduced to a puddle. On his way back to Rigby's with a fistful of spoons, Bob suddenly remembered an East Hampton wedding we had attended at a magnificent beach house surrounded by lush green lawns and immaculately trimmed hedges. Several hundred of New York's most discerning, dressed in beachy fashions, gracefully plucked smoked salmon and caviar canapés from silver trays; waiters in black and white glided quietly through the crowd with champagne. Bob smiled, picturing wedding tents set up in Rigby's rocky yard, where the goats could try the canapés. He was honored to be sharing fish *suup* with these men.

Rigby and his friends couldn't wait for the spoons. They were making short work of the sorbet, and as Bob climbed up to join them the fat man offered a glass and said with a smile, "Piña colada." As Bob took the glass, he realized they had poured the Mt. Gay over the coconut sorbet and were all enjoying tropical drinks. After finishing his piña colada, Bob went home and called to tell me about his first Anguilla dinner party.

Jesse's semester ended and he joined me in Florida, where he was quickly immersed into the trucking business. We still had eight vanloads to be taken to the loading dock, invoiced for customs, and shrink-wrapped on wooden pallets to be handled by forklifts. It took us three days—lugging, documenting, and packing. We were quite a spectacle: mother and son packing tons of restaurant equipment and Rubbermaid plastic containers on skids.

After almost a month of marathon shopping, I longed for the beach in front of our restaurant. I couldn't wait to get out of the traffic and away from the malls and superstores. Even our bunker of a house in Anguilla seemed to me a paradise compared to a Marriott in Florida. Jesse and I made a pact to spend a day relaxing in the sun as soon as we arrived on the island, before jumping into construction.

I was nervous about the amount of luggage we had, but when we reached the check-in for San Juan I remembered that flights to Puerto Rico always pushed their baggage capacity to the limit. An unruly crowd of people, apparently returning home after a visit to the States, jostled and shoved, trying to reach the counter first. Huge cardboard boxes and oversized suitcases held together with duct tape were being skidded toward the scale; many were overweight and needed to be opened and repacked. They had boom boxes, TVs, camcorders, computers, tools, hair dryers, clothes, toys, and even plumbing parts. The man ahead of us was trying to send a toilet through as baggage, and the ticket agent flatly refused. He dragged his toilet off to the side and moved to a new line, hoping to get it aboard with someone more lenient.

We checked in amongst a throng of screaming children hauling giant carnival-like stuffed animals and wearing Disney World shirts and Mickey Mouse hats. The mob scene continued at the gate, despite the announcement to board by seat number only. As soon as the flight number to Puerto Rico was announced, all three hundred people leapt from their seats and jammed into the boarding area. After every square inch of storage space on the plane was crammed full and the zealous mob forced to sit down, we were finally ready to depart. Jesse and I slept the whole flight, waking to the traditional roar of applause as the plane touched down in San Juan. It always made us laugh.

The small American Eagle flight to Anguilla was momentous; for the first time, we were not arriving as tourists, but going home. Bob was waiting at the airport, anxious to surprise us with the car he had bought for $2,500. After hugs and kisses, we wheeled the luggage out to the parking lot and up to the smallest automobile I'd ever seen.

"Where's the rental jeep?" I asked.

"This is our new car," Bob said proudly. "It's a Suzuki—ten years old, but runs like a charm. The hatchback gives us a *little* extra room for hauling things around." It gleamed in the sunlight from a fresh coat of wax, even though the red paint was a little faded here and there.

"I love it," I said.

"It's cute, Dad," Jesse added generously.

We had trouble fitting our luggage in, but as we drove away I exhaled a long sigh of relief. Bumbling along at 25 mph in our tiny car was far more agreeable than defending myself at 75 mph on Interstate 95. The briny smell of a salt pond drifted in through the open windows, and I felt every strand of muscle in my body relax.

"Let's go to the beach," I said.

We ran in the house, rooted through piles of boxes for bathing suits and towels, and drove to Meads Bay. The afternoon sun was still scorchingly hot, and Jesse and Bob dove into the water to cool off. I watched as a split-tailed frigate bird circled lazily, coasting on the wind currents somewhere way, way over my head. The waves rolled in against the beach, continuing their gentle but relentless foray, as if the grains of sand forever needed reorganizing. Covered with suntan lotion, safe upon my towel, my eyes closed as I surrendered to the rhythm of the sea.

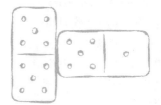

Chapter 4

ISLAND TIME. It slowed our heartbeats and eased our blood pressure. In this easy-glide rhythm, stress evaporated—things worked themselves out. We had pictured ourselves propped against a sprawling shade tree, eyes half shut, the world turning slowly under us as it has for millions of years and probably will for just as long.

Slowing to this tempo was not as easy as it looked. Our containers had arrived, but they were padlocked by customs. Tippy the customs broker was an expert at clearing containers and promised to have our entry completed in just a few days. After a week, not only had he neglected to call us, but he was nowhere to be found. His girlfriend, tired of our increasingly panicky calls, finally directed us to the domino game under the mahogany tree by Ashley's Grocery. Sure enough, there was Tippy playing dominos.

"I was gonna call you this afternoon," he said as he shook our hands.

"Tippy," Bob began, "where's our entry? It's been a week. You said a couple of days."

"Too mucha pages," he said. "An I ain' know what all this stuff is made of."

"What do you mean, made of?" I asked, following him to his car, where he handed us the stack of invoices we had given him from which to calculate the duty.

"You gotta say what everything here made of." He held up the mile-long cash register tape from Home Depot. "See this?" He pointed to the first item. "What this is?"

"Fencing . . . eight hundred twenty-six dollars," I read out loud.

"But what's it *made* of?" Tippy insisted.

"It's a wooden fence," Bob said.

"Okay, you gotta write down what every item in that container is made of. The dishes: pottery or china? Wine racks: metal or wood? If they's metal, what kind? Brass, aluminum, or what? See, everything gets charged at a different percentage."

We stared in disbelief at the hundreds of items on the receipts. "You have to be kidding," I said.

"Customs don't kid about nothin'," Tippy said. "They pretty serious fellas. You got a lotta papers here—this gonna take a lotta carbon paper."

"Carbon paper!" I lost it. "You can do all this on a computer, right?"

"No, man. Customs makes you show all your figuring in long division on a separate paper. And they makes you fill out all the forms in triplicate using carbon paper." He handed all the receipts back to me, said to bring them back when everything had been identified, and returned to the domino game.

We stayed up until four in the morning, trying to reconstruct everything I'd purchased. Home Depot receipts were time-consuming but fairly easy. We just had to decipher their cash register codes for each item. Some purchases, however, were not as straightforward. It wasn't clear how to categorize artwork, for example. Was it made of paper? Or did we have to note the material of the frame? And what about the chairs—did the total cost get separated between the rattan and the seat cushion, or was it just counted as a chair? And what about the brass tacks where the fabric was upholstered? And was the cushion stuffed with foam or polyester? We had no idea and could picture the customs officials tearing a chair apart to determine its contents. We broke everything down as much as we could and labeled every receipt with a thorough description.

Tippy's stellar reputation as a customs broker was nothing compared to his fame as a domino player. Clearly the game had priority, and though he assured us that progress was being made on the paperwork, he could always be found under his favorite tree. Our containers remained padlocked in front of the restaurant while Bob and the Davis brothers sulked around aimlessly with no materials. Tippy played dominos.

In Anguilla, the game of dominos requires only a table, something to sit on, a set of dominos, and, most important, shade. A domino tree is centrally located in almost every village, strategically placed where taxi drivers congregate, in front of a grocery store or even at a gas station. The game's popularity is understandable in the eighty-five-degree weather, and besides, it's easier to drink a Heineken while playing dominos than, say, soccer.

But it is serious sport. There are week-long domino tournaments. There are domino teams with uniforms. There are traveling domino teams that fly or boat to other islands, claiming international trophies.

I used to think dominos was an easygoing diversion in which players ponder a move and quietly place their pieces on the table in an orderly, even reserved, fashion. Not in Anguilla.

The technique for slamming is highly developed and practiced. Dominos are discreetly hidden in one hand—held like playing cards—and once a play has been determined, the chosen piece is raised slowly above the table, as if the player were sneaking up to assassinate a fly. Once this slow, methodical arm raising has created sufficient suspense, *bam*—the domino is slapped down on the table, often with enough force to bounce the pieces several inches in the air.

The exuberance and gusto with which the pieces are slammed down actually makes it a lively spectator sport. Heated games often last long into the night, with small crowds of anxious onlookers waiting to get a turn. Sometimes several tables are lined up in a row and players rotate between games. Bets are placed, money changes hands, and the slamming rhythm intensifies as the stakes rise. Instead of a throbbing head from too much partying, a domino champion wakes the next morning with a throbbing hand.

Finally, after two more weeks, Tippy had finished the entry and I went to the treasury to pay the duty. The outdoor waiting area was filled with people waiting in lines at various windows as if buying tickets at Grand Central Station. Instead of destinations such as Boston or Philadelphia, the signs over each window read DRIVER'S LICENSES, STAMP DUTY, TAXES, MAIN CASHIER, ANGUILLA NATIONAL LOTTERY, and, over mine, CUSTOMS DUTIES. This was where the island did its business—everyone came here at one time or another. In line with me was a barefoot fisherman, a heavyset man in a business suit, and a smartly dressed young woman with a Cap Juluca name tag on her jacket.

"I'm here to pay the duty on the Blanchard's shipment," I said to the woman behind the glass window.

"You got a real Sears catalog here," the woman said as she began stripping staples from the two-inch-thick bundle of papers that Tippy had assembled for her. She separated pink from blue from yellow, stamped them all furiously, and initialed each stamp. She slid one copy out through the slot in the window, apparently for me to examine, and I asked if I was paying in U.S. or E.C.

"That'll be $26,240 U.S.," she said, "or $70,323 E.C. Take your pick."

After I had caught my breath again, I slid the check under the window and asked, "Now, how do I get the containers unlocked?"

"You have to call and make an appointment for the field agents to inspect the merchandise as you unload it."

"But I wasn't going to unload everything until we need it. The stuff will just be in the way."

"Once the containers are opened, you have to take everything out so customs can check it against the entry," she explained patiently. "You can put it all back if you want." I drove away trying to think of a way to break this news to Bob. He would not be happy about spending a whole day unloading the containers, only to load them again.

The field agent couldn't come until the next day, and I knew once Bob got his hands on the lumber, there'd be no more free time—so we took a beach walk while we still could. At Maunday's Bay, where Cap Juluca's white villas stretch its entire length, the sand is flat and hard and the water is calm, shallow, and extra green. Bob, Jesse, and I left our shoes in the car and walked the mile-long beach with our feet in the water, watching sand crabs scurry into their holes as we approached. Across the channel, St. Martin's verdant mountains poked up out of the sea, and to the west, the extinct volcano that is the island of Saba rose majestically 2,900 feet, its head in the clouds. Resort guests were sunning on lounge chairs in front of their villas and a beach attendant was offering them small cups of lemon sorbet for an afternoon cool-down. Another attendant passed with a tray of cold washcloths, which people lazily spread out on their parched faces and tummies.

"It just hit me," Bob said, "that all these people might really come to our restaurant. Look at them. You know, this is a tough crowd. These people are used to the finest restaurants in the world."

"You sound a little nervous, Dad," Jesse said. "Don't you *want* them to come?"

"Of course I want them to come. But did you see that woman who just passed us with the big white Gucci sunglasses? She's not gonna be easy to please, you know."

The restaurant slowly began to take shape. With the customs ordeal behind us and the containers beginning to empty, we settled into a daily schedule of construction and landscaping. We worked from dawn to dusk seven days a week, taking dips in the sea to cool off—sometimes hourly. The heat was unrelenting. I had always loved long days reading a good book on the beach. The sun's soothing warmth had felt like a massage. But working under it for twelve hours was quite another thing. We knew now why the locals craved shade.

I did much of the gardening in my bathing suit, and my skin quickly took on an Anguillian hue—Clinton teased me about looking as dark as a local. Bob went through quarts of sunblock, and after the first few weeks of redness even he began to bronze. We learned how to pace ourselves to get through the day; we consumed gallons of water and came to respect the slower, unhurried, but deliberate tempo of the Davis brothers.

The landscaping transformation was magical. Tangled, overgrown vines were replaced with white beach lilies, pink oleander, ferns, palms, yucca, and bougainvillea in pale yellow, apricot, and fuchsia. A huge, gangly sea grape was pruned and converted into a generous shade tree; wart fern carpeted the ground beneath it. We laid a stone path that wound its way under the sprawling branches of the sea grape and down to the beach. A picket fence bordered the gardens near the front entrance, and within only a few weeks, the bougainvillea's creeping vines were weaving in and out of the white boards, spilling over on both sides of the fence with bunches of contented blossoms. We planted two lime trees in hopes of providing juice for daiquiris at the bar. A bed of allamanda sent leggy stalks skyward, with large yellow flowers that popped open at the end of each, and a bed of Mexican firecracker grew like a weed, covering itself with tiny red buds.

The owner of the nursery in Florida where I had bought the plants gave me his only rule for gardening in the tropics. The recipe was simple, the man said: "Just add water and bake." The reliable Anguilla sun easily handled the baking. Water was the problem. A rare and precious commodity, water was in short supply. June and July had brought no rain. To fill our cistern from the island's desalinization plant took three truckloads of water—about 7,500 gallons—and cost us $300. Our thirsty garden drained the cistern and our checkbook every five days. Shabby and Clinton watched with mild disapproval as we diligently drenched the ground surrounding the restaurant. We had created a garden monster.

The Davis brothers were skilled masons but enjoyed learning to build with wood as much as Bob liked being educated in the local patois. But Rocky, the oldest brother, needed more translation than the others. Perhaps he watched less TV, or maybe he had less contact with tourists; whatever it was, Rocky's conversations were impossible to interpret. "Busithoffhelongtoo," he said with lightning speed, handing Bob a piece of wood.

As Bob continued to stare blankly, Rocky slowed down a little. "Busit hoff he long too."

Clinton translated. "Bust it in half, he want it shorter."

Shabby chimed in. "He wants you to cut that piece of wood for him. It's too long."

The days were hard and hot, and we couldn't bear the thought of cooking dinner. We became regulars at a local barbecue place half a mile up the road. Bernice was the proprietor of this low-budget, backyard operation made up of a homemade grill like the one we'd cooked our lunch on in Barbados years ago, a fryer, three plastic tables, and an Igloo cooler filled with ice-covered drinks. Extension cords stretched overhead to several bare lightbulbs that dangled from the fronds of a palm tree swinging in the breeze.

When we arrived, the grill would be heaped with ribs and chicken legs, and the island staple, rice and peas, was always simmering in a slow cooker on a nearby plywood table. Bernice, in her oversized Calvin Klein T-shirt, wielded a cleaver in one hand and a family-sized bottle of Kraft barbecue sauce in the other. There was no need to advertise here: a big speed bump in the main road in front of Bernice's house did the job. Each passing car—after much tooting and waving—slowed to a crawl to clear the bump, getting a whiff of the smoky barbecue aroma. Madison Avenue couldn't have created a better marketing campaign.

I loved gardening and helping with the construction. The menu was beginning to scare me, however—especially when I pictured the fashionable and unforgiving crowd that might be waiting to test my culinary skills. I was familiar with their expectations, having eavesdropped on nearby tables in the Malliouhana dining room. Firmly believing that the entire kitchen staff was at their personal disposal, diners would ask, "Would the chef mind terribly preparing something special for my wife tonight? Tell him it's for Mrs. Lawrence. She has a craving for veal piccata; make sure he pounds it extra thin, though. Be a dear and see what he can do."

I knew it was time to stop playing in the dirt and turn my attention to food. Comfortably settled on the couch in our living room, I surrounded myself with dozens of my favorite cookbooks, restaurant menus amassed over the years, and piles of *Bon Appetit* and

Gourmet magazines. Four blank pads of paper were neatly lined up on the coffee table—one each for appetizers, salads, main courses, and desserts.

I poured through hundreds of recipes, sorting, studying, evaluating, and choosing those worthy of a trial run. I rejected any dishes with heavy sauces and time-intensive reductions, while those with fresh salsas and flavorful herbs and spices went on my test list. Desserts required sublists for baked, frozen, fruit, and chocolate.

Fascinating articles about food trends distracted me, though I don't think of myself as trendy. Food, however, is an *entirely* different story. I will go to great lengths to taste something new. *Extreme* lengths. When the day came to send Jesse off to college, we could have bought him a plane ticket from Vermont to Walla Walla, Washington. Instead, the three of us drove over three thousand miles on back roads. You miss everything at 70 mph, and fast food along the interstates was of no interest to us. Following tiny gray lines on the map, we meandered across the country for almost a month tasting the regional foods of America. We arrived at Jesse's dorm five pounds heavier, having sampled our way from New England to the Pacific Northwest. We can tell you where to get melt-in-your-mouth biscuits with fresh peach preserves in Memphis, the finest barbecue in San Antonio, the crustiest sourdough in San Francisco, and a wondrous cedar-smoked salmon in Seattle.

Food is an obsession, perhaps even an addiction, that started in seventh grade when I would rush home to watch Julia Child prepare beef bourguignon. Her enthusiasm was contagious. Creating the menu for my own restaurant in Anguilla made me feel like Julia. I was inspired just reading recipes for chili-crusted sea scallops and Jamaican jerk sauce. Lists evolved day by day.

The testing began. Thomas was kind enough to bring me several lobsters that arrived in a lively, squirming burlap bag. I peeked inside, debating the best form of attack. What is it about lobsters, anyway? In Maine they have vicious claws that snap at your fingers.

These had no claws but were completely covered with spines and were just as treacherous to handle. With two giant oven mitts, I grasped the first creature by the antennae and lowered it gingerly into a pot. Scalding water showered the kitchen, but I bravely emptied the bag.

I rolled out dough for dumplings—very thin so they'd be tender, almost transparent, when cooked—and cut them into circles. With the lobster meat cooled and diced, I added wild mushrooms, shallots, ginger, and a tiny bit of goat cheese to hold the mixture together. I dropped a spoonful of filling into the center of each circle and crimped the edges into little half-moons ready for steaming. I glazed the tiny bundles with fresh lemon juice, more ginger, a little garlic, a spoonful of sugar, and some soy sauce. The first batch didn't have enough lobster, the next had too much lemon. My crimping technique slowly improved. Sometimes the dough would tear or the egg used to seal the dough wouldn't stick. But after repeated attempts I had perfected my first appetizer.

The Caribbean is known for its jerk sauce, and I tested eight different recipes before concocting my own variation. The final list of eighteen ingredients included ten different herbs and spices, fresh lime and orange juice, and that hottest of hot peppers, habaneros. Those fiery little devils came in a rainbow of colors, which I initially suspected might reveal their level of heat, but I was wrong—they were all hotter than hell. My eyes watered and burned; my fingertips were on fire for days.

Grilled Tuna with Coconut Rice Cakes

My love of Asian food prompted me to come up with an easy marinade for grilled tuna served with crispy coconut rice cakes. For two recipes so easy, the contrast of flavors and texture was a great discovery.

Make the rice cakes first. You will need a jelly-roll pan approximately 10 by 15 inches. In a saucepan, bring 7½ cups water and 1½ cups unsweetened coconut milk to a boil. Add 1½ teaspoons salt and 4½ cups jasmine rice. Cover and reduce heat to very low. Cook for 20 minutes or until liquid is absorbed. Transfer rice to a bowl and stir in 4 minced scallions and ¼ cup toasted sesame seeds. Press mixture firmly into jelly-roll pan. I cover it with plastic wrap and use a rolling pin to make it even and compact. Chill well. When ready to serve, cut into 3-inch squares and then in half into triangles. Brush with olive oil, dust with bread crumbs, and sauté until golden brown on both sides. Makes 30 triangles.

Have 6 tuna steaks cut 2 inches thick so it's easy to cook them rare. Marinate the fish for about an hour in 1¼ cups teriyaki sauce, ⅓ cup cooking sherry, 1 tablespoon minced ginger, 4 minced scallions, 1 teaspoon minced garlic, ¼ teaspoon cayenne pepper, ½ teaspoon black pepper, and 2 tablespoons fresh lemon juice. Grill quickly over hot coals and serve immediately. Serves six.

Grilled whole snapper on a bed of sauteed corn and spinach with Thai curry sauce; smoked salmon bundles filled with crab salad and a lemon-chive crème fraîche; crispy coconut prawns with homemade apricot chutney; lemon-buttermilk pound cake topped with homemade vanilla bean ice cream and fresh berries; mangoes and cream with cinnamon and a little brown sugar . . . relentless trial and error. Bob and Jesse eagerly sampled everything, arriving nightly with ambitious appetites, ready to evaluate my latest experiments.

I took a break one afternoon to give Betsy and Gary an update. I longed for our weekly dinners together in Vermont and thought a letter might help assuage my homesickness.

Greetings from paradise,

Thanks for the water balloons. I'm using them for a dessert we dubbed "cracked coconut." I make a mold by rolling the bottom half of the balloon around in melted chocolate, cover it with toasted coconut, and let it harden. Then I pop the balloon and the remaining chocolate shell looks exactly like half a coconut. I fill it with coconut ice cream and surround it with Kahlúa custard sauce and another shell is propped on top, so it looks like it was just cracked open. Lots of work—sometimes I think I've cracked—but the end result is so much fun I couldn't pass it up.

Today I'm trying to thicken some corn chowder without using cream. I think I'll try pureeing some of the corn and see if it's the right consistency. Last night we grilled local lobsters with olive oil and Cajun spices—also, grilled pineapple slices sprinkled with cinnamon. Wish you could have joined us!

My biggest problem is getting ingredients. Luckily, the French side of St. Martin has some wonderful gourmet shops, but I have trouble translating words like **sesame** *and* **beets** *into French. I'm in pretty good shape now, but if you could send some Chinese dumpling wrappers, that would be great. Don't forget to include a receipt for customs. Otherwise I'll never get them out of the warehouse.*

Don't forget about us down here—keep in touch!

Love,
Mel

Bob, Jesse, and I tasted for weeks. We brushed grilled bananas with Myers's rum, compared the virtues of regular chicken to free-range, and one night, we sampled fourteen flavors of ice cream and sorbet. We had regular discussions about how many spicy dishes we should serve, and whether or not pasta was too mundane.

Rum Punch

We tasted rum punches around the island and worked together to create the perfect mixture. Some, we agreed, were too sweet and bright red with grenadine. Others didn't have the fresh taste we were looking for. Guava juice, we discovered, was the missing ingredient from most we tried, and freshly squeezed orange juice was a must. Still, our final recipe was simple.

Combine equal amounts of pineapple juice, guava juice, freshly squeezed orange juice, and Mt. Gay rum. Add just a dash of grenadine and another of Angostura bitters. Pour over ice and top with a sprinkle of nutmeg.

The menu evolved into a collection of foods we fancied, impossible to categorize—no simple label would describe our cuisine. This, in the weeks to come, became a sore point. "What kind of food will you serve? French? Italian?" everyone asked. I had no choice but to list everything on the menu.

Working at a table on our porch, I created a complete ingredient list of produce, meat, fish, and dairy, detailing one recipe at a time. The number of items needed was formidable. Shading my eyes from the blinding sun, I watched a barefoot man walking by carrying a machete and eating a banana. If his pace were any slower, he would have been standing still. No hurry. No stress. *That man couldn't care less about portobello mushrooms and goat cheese,* I thought. Beyond him, I heard the sound of dominos slapping down on the table at the gas station. Had I been on vacation, it might be a charming neighborhood scene. Instead, it sent a wave of terror right through me. *Look where we are, for God's sake! How on earth are we going to get what we need to run this restaurant? I can't continue running to St. Martin and paying gourmet shop prices.* Shaking my head, I went back inside, plopped down on the couch, and called Bob.

"Hi. We're sanding the floor in the bar. How's it going there?"

I could tell he wanted to get back to the bar floor, but I needed to talk. "Bob, I'm afraid we might be in trouble. I can't imagine where we're going to get these ingredients. I think we might have really lost our heads this time."

Bob assured me we'd figure it out. I told him I was going into The Valley to see what I could find, and we agreed to have lunch at Cap Juluca when I was done.

It was a magnificent day—the sky was a brilliant blue, all the windows were down in the car, and the air temperature felt neither hot nor cold. My first stop was going to be easy. Following directions to Glenford's Dairy, I parked in front of a building that looked like it *used* to be Glenford's. The painted sign on the building had faded from the sun, and the yard was empty except for a family of goats dining on scattered trash.

A man poked his head out the door. "Good morning," I began. "My husband and I are opening a restaurant and I was hoping to get a price list—"

"Price list finish," he interrupted.

"Well," I said calmly, "when do you think you might have another price list?"

"What are you looking for?" he asked.

I showed him my list and he said he could special-order anything I wanted from St. Thomas. "I gonna back-check my supplier and see what he say." But he was pretty sure it would take two to three weeks for all my special requests. Right now, though, all he had was milk.

The rest of the morning continued in the same manner. I tried all the grocery stores in search of ingredients. They actually had a few things I needed, some shredded coconut and basics, like salt and sugar, but the prices were prohibitive in small retail packages. And the meat was not even a consideration. There was no beef or lamb, and the chicken was in yellow cardboard boxes labeled GRADE C.

I went to see Joshua and Evelyn, which turned out to be my most successful stop. They had gallons of extra-virgin olive oil, canned juices for the bar, huge packages of paper towels, and a surprising number of the odds and ends on my list. I loved spending time with them, so I sat for a while and gave them an update on our progress and listened to their latest news.

"Gloria big, you know," said Evelyn. "She makin' a baby."

"How many grandchildren will you have then?" I asked.

"Over forty," she said, and began counting with her fingers in her lap. "Carroll the mechanic, he have six by his wife and four out of the marriage. Lincoln, the one at the airport, he have two. Bernice, she have two, and Vernal, he have a next one."

Just then, two of the forty came racing out of the kitchen. Amalia and Kim-Misha were chasing each other, laughing hysterically, and interrupted Evelyn's tally. "Them disgusting li'l childrens," she said with undeniable affection. "Them keepin' me full speed."

Three generations filled her house with energy and love. She couldn't fathom my life as an only child, visiting grandparents on occasional weekends and holidays. She hugged me with her large black arms. Joshua called out as I was leaving, "Daughter, don't work too hard. Even the Lord rested on the seventh day."

I stopped at the market on the way back. Envisioning cartloads of tropical fruits and vegetables, I expected to become friendly with the local women selling produce and spend time learning about things such as guava and breadfruit. Dreamland. A few robust women were surrounded by piles of boxes filled with mangoes, lemons, pineapples, squash, and potatoes. But there were no peppers, tomatoes, onions, lettuce, berries, or papayas. One woman explained their produce came by boat from Santo Domingo every two weeks and I should come back on Thursday for a better selection. *If the restaurant was open now,* I thought, *how could I wait for produce until next Thursday?*

Over lunch at Cap Juluca I recounted the morning's events to Bob. "So basically," I said, "I found no fish, no dairy, no meat, and no produce. Oh, actually, I did have a little luck. Joshua had olive oil and vinegar," I added.

"Great," he said sarcastically. "We can make salad dressings again."

"At least this time," I said, "we have a view. Look where we are. *This* is the place for a board meeting." We were fifty feet from the water, surrounded by tanned people in bathing suits, sitting under a Moroccan-style tent. We ordered a salad with shrimp and avocado and a grilled swordfish sandwich and wondered where the ingredients came from. Our spirited waiter, whose name tag introduced him as Wayne, was extremely accommodating when we asked about the food. He brought George, the chef, out to meet us. George was delightful—a young Anguillian eager to make great food and just as willing to share his purchasing secrets with us. "You gotta go off island for this stuff, man," he said, so I made a list. He gave us names of suppliers in St. Martin and Miami, and we left feeling as though we had finally broken some sort of code. The puzzle was not solved, but at least the pieces were coming together.

Leaving Cap Juluca, we followed a truck haphazardly loaded with used air conditioners and cardboard boxes. Three men were in the back of the truck holding on for dear life, arms stretched wide to keep their cargo in place. A box of nails tumbled onto the road, immediately giving us a flat tire next to a salt pond. Bob and I got out of the car to change the tire.

"It's fluffing," I said. "It's like a gigantic outdoor bubble bath."

"What?" said Bob distractedly as he searched for the jack.

"It's fluffing," I repeated. "The pond is fluffing." Bob looked at me like I was crazy, and while he loosened the lug nuts, I tried to figure out why all the white balls were blowing off the pond. A family of ducks swam in circles, and dozens of orange-legged birds darted in and out of the tangled roots against the shore. Large, sudsy balls were breezing past us, but Bob didn't appreciate my jokes about being in the middle of a Caribbean snowstorm. He was hot and sweaty from changing the tire and anxious to get back to work.

Clinton and Shabby were building shelves in the coffee area when we returned and I told them about the "fluffing."

"Mel," Shabby said. "That's salt."

"Salt?"

"Haven't you seen salt ponds all over the island?" Clinton asked. "Until 'bout fifteen years ago, they harvest salt outta the ponds and ship it all over the Caribbean—even England. It was how everybody earn a living here before we had tourists. When you see the foam it mean the pond ripe for pickin. It mean there's plenty of salt."

"What did they do, collect all these bubbles and dry them out?"

"Mel. You wanna hear about pickin' the ponds, you gotta talk to Mammy. She work in the ponds for years, and she love to talk."

Just then Mac stopped by in his taxi to ask if we could find a job at the restaurant for his girlfriend, Garrilin. When I told him to bring her by, he said, "She right outside in the van."

My first "interview" thus took place on a pile of lumber. Garrilin and I talked easily—more about our families than work experience or references. I could tell by her stories that she had the gift of gab—in a matter of minutes, I learned her sister was about to get married in Nevis and her little niece was getting straight A's in school. I showed her the menu. "I ain' know what most a this stuff is," she said, "but if you show me what to do, I can do it."

Still curious about the salt ponds, I asked Garrilin if she knew Mammy.

"Yeah, man. Everyone know Mammy. You wanna meet her? We go see Mammy together. The onliest thing is I can't go today. How tomorrow?"

Garrilin gave me directions to Mammy's house and told me to meet her there at ten o'clock the next day.

Clinton stopped hammering and stroked his chin as if deep in thought when I asked where we could find fresh fish. "Mel," he said, "Island Harbor. That where the fish be." He chugged some water out of a nearby Evian bottle. "The fishermen all be up there every afternoon. You go Island Harbor four o'clock and there be all kinds a fish. Ask for Cleve—he a big-time fisherman. He caught the big fish you see hangin' in the airport."

Later that afternoon we drove the island from west to east, tip to tip. We always loved this little excursion. The eastern end was wilder, less developed. There were no hotels, no real landmarks, just an occasional sign denoting the tiny villages: Water Swamp, Little Dix, Shoal Bay, Canafist. Most villages had a church, and we passed an occasional grocery store and other home businesses where signs read LICENSE PLATES MADE HERE, ALTERATIONS, and the most popular, ISLAND TOURS. As unhurried as life was in our western end of the island, here it slowed even more.

Island Harbor is the quintessential fishing village: small boats painted bright primary colors and varnished to a glossy sheen, little boys helping their fathers unload the day's catch, women haggling over the price of snapper, clear green water ribboned with white foam where the coral reefs broke the surface.

There was much to see, though the scene was not a flurry of activity. The fishermen were calmly going about their routine, unaware of the romantic picture they painted. Cleve wore no shoes, only a hat and old shorts, and like the other fisherman, he was anchoring his boat for the night. When Bob asked him about fish, he introduced us immediately to his brother. Between the two of them, he assured us, they could supply us with all the fish we wanted. Wahoo, tuna, snapper, mahimahi—as soon as we gave them the word, they'd deliver fish to our door.

"Success," I said as we drove back to the bustle of the west end. "Fresh fish anytime we want, and delivered to the restaurant." I was eager to start cooking.

Garrilin and I pulled into the parking lot of the old clinic in South Hill just before ten o'clock. She nodded toward an older woman hanging shirts on a clothesline at the house next door and said, "That Mammy. She gonna tell you all about pickin' the pond."

Mammy Garrilin and I sat on the porch. Soon Mammy's sister joined us, explaining that she too worked in the pond. I wasn't sure where to begin, so I asked how many years they had picked the salt.

"I mussa wen' in the pond from twelve years," Mammy said. "Me and my mother, we used to get caps on our fingers. The salt done burn, ya know. It cut your hands. We tie pieces a old bicycle tubes on our fingers or sometimes we wrap our hands with cloth. Anything to keep the salt from burnin'."

I winced at the description but by then Mammy and her sister were enjoying the memories.

"Me and my mother," Mammy continued, "we walk down the hill to the pond at Sandy Ground. It too hot in the sun, so sometimes we go down from midnight and make day. We work all night long. I had love the fun of it. We walk out in the pond and the water come up over my hips when I was young."

Mammy's sister continued. "We scoop up chunks of salt with our hands and puts 'em in a basket and carries 'em over to these big wooden boxes. We call 'em flats. Inside the flats they had maybe eighteen small barrels line up."

Mammy interrupted. "We rinse off the chunks a salt in the water and a fella would liff me up so I can throw 'em in the barrels. Some flats have up to nine, ten, eleven people working on 'em, and we share up the shillings for the work when done. I remember when I make nineteen shillings for the week. The salt would cover my skin. And man, you couldn't sit down in the pond. If you fall down an' the salt get all through your body, it burn you up.

Sometimes when we fall we have to run to the sea to freshen. If it real bad we run all the way home to wash it even more.

"Once the flats was full with salt, I done put a cutter on my head and carry the barrels out to the salt heap onshore." Mammy's sister could see I had no idea what a cutter was and dashed into the house for a visual aid, returning with an old threadbare towel she twirled expertly into a series of concentric rings. It looked like a terry-cloth coil. She placed it on her head, demonstrating how they used to tie it on with string, and patted the top, showing me how it protected her from the weight of the barrels.

"The salt heap would get high, high, high, and we shovel it into bags and sew them closed. Then we put the bags on our heads and walk out into the sea. There was no wharf back then, and we had to take it out to the boat that would carry it away. Oh, yes, we had fun. Sometime we get no sleep a'tall. We walk back up the hill from Sandy Ground and jus' go home, rinse our clothes, bathe our skin, and walk to the pond in West End. Then we fill more flats the same way again."

Garrilin enjoyed the history lesson as much as I did. After we left I pulled out a towel from my car, twirled it into a cutter, and placed it on top of my head. Garrilin put a book on the towel, and I walked around balancing it carefully and imagining carrying a heavy pail of salt instead. "You could do it, man," she said. "You could work the pond with Mammy."

September 10 and it was time for Jesse to go back to school. He and I spent the morning together, packing and talking at home.

"Mom, I know this probably isn't the best time to say this, but I've been thinking about transferring. I'm not sure Whitman College is really where I want to be."

"Now? Don't classes start in a couple of days?"

"I wouldn't be able to do it this semester, but I just don't know if it's the right place for me."

"Is there some problem that I don't know about?" I was starting to get worried.

"No. No problem. There just aren't any classes I want to take except art, and I think I might be happier at a bigger school." His voice was soft and quiet, and I could tell he was upset. This was no minor issue.

My heart sank, and my stomach was tied in knots. We had spent the past three months together every single day, but Jesse hadn't mentioned school until now, just hours before his flight. It was as if he had been waiting for exactly the right moment, and when it never came, he finally just blurted it out.

I felt like the worst parent on earth. Jesse had devoted his entire summer vacation helping us get our new Anguilla lives in order, planning and building. Bob and I had been totally consumed with the restaurant and hadn't realized Jesse was going through his own crisis. We sorted his clothes and packed in silence for a few minutes until Jesse changed the subject. "Let me know how the opening goes," he said quietly.

And then it hit me. Tears trickled down my cheeks as I realized we would be far away from each other. Jesse had adored the summer's adventures, learning to build with Bob and exploring this wonderful little country with me. I could tell he was sad about leaving.

"The opening is still weeks away," I finally said. "We'll talk a lot before then. Jesse, we can't let the distance change how close we are. You can call us anytime, day or night, about anything whatsoever. And I'll keep you posted on everything that happens here. I promise."

We had already agreed that flying from Walla Walla to Anguilla for Thanksgiving would not be practical. The connections were bad, and by the time Jesse got here it would be almost time to leave. It would be our first holiday apart, but he assured us that he wouldn't be alone and would have plenty of invitations from friends for turkey dinner. Being so far away was going to take some adjustment for all of us. Jesse was growing up, and our moving to Anguilla didn't make it any easier.

Jesse and I picked up Bob for the trip to the airport and drove without much conversation. American Eagle took off, and I cried hard. Bob and I went home for the afternoon and spent the rest of the day tracking Jesse's journey. First San Juan, then Chicago, then Seattle; finally, twelve hours later, he called to say he was safe and sound in his room at school. "Say hi to Clinton and Shabby and everyone for me," he reminded us.

"Call us tomorrow," Bob said. "We want to know what classes you end up getting."

"Okay. I love you."

"We love you too. Sleep well."

Bob and I anguished over whether we had made a hasty decision moving to this remote island, so far from friends and family. We'd get through it, but I was still fighting back tears as I fell asleep.

Chapter 5

A ROOSTER CROWED IN THE DISTANCE, and I woke feeling empty and far away. Jesse would be fine, I told myself; he was in college and Walla Walla, Washington, would seem just as far from Vermont as it did from Anguilla. I knew I wasn't a bad parent—just a protective mother. If I could only shake this damned guilt. Bob returned to work with the Davis brothers, and I had plenty to keep me busy.

From the outside, Scotiabank looked like any other building in Anguilla. Inside, I was transported to another world; it could have been a Chase Manhattan branch on Lexington Avenue except for the two barefoot fishermen filling out deposit slips. There were sleek gray counters, orderly lines of customers, and even air-conditioning. I was immediately aware of the repetitive thud of rubber stamps, as tellers whomped every piece of paper that crossed their path—I had discovered a new Caribbean rhythm.

The morning sun angled in through a window, highlighting the two women in customer service. Ruth was tall and slender, with her hair neatly pulled back into a French braid and a stunning gold necklace displayed over her red uniform. Carlyn could have easily been a model had she not chosen to help people open bank accounts. They jumped into the stamping rhythm, manually applying an account number to each one of my checks.

There was a charisma about Anguillian women that was almost startling, I thought, looking around the bank. They walked slowly, with exceptional posture. They had high cheekbones, smooth chocolate skin, and smiles that illuminated the room around them. One young girl had her hair braided in what must have been a hundred strands gracefully hanging down to her waist. Another had long fingernails intricately painted with tiny gold stars that shimmered as she counted out money for a customer next to me.

Anguilla has always been an offshore tax haven. Though money laundering is against the law and the source of any large deposit is closely scrutinized, substantial sums of money from all over the world do pass through the handful of banks here. A customer service person has to be quite knowledgeable about international banking and foreign currencies. It is common for them to handle wire transfers and bank drafts in U.S. or E.C. dollars, pounds, francs, guilders, or marks. It was a sharp contrast between this cool, sophisticated Scotiabank and the simple, less complicated world outside. A bank job in Anguilla was like a bus ticket out of small-town Kansas. It wasn't vanity that made these women beautiful, it was pride.

From Scotiabank, I went to open accounts at Caribbean Commercial Bank and National Bank of Anguilla. Unlike Scotiabank, which was based in Toronto, the others were locally owned and operated, and every bit as refined and professional. We needed accounts for the restaurant in all three: one for Visa, one for MasterCard, and the other for American Express. They each had their specialty. I preferred doing business in the local banks, feeling it supported the island economy that much more. As it turned out, everyone, including locals, has accounts in more than one place. Barclays Bank was there as well, but four accounts seemed like overkill, given that we hadn't earned anything yet.

I was getting nervous about money. Though I had diligently recorded our expenses, I had not yet taken the time to calculate how much was left. The day of reckoning had come.

I was surrounded by receipts, and the columns in my green ledger book filled up quickly. Lumber, freight, and duty topped the list, but dozens of other expenses added up to alarming numbers. Thousands of dollars went to Cable & Wireless and labor for the Davis brothers. Little Joe the electrician and Charles the plumber were no bargain. Deposits on the house, hurricane insurance, buying the car, and countless other expenditures brought us to a grand total of $260,000. We were left with under $10,000. That was it.

I suddenly needed to get away from the adding machine and put my feet in the water. On the way to Shoal Bay I couldn't resist a group of schoolchildren, not more than five or six years old, who flagged me down for a ride home. They stood on the side of the road in their tiny pink uniforms with huge backpacks that hung down past their knees. "A lift," they called out. "A lift. A lift." Our little Suzuki barely held four adults, but by the time everyone was settled inside, eight children, backpacks and all, were crammed in. It was like the circus Volkswagen filled with countless clowns. The biggest boy claimed the front seat and put a little one on his lap. The backseat held four across, with two more on top. They had trouble closing the doors, but after much squirming and wiggling, they succeeded and off we went.

Just as the giggles and teasing started distracting me from my troubles, the real laughter began. I was so preoccupied that I neglected to slow down for a speed bump, and *wham*—everyone's head hit the roof of the car. My small passengers were having the time of their lives. "White lady hit the bump," I heard from behind. "Do it again," said a little voice next to me. I couldn't help but join in the laughter.

You loves Anguilla, don't you? Joshua's words echoed in my head as I dropped my tiny friends off in Blowing Point, turned around, and went straight to the restaurant. *It's only money,* I said to myself. *It will work itself out once we're up and running.* I spent the rest of the afternoon upholstering bar stools. *Hard work is good therapy,* I reasoned.

The restaurant was coming together. The Davis brothers worked from nine to four, but Bob and I continued to work killingly long hours. We stopped to eat sandwiches, and I frequently ran up to a little grocery store for candy bars and cold drinks. I looked forward to my daily visits and loved to chat with Christine, the owner. Christine was cut out to be a shopkeeper even though she had worked for thirty years at the Mars candy factory in Slough, England. A very large woman, her benefits had undoubtedly included plenty of samples.

"You work too hard," she would say, eyeing the paint and dirt that usually covered my clothes. "Don't you ever take a rest?" She'd then shimmy her shoulders with a large, sexy wiggle and say, "Mrs. Blanchard, we all need to get out and dance a little sometimes."

"Christine, do *you* ever take a rest?" I would retaliate, knowing the answer. She, her daughter Sandra, and her niece Pat were in that store from six in the morning until eleven at night. Always happy to see me, Christine had become my confidante. We exchanged war stories, hers of candy bars, mine of salad dressing. While we talked, little children clutching fistfuls of coins came to buy whatever candy they could afford. Christine would help with their math, while I marveled at the selection of goods for sale: cod liver oil, ginseng extract from China, rum, condoms, cakes, and canned goods.

Our kitchen staff was taking shape. In addition to Garrilin we had hired Shabby as a grill cook, and Clinton had said, "I could try a little thing in the kitchen too." They were planning to continue doing construction with their brothers during the day and work with me in the kitchen each night.

With only three weeks to go until opening, we were grateful when people began stopping by looking for jobs. It was a simple process compared to back home—no advertising, no applications, no formal interviews, and no references. When the restaurant started to look presentable from the road, people appeared daily in search of work.

Dressed in khakis and a light blue oxford shirt, one of our first applicants came with the obvious intent of making a good impression. He was surprised to see me, the boss, splattered from head to toe with pink paint. I immediately felt as if I were the one being evaluated when he asked if I'd been in the restaurant business before. He handed me a resumé and explained that he had worked in dining rooms in New York and Miami. He could run the whole restaurant, he assured me, and was certain we would never find another Anguillian with such a strong professional background. Perhaps not, I thought, but it felt unsettling to hire someone whose innocence had been lost in New York and Miami. I ended the conversation with a simple, "Thank you, we'll give you a call." I hoped we could do better than that.

I was wrestling with a thorny bougainvillea when a white jeep pulled up and a tall, wiry young man hopped out and offered to give me a hand. After we had the plant safely in the ground, he continued to follow me around, helping in the garden. Lugging burlapped root balls of hibiscus, small palms, and lime trees, we set them beside their respective holes ready for planting and talked nonstop as we worked. I learned his name was Lowell Hodge and he lived right up the road in Long Bay, near Christine's shop.

"Are you looking for any waiters, or am I too late?" Lowell asked.

He helped me load the wheelbarrow with some smaller plants. "Actually, we don't have *any* waiters. We've hired a few people to help in the kitchen, but so far that's it. Have you worked as a waiter before?" I asked, hoping he wasn't going to tell me about his last job in New York.

Lowell smiled. There was an honest, accomplished look in his eyes. "I work at Coccoloba Hotel since I sixteen, but I ready to make a switch."

"Are you having some sort of problem there?"

Lowell paused for a minute, assessing my dirty hands and torn T-shirt. The sun was hot, and I could feel the sweat streaking my face with dirt.

"I'm sorry, I didn't mean to stare. You never stop, do you?" he asked.

"No. I like to work. Are you sure you want to get tangled up with me? I guarantee I'll be working just as hard in the restaurant as I am out here, and I'll expect everyone to do the same." Then I realized he hadn't answered my question. "So, is there a problem at Coccoloba?"

"No, not really. I just have a good feeling about this place. I think you're going to be real busy."

Surprised that he had such a positive opinion about our project, I asked why he thought we were going to be busy.

"Everyone talkin' about you guys. You put this place up *fast,* and you workin' so hard. My brother a waiter up Malliouhana and they all talkin' about it. Everyone I see at Christine shop talkin' about it too. Just wait till the season. You gonna be packed."

"And you want to be here when we are."

"I a good waiter. You'll see. Give me a chance."

I liked this young man. When I said he was hired, he offered to be at our disposal until the opening. Both of us, now equally covered with dirt, went inside to see Bob.

Lowell introduced himself with confidence. "Hey, Bob, I Lowell. The place looks great." They shook hands, and after just a few short words I knew Bob agreed we were lucky to have Lowell on our team.

Every morning for the next few weeks Lowell and I worked side by side. The barren, sandy yard continued to transform into an enchanted garden. Bob and Clinton sometimes came outside to help. We built two oval-shaped fountains out of rocks outside the dining room, visible from almost every table. In each a series of water jets was installed along with underwater lights to illuminate them. The winding stone path to the beach meandered alongside one of the fountains. It continued through the dappled shade of the big, gnarled sea grape tree and then down to the sea.

I wouldn't have blamed Charles the plumber had he wanted to strangle me. I wanted a trickle, not a splash, in the fountains, and it took countless attempts to adjust the spray of water. First he had five-foot-high jets that gushed into the air. Then came short, fat, foamy bubbles, barely visible from the restaurant. "No problem," Charles assured me. "We gonna get this water just the way you wannit." We settled on something that looked like a mushroom or bell on one side and a multitude of fine sprays on the other.

Our only source of disagreement was aesthetic. Charles really wanted colored lights in the fountains, thinking this would make it more spectacular. He was disappointed when I said I wasn't looking for spectacular—just a calming sense of peace and serenity. "Whatever you want," he conceded.

My mom always called me a tomboy, and I guess I've never changed. The only way I could seem to mix the dirt with the fertilizer was with my hands. I dumped the dirt in the wheelbarrow, added some fertilizer, and gathered up armloads at a time from underneath, blending it thoroughly. Lowell hosed in enough water to make a thick, muddy concoction—perfect, I declared, for filling in the holes around the plants. Not wanting to ruin my sandals, I did the entire job barefoot, and by the end of each day I was coated with black mud between my toes, under my fingernails, in my hair, and basically all over my entire body. "Pigpen Mel," Bob called me.

Lowell and I painted the shutters, along with several trees and anything else that got in our way. We used teal paint to match the deepest part of the sea. I had bought a Wagner paint sprayer just for that purpose and was surprised at the excitement it created. Shabby called down from the roof, "Is that a Wagner?"

"Yes," I said. "Have you ever used one?"

Before I knew it, Shabby, Clinton, and Little Joe had gathered around watching me spray the shutters. For some reason they loved the paint sprayer. "Clinton," Shabby said, "I see the Wagner on TV, and man, it can paint a whole house in a day. It the best." From the roof, Bob asked if anyone was coming back up to help him finish the shingles. They oohed and ahhed at the Wagner one more time before reluctantly going back to work.

Lowell brought over his friend Miguel, whom he introduced as a lunchtime waiter at Cap Juluca. His black beret tipped stylishly to the left, Miguel seemed a bit of a lady's man. Keeping his shades on, he wandered inside to speak with Bob.

"Hey, Lo said you might need another waiter."

"We might," Bob said, not wanting to commit himself.

"Cool," Miguel answered softly.

Bob stepped down from his ladder and shook Miguel's hand. "Do you have any experience?"

"I work Cap Juluca for lunch. You don't recognize me, man?"

"Sorry, maybe it's the hat and the shades."

"That cool. That cool," said Miguel. "I see you at lunch. Swordfish sandwich and Carib beer."

"Do you know anything about wine?"

"No, but I'd like to learn. So many guests over Cap Juluca ask me questions about wine, and I have to fake my way around it. It'd be nice to know what I talkin' about."

By the end of their talk, Miguel had joined the Blanchard's team. Bob explained that he didn't have time now, but once we were up and running, they'd spend time together tasting and evaluating the wines on our list. "Maybe you could come help organize the wine cellar before we open," I suggested.

"Cool."

"Cool," I said, and waved goodbye.

Lowell and I were cleaning the kitchen floor with muriatic acid and steel wool when I noticed a skinny pair of legs rising out of the bulkiest pair of Nikes I'd ever seen. "I work for you?"

Still focused on the big sneakers, I asked, "What's your name?"

"Marcus," he said. "I could work for you?"

Marcus was a sixteen-year-old beanpole of a kid who didn't see the point in tying his shoes. Hoping he wasn't looking for a waitering job, I said, "What exactly did you have in mind?"

He sat up on a table and thought for a while. "I wash the dishes," he concluded.

His accent sounded unusual to me, and I asked if he was from Anguilla.

"I from St. Kitts but my mudda from here. Don't need papers."

"You mean you don't need a work permit?"

"No. My mudda from here so I okay."

"Are you in school?"

"No. I can work anytime."

"Okay, how about if you work mornings with me and Bob? You can help peel and slice vegetables and do the dishes from the prep work."

"Irie. That cool," Marcus said.

"Give me your phone number so I can call you when we're ready."

Awkwardly he said, "No phone."

"Why don't you stop by in a couple of weeks, then, and we'll take it from there?"

"Okay, thanks."

Construction continued day after day, and everyone was enjoying the challenge. Our crew was proud of our progress and bragged to taxi drivers who stopped by. "Check us out," they'd say. "Blanchard's going to be the best restaurant on the island." The buzz was spreading.

We hired Alwyn as a waiter, who had worked at Malliouhana and was ready for a change. We decided only two more people were needed, a dishwasher and one more person to prep in the kitchen.

The dishwasher position filled quickly. Clinton and Shabby introduced us to their friend Renford. "Call me Bug," he said.

"Bug?"

He smiled, and his voice went up several octaves. "Yeah, call me Bug. I loves to wash dishes."

Last but certainly not least came Ozzie. Ozzie pulled up in a bright purple jeep and hopped out with a lively bounce in his step. Barely more than five feet tall, he came dressed in old shorts and wore rubber thongs that prominently displayed his blue-painted toenails. He said his girlfriend, Sweenda, had done the handiwork.

"Sweenda?" I said. "Is that Cora Lee's daughter?"

"Yeah, man. That who toll me 'bout you. Would you be willing to give me a do?"

Ozzie, it turned out, had been working in the Malliouhana kitchen and, like Alwyn, was ready for a change. He was a particularly industrious young man and worked for his uncle during the day in a startling number of family businesses. Uncle Moran had a funeral home, car rental agency, septic pumping truck, garbage removal business, and flower shop. Ozzie helped with them all. We decided to "give him a do," as he said, and that completed our hiring process. No advertisements, no applications, no references, and we had a staff of eight.

Bob and I were making frantic trips to St. Martin to get last-minute odds and ends for the building and line up food suppliers. Stops at our favorite patisserie were routine now, as was lunch at Tropicana. We had located wine vendors, suppliers for meat, fish, and produce, and a little French distributor for dairy products. We rarely needed a map over there anymore, and my high school French was improving all the time. The suppliers were accustomed to shipping things to Anguilla and made regular deliveries to the

Lady Odessa. Getting ingredients no longer seemed overwhelming—a little cumbersome, perhaps, but at least we could get what we needed.

By the end of September I had sprayed and rolled on over two hundred gallons of paint. Even though a significant portion of that was washed from my body each day, most of it was where it was supposed to be. The lumber pile was gone, and we were down to the final touches. Bob was sanding and finishing the mahogany bar he and Jesse had built, and the Davis boys were getting ready to go on to a new job.

We were all moving kitchen equipment around on a particularly hot day, and I had just returned from Christine's with a load of cold drinks. "Aya, Lawd," Clinton said, staring at the huge stove we were about to move. I knew what he meant was "Oh, my God."

"What's the matter, Clinton?"

"Aya, Lawd," he exclaimed again.

"Bubby"—that's what he called Bob—"we ain' got no gas."

"What do you mean, we don't have any gas? Wasn't there gas here before?"

"Yeah, man, but they took the tanks."

"Well, what do we do?"

"Jeremiah Gumbs."

"What?"

"Go see Jerry Gumbs," Clinton said.

"Who's Jerry Gumbs and where do I find him? Is he related to Joshua Gumbs?"

"All them Gumbs related, Mel. He live near we."

"In Blowing Point?"

"Yeah. Follow signs down to Rendezvous Bay Hotel and ask for Jerry. We need Jerry before we can hook up this stove."

Leaving behind instructions on how to arrange the new stainless-steel tables and various pieces of equipment, Bob and I drove to Blowing Point. Rounding the salt pond in West End, we spotted a white hearse—about a 1969 vintage—parked in front of

Gee Wee's Bakery. The driver's-side door was open, and Ozzie was nonchalantly leaning on the door eating a sandwich. "Only in Anguilla," Bob said as we drove by the hearse and waved. Ozzie was thrilled to see us and tooted his horn. "Only in Anguilla," I repeated. "Do you think there's a body in there?"

Unlike Malliouhana and Cap Juluca, Rendezvous Bay Hotel had an old-world charm that took us back to another era. The word *luxury* did not come to mind as we studied the camplike main building, with a huge veranda stretching from one end to another. Worn rocking chairs made of wicker faced the sea, and a long picnic table was set for twelve with mismatched tableware. Across the driveway were two motel-like buildings that we guessed housed the rooms.

At one end of the veranda a man was napping on a lounge chair, and as we walked closer we were certain he was the Anguillian Santa Claus. His bare belly rounded upward as he dozed, and his long, bushy white beard came halfway down his chest.

Sensing we were hovering over him, he opened an eye. "May I help you?" he said in a deep, deep voice, not unlike Joshua's. Baritones, apparently, ran in the Gumbs family.

"Are you by any chance Jerry Gumbs?" Bob started.

"I am."

"I'm Melinda and this is Bob. We're opening a restaurant on Meads Bay, and we were told you're the gas man."

"Well, you come to the right place. It's hot today. Would you like something to drink?"

Surprised at the hospitality, we took a minute to answer yes.

"How about a Ting? Ting the best drink."

"What is it? Does it have alcohol?"

"No, no, no. Ting is a grapefruit drink from St. Kitts. Come with me and we all have a Ting."

Jerry slowly got up from the lounge chair, slipped on a pair of well-worn Birkenstocks, and led us down the veranda into a kitchen. There were no doors on the way—everything just opened to the outside. The refrigerator was from the fifties, with rounded corners and a latch handle. Jerry pulled out three green bottles with a yellow label.

"Let's sit," Jerry said.

Bob and I followed him back to the lounge chair and sat down at a nearby card table. There was something curious about Jerry Gumbs, almost magical. We wanted to know him.

The three of us drank our Tings and talked for hours. Bob and I were riveted by his tales. The son of a fisherman, Jerry was born in 1913, and in his youth he had been the only tailor in Anguilla. He made uniforms for the boys on the racing boats and suits for people from other islands. I conjured up images of men arriving in tattered clothes on small, handmade fishing boats, leaving a week later with a three-piece suit ready to propose marriage to a loved one at home.

He opened Rendezvous Bay in 1959 as the first hotel in Anguilla, but before choosing to live a cloistered life in a cabin on the hotel property, Jerry Gumbs had been around. At age twenty-five he had emigrated to Brooklyn and studied at the Metropolitan Vocational High School, following which he won a scholarship to City College of New York. In 1941, after Pearl Harbor, Jerry joined the United States Army and was granted American citizenship. He studied accounting at the New York Academy of Business and engineering at the University of Pennsylvania. In 1951, he proudly told us, he built the first ranch house in Edison, New Jersey.

And on August 14, 1967, Jeremiah Gumbs was the *New York Times* "Man in the News" as a leader of the Anguilla Revolution. This upheaval was what had allowed Anguilla to grow to what it is today. Up until then, the islanders were relatively poor and at the mercy of outsiders. The British Colony of Anguilla, St. Kitts, and Nevis was administered in St. Kitts, where the legislative council allowed one vote to Anguilla, two to Nevis, and seven to St. Kitts. Anguilla had little in the way of health and education facilities; there were no paved roads, no electricity, and no industry; and people were forced to leave the island to earn a living.

Jerry, along with eleven other determined Anguillians, formed the vanguard of the Anguilla Revolution and won the island's position as a British Dependent Territory, successfully separated from St. Kitts and Nevis. The newly acquired direct link to Britain gave birth to the development and progress of Anguilla.

But Jerry had other stories to tell.

"In 1957," he said, "Castro's people came to my house in New Jersey all the time."

"Castro? What on earth for?" I asked.

"He wanted to buy Dog Island from me for a base. You know Dog Island?"

Bob answered, "Isn't that the flat island we can see from Meads Bay?"

"That's right," Jerry said.

"Are you saying Fidel Castro was trying to make Anguilla another Cuba?"

"They offered me a penthouse at the Cuban embassy in New York in exchange for Dog Island." He paused and continued with pride. "I never took a dollar from anyone. Not me."

Bob asked if he had ever actually met Castro.

With a laugh, Jerry said, "We were both staying at the Theresa Hotel in New York, and he brought in a *live* chicken to cook at the hotel. He walked into the lobby with a live, squawking chicken. Yes, all of us at the hotel knew Castro."

We finally got around to asking Jerry about the gas again.

"Oh, that no problem. I'll have two full tanks delivered first thing in the morning. Is that fast enough?"

"Yes, of course," I said. "That's great. Will you come eat at the restaurant? We'd love to have you as our guest."

"Sure. I'll get down there sometime," he said, accepting our thanks for the Tings. By the time we returned to work everyone had gone home, and we decided to do the same. Bob made us an omelet, and I did some paperwork. Before sleep, I wrote a letter home.

Dear Nina,

It's after midnight and I'm exhausted. I'm so sorry I couldn't talk when you called. There just aren't enough hours in each day.

Remember when we used to fantasize about living on an island? I had images of sitting on my patio under a palm tree, rum punch in my hand, looking out at the sea. Bob and Jesse would go for an early morning beach walk while I baked banana bread and arranged platters of fresh pineapple and mango for breakfast.

You'd come visit with Michael and the kids and we'd go to the beach all day. Then for dinner, as the sun set over the water, we'd grill a giant red snapper after stuffing it with fresh herbs from the garden and lemons picked in our backyard.

So far, life hasn't been exactly *like that dream. Customs is a major hassle, our house faces a gas station, and the pineapples come from Santo Domingo. Not to worry, though—Anguilla is turning into a different sort of dream. It's as much about the people as the beach and the views. When you come down, you'll meet Clinton, Lowell, Ozzie, and the others and you'll see what I mean.*

We're working harder than ever and money is tight but we're happy to be here. As they say in Anguilla, everything cool, man.

Love,
Mel

Five days before the opening, the pace had shifted to a dead run. The last little details were being finished on the building, and all the food and wine was on order. Clinton and I were adjusting lights out in the garden when he asked, "When the rest of the staff comin' to work, anyway?"

"Bob and Lowell are getting the food and wine at Blowing Point tomorrow, and everyone else is coming the next morning. That will give us three days with the whole crew before we open."

Lowell had borrowed a pickup so he and Bob could get the final supplies from the port when they arrived. The *Lady Odessa* was running two hours late. As they waited at the pier, Lowell was cool and patient while Bob paced, counting things that had to be done before the opening. *Island time,* he scolded himself. *I've got to adjust to island time.*

They watched the *Lady Odessa* tie up, and its crew unloaded a jeep, three goats, an engine, and some car fenders. Our food was then lifted out of the cabin and stacked on the pier. It reminded Bob of the dripping boxes of chicken on the pier the day he'd met Shabby. Our suppliers had used a lot of ice, at least, but Bob knew he didn't have much time before the sun did its damage. With the help of a porter equipped with a wheelbarrow, Bob and Lowell made twenty-two trips carting boxes of wine, produce, and meat up to customs at the ferry terminal.

"You got a bond number?" asked the customs officer.

Relieved that someone at the bank had told him about this process, Bob confidently said, "Yes. It's three-four-zero-three." This allowed him to bring food orders in without going through the paperwork process beforehand.

The officer inspected the boxes and told Bob and Lowell they were free to go with everything but the wine. "Wine gotta go in the warehouse," he said.

"What?" Bob felt his face redden.

"Your bond is good only for perishables, not wine. You gotta do an entry and leave it in the warehouse until you pay the duty."

"Some of this wine is very perishable. I have old Bordeaux that will spoil in the warehouse. It's an oven in there. And our restaurant opens in two days." Without that shipment, our new glass wine cellar would look ridiculous, and Bob thought we might have to postpone the opening. But, we already had reservations, and he wasn't ready to give up.

"Lowell, what do we do?" Bob asked, exasperated.

"Hold on," he said, and disappeared behind the customs window. Bob could see him talking with another officer. After a few minutes they both came back out, and the officer shook Bob's hand. "This my brother Glen," Lowell said. "He gonna help."

"I can't release the wine now, but if you take these papers to your broker and get them back here before I leave at six, we'll clear the wine," said Glen, saving the day.

"Thank you so much," Bob said. "Lowell, you finish loading the food and I'll go look for Tippy under the domino tree. Put everything in the walk-in cooler and meet me back here for the wine."

"Yeah, boss. No problem," Lowell said.

Luckily Tippy was in his usual spot and helped out with the emergency entry. Bob and Miguel spent the next day organizing the wine cellar, sorting bottles by region and labeling each with a bin number. The wine racks were filled from floor to ceiling with selections from 350 vineyards stretching from Napa to Bordeaux. The doors of the cellar had small-paned glass windows, and we dimmed the lights inside so that the bottles glowed, quietly adding a sense of luxury to the dining room. We couldn't wait for guests to arrive.

In the kitchen, Clinton and Ozzie danced as they chopped, sliced, diced, and riced. Shabby took charge of the grill. Garrilin helped with salads and desserts. And Bug was a born comedian; he could wash dishes and keep us laughing all night.

We went through some trial runs. We made all the sauces, salad dressings, and soups. The gazpacho was just as chunky as I'd envisioned.

Gazpacho

Coarsely chop 5 large plum tomatoes, 1 red pepper, 1 small onion, and ½ of a seedless cucumber. Add to the vegetables ½ cup red wine vinegar, 2 teaspoons fresh lemon juice, ½ cup extra virgin olive oil, and 1¼ cups tomato juice and mix well. Season with a pinch of cayenne pepper, ½ teaspoon salt, ½ teaspoon black pepper, and ¼ cup chopped fresh dill. Serves six.

We cut the meat, cleaned the fish, and made ice creams, sorbets, and cracked coconuts. The chicken was marinated, and the jerk sauce was, as the menu stated, hot hot hot.

Bob reviewed the dining room layout with the waiters, assigning a number to each of the eighteen tables. He'd gone over serving, clearing, and resetting, and I had explained the menu. He and Miguel practiced locating, presenting, opening, and pouring wine. Alwyn polished silver.

Blanchard's Restaurant was about to be born. At twenty minutes after midnight the night before we opened, we pronounced everything ready. We had twenty-two reservations for opening night, and as Bob and I said good night to our new family of staff, I didn't know if I was more tired, excited, or just plain scared to death.

We collapsed into bed, and Bob said, "Can you believe this whole thing started with a simple trip to the beach?"

Part Two

Chapter 6

SIX O'CLOCK ON OPENING NIGHT. Our staff was in high gear. A bond had developed among everyone; in just a short time, the common goal of creating and building this restaurant had brought us all together. The first day of unloading containers with the Davis brothers was history now, as were the long, hot days of construction, the endless testing of recipes, and the unnerving search for ingredients. Opening night was the culmination of what had become a collective dream, and each member of our staff had played their part. Blanchard's was *their* restaurant now as much as ours.

In the kitchen, everyone was in clean, starched chef's jackets and ready to cook. Garrilin washed the bush, as she called it, for salads. Shabby had the grill hot and ready to go, and the rest of us nervously waited for our first order.

The wait staff bustled about, looking strikingly handsome with their crisp white dress shirts contrasting their smooth black skin. They were proud of their Blanchard's logo embroidered over the pocket. With meticulous care, the stemware had been polished until it sparkled, and each glass was held up to the light, ensuring that no smudges or spots remained. The mahogany bar top was burnished to a glowing sheen, and bottles were straightened repeatedly on the back bar until each was where it belonged. The bar refrigerator was stocked with freshly squeezed orange juice for rum punch, icy cold Heinekens, Caribs, sodas, and Perrier. The ice bin was full, and in it, bottles of sauvignon blanc from the Loire Valley chilled next to chardonnay from Sonoma, ready to be poured by the glass.

Lowell, Miguel, and Alwyn checked the dining room with Bob again and again, straightening place settings, moving glasses an inch to the left, then to the right, then back to the left. They recited the table numbers and seat numbers and reviewed the menu and the wine list for the umpteenth time.

We had arranged flowers in bud vases for the tables, picking blossoms from the garden. Some had green furls made from a leaf, a brilliant yellow allamanda tucked in the middle, and a tiny dot of red in the center from a firecracker plant. Others had long, leggy green shoots—almost Japanese in nature—and pink hibiscus floating in the center.

Bob and I stood in the middle of the dining room and looked around in awe. The floor-to-ceiling teal shutters were flung open, and beyond them the gardens twinkled as a gentle breeze shifted the plants and flowers that were illuminated from below. The fountains shimmered as underwater lights bounced off the water columns dancing in the air. Beyond the gardens, the sea crashed against Meads Bay; our stone path, lit softly on each side, meandered toward the waves. In the dining room, potted palms rustled under lazily spinning ceiling fans. The white rattan chairs sat ready to be broken in, and our dishes, silver, and hand-blown crystal flickered in the candlelight. The sound of Vivaldi filled the room.

I felt a rush of excitement ripple through my body, and I squeezed Bob's hand. It was like waiting for the curtain to go up on Broadway.

"What if they don't like my food?" I asked him.

Bob looked into my eyes and said, "I've worried about a lot of things: making this shack look like a restaurant, running out of money, putting together a good staff. But there's one thing we absolutely don't need to worry about, and that's your cooking."

"I wish I could be as sure."

With several minutes left before the first guests were due to arrive, Miguel made us each a sample of his favorite frozen drink. Banana cabana, he called it. Carrying our drinks, Bob and I walked through the bar and out the front door and followed the path down to the beach. It stopped where the white sand began, and I stood next to Bob, arm around his waist, watching the last bit of orange light disappear into the west. Above, the sky was already full of stars and the small crescent of a moon lay on its side, clear and bright against the navy blue sky.

Bob took a long sip of Miguel's thick banana drink. "Mel, this is fantastic. I love it. It's much better than a piña colada and not nearly as sweet. People are going to go crazy for this."

Banana Cabanas

To make two banana cabanas, put ½ cup Coco Lopez into a blender. Add ½ cup Baileys Irish Cream, 2 ripe bananas, 2 cups ice cubes, and, if you like, 2 ounces white rum. It's great with or without the rum. Blend on high speed until smooth and creamy.

"I should go check on the kitchen," I said. But Bob wouldn't let go.

"Let's always remember this night," he said. "Our new life is officially beginning right now."

"It's going to be an unhappy life if I don't go check on the kitchen," I said. We turned away from the sea and walked back to the restaurant, anxious to begin.

By six-thirty we were ready. There was nothing left to straighten, polish, prep, bake, check, or recheck. Bob dashed in and out of the kitchen and I went over the menu one last time with the staff.

"Follow my lead," I said. "As soon as orders come in, we'll take one at a time and do it all together. Once we get the hang of it, there won't be anything to worry about."

Lowell and Miguel tried to look busy in the dining room, but mostly they peered through the shutters, watching for headlights.

"People comin'," Lowell finally said. "Yes. People comin'."

The first guests arrived a few minutes before seven. We had twenty-two reservations and didn't expect more, which was fine with us. It was October and the island was quiet—a perfect time to smooth out any wrinkles before the season really started. Twenty-two felt like just the right number.

Within an hour, forty-eight people were seated and my orderly kitchen had fallen into total chaos.

"Lowell," I shouted, "tell everyone we're out of lobster. We can't grill them fast enough."

"But what about table five?" he asked frantically. "They order three lobsters!"

"Lowell," I repeated in a panic, "*please.* Just tell them I'm sorry. We can't handle it."

Bob came skidding into the kitchen to return a tuna and a tenderloin. "These are both supposed to be rare," he said, looking at Shabby, who was manning the grill. "They're completely cooked through."

"Shabby," I explained, "when the order says rare, you hardly cook it at all."

"But Mel," he said, "I cook the steak till it have no more blood. And you can't send out raw tuna."

"Shabby, you do know what *rare* means, right?" As the words came out of my mouth I wished I had stopped myself. The devastated look on Shabby's face went right to my heart.

"Yeah, but—"

"Shabby, it's too crazy to talk about it now. Let's redo these orders together and get the people some dinner, okay?"

"You gonna send it out raw?" he asked, staring at me.

The kitchen was beastly hot, but as soon as we opened the back door, all the order slips flew around the room and out of sight. I was flat on my stomach searching under the stove for the last missing order when Garrilin announced, "Mel, I outta dumplings. Where the rest be?"

"The rest? You served *all* those dumplings?"

Before I could solve the dumpling crisis, Shabby said, "Mel, I flip the tuna below. The one above not ready yet. I think this one rare now. You want me to put it on the plate?"

"That would be great," I said. "Just put a flat layer of orzo down first like I've been doing all night."

"Cool," he said.

As I showed Ozzie how to make more dumplings, I saw Shabby's plate of tuna heading out the door. The fish was perched atop a veritable mountain of orzo, reminding me of Cora Lee's mound of rice and peas—enough to serve a family of four. I let it go and knew there were training days ahead. "Ahh-la-la," Ozzie said. "Ahh-la-la," a term he had apparently picked up from working under the French chef in the Malliouhana kitchen.

"Hey, Mel," Bug said halfway through the evening, "them people really likes the food. These plates comin' back so clean, I don' need to wash 'em."

"If we could only keep up, I'd be a lot happier," I said.

The scene in the dining room was frenzied as well. Bob loved talking with the guests and had a difficult time pulling himself away when the waiters needed help. Everyone wanted to know where we were from, what we had done before, and how we ended up in Anguilla. The wine list also required Bob's attention, and several tables wanted to discuss specific vineyards and grape varieties at length. He had difficulty cutting short a debate over the virtues of Oregon Pinot Noirs versus Burgundies and could have talked for hours about why American vintners insist on making chardonnay so oaky. Alwyn whispered in his ear, "Bob, the people at table two leave."

"They left? Without eating?" Bob asked.

Alwyn shook his head. "Yeah, man, they just leave. They say nobody take their order."

That night in bed, Bob and I went over the evening's events and talked about ways to improve. Just as we were falling asleep, I flung off the covers and screamed, "Get out of bed!" Something was tickling my foot.

Bob leapt up with a jolt and saw a centipede making its way across the sheets, completely ignoring our antics. Its hundred little legs wormed slowly along until Bob's shoe stopped it dead in its tracks. We'd seen them before, along with scorpions and a host of other little creatures, but never before had one joined us in bed. We religiously checked shoes each morning—these bugs love to hide in the cool toe of a sneaker—but the bed was different, a real intrusion. We spent a restless night, waking to every little noise, and called the exterminator first thing in the morning.

I learned a lot about fish in those early weeks. I discovered the difference between black grouper and gray grouper, yellowtail snapper and red snapper, which fish needed to be scaled and which skinned. A favorite throughout the Caribbean is a fish called wahoo. Bob heard they're great fighting fish to catch, and we concluded their name came about because the only thing you can do is yell "Wahoo!" when one takes your line.

Cleve introduced us to our first wahoo. The last time I had seen a fish of that size was at an aquarium. He came in the kitchen through the back door and placed the whole fish—maybe forty or fifty pounds—on a table with a loud thud.

"Cleve, it's giant," I said, eyeing the large gray head, not knowing if I had it in me to turn it into dinner. I paid Cleve in cash and continued staring at the fish. It was over four feet long and resembled a torpedo.

Shabby arrived a few minutes later, impressed with the delivery. "Mel, that a beautiful wahoo. Can I cut it up?"

"I was hoping you'd say that," I said with a big sigh of relief. Shabby assumed the fish-cutting responsibility from that day forward. I took over once he presented me with manageable fillets. We made a good team.

The dining room started to run more smoothly, though we still had our problems. One evening Bob came into the kitchen during dinner to ask me if I had taken a reservation for six people under the name of Gucci.

"Yes," I said. "I think it was for eight o'clock."

"Well," he added, "did you take one for Lucci as well?"

"What are you talking about?" I asked.

"Lowell seated a table of six half an hour ago whose name is Lucci. They speak Italian—no English at all. When they said their name, Lowell assumed it was Gucci, since it was so close."

"Yeah. So?"

"The Guccis are now standing in the bar waiting for their table, and I don't have room for another six. *They* speak English quite well and have made it clear that they will tell the concierge at Cap Juluca how poorly they've been treated. Mr. Gucci is pounding furiously on the bar and yelling about our terrible service."

Bob was beside himself. "Luccis. Guccis," he said. "When the second one called, we must have thought it was the first one reconfirming. Who would think we'd have two Italian tables of six with such similar names on the same night? What should I do?"

Bug answered before I got a chance. "Tell one of 'em they can come in here and eat with us. We don' care if they Succi, Mucci, or whatever. Tell 'em we likes Italians back here in the kitchen. We set up a table right here nex' to me."

Just looking at Bug made us laugh. He had soapsuds up to his elbows and was wearing shorts and black leather dress shoes. He continued to sing a little tune about the Guccis and the Luccis while he washed the piles of dirty dishes. Bob left to deal with the situation with a fresh outlook, trying to keep the Gucci/Lucci crisis in perspective. Mr. Gucci stormed out of the restaurant. Bob looked at Lowell and said, "I don't think the Guccis will be back, do you?"

"No, man," Lowell answered. "They ain' havin' a good night a 'tall."

Our St. Martin suppliers were not working out as well as planned. The patois there, a mixture of French, Dutch, and Caribbean, was much more difficult to interpret than the Anguillian version, which was at least based on English. We ordered 250 pounds of flour and received 2,500 instead—perfect if we were opening a bakery. I ordered a case of radishes and received twelve radicchio. Sun-dried tomatoes were missing from an order and replaced with pink ice cream cones. We were also at the mercy of Mother Nature: The *Lady Odessa* stopped running for three days in a row because of a ground sea.

"Sorry," they said. "The waves are too rough to cross the channel."

No one was able to define the term *ground sea,* but it is an oddity that seafarers must know in their souls. It was an underwater storm that assaulted the beach in front of the restaurant. The noise was deafening as ten-foot waves crashed against the sand, drowning out all conversation in the dining room. Yet the sky overhead was clear and blue, and relaxed island pelicans stood patiently on the rocks, backs to the wind, waiting for the sea to calm down so they could resume fishing.

The customers loved it. At Cap Juluca the waves crashed right through Pimms, and the beach bar floor was covered with water. Malliouhana's dining room, perched on its promontory, was dry but dramatic as enormous swells collided with the craggy rocks below. With each crash salt spray was propelled into the air, sometimes soaring over the roof, creating a curtain of color as the sun's rays rainbowed through the airborne water. Guests sat for hours mesmerized by the show. Meanwhile, we were out of almost everything on the menu. The seven-mile passage between Anguilla and St. Martin became impassable.

We hadn't seen Thomas in days. He had become a regular part of our day, arriving barefoot and salty from the sea with his burlap bag of squirming lobsters. During a ground sea it was impossible for him to go out and pull up his traps. "This ground sea," he said, "she gonna mash up my pots. It'll take days to fix 'em up again."

"How long do these ground seas last?" Bob asked Rupert, the captain of the *Lady Odessa*.

"Usually a couple a days," he answered as the two stared across the channel to St. Martin. "A week at the most."

"A week!" Bob said. "We'll be out of food and closed in a week. What am I going to feed my customers?"

"I'm *already* out of business," Rupert said. "My boat ain' makin' no money tie up out there. We always get a couple a ground seas in December. This one early, though; she a bad one."

They both scowled at the waves as the *Lady Odessa*, firmly tethered in place, rode up and down, rocking with the swells. The taxi driver tree shaded a lineup of unhappy men, and even the domino table sat idle; the ground sea had put a temporary stop to everyone's business, and spirits were low. Bob scoured the stores, gathering scraps for our empty walk-in cooler—a head of lettuce here, a few tomatoes there. He returned with a backseat full of food but only half the shopping list crossed off. "Shiitake mushrooms are not an Anguillian staple," he declared crossly while unloading the car.

We watched the unrelenting surf at Meads Bay; it was awesome, formidable, and showed no signs of subsiding. The waves roared so loudly it was difficult to speak. "We won't have anything to serve in two more days," I yelled. "We'll just have to close."

Three days later the waves returned to normal, the sky never once hinting that we'd had bad weather. The underwater storm had come and gone. We had hidden our regular menus at the restaurant and managed to eke out enough specials to remain open until the *Lady Odessa* and ferryboats were running again.

I went back to see George, the chef at Cap Juluca, who suggested I call his supplier in Miami if I wanted a more reliable source of food. "They can get anything," he said, "but it's expensive—everything comes by air. But man, when you get a ground sea, you don't need to worry."

Expensive was an understatement. Tourists continually asked why prices in Anguilla are so high. If they spent only one week trying to supply a restaurant, they'd understand immediately. Our menu prices had to go up as soon as we made the switch to Miami, with freight costs of over a dollar a pound and duty reaching astronomical numbers. The freight wasn't bad with expensive items such as veal chops, but for a fifty-pound bag of potatoes that cost $11 in Miami, it was another story. Add $50 in freight, plus the duty, and that bag of potatoes costs $70. But the accessibility of ingredients improved drastically; shiitake mushrooms, fresh herbs, raspberries, spring roll wrappers, and all those other hard-to-find items came with *relatively* little hassle.

Calculating how much to order was the hard part. We needed a crystal ball. We had to guess how many dinners would be served and which menu items would be the most popular. One night practically everyone in the restaurant ordered veal chops. That left us with too much snapper and tuna, which had to be thrown away. Two nights later, having loaded up on veal chops, we had a run on lobster. Trying to predict the future, I made daily lists and faxed them to Miami.

Then the relay race began. Our food was packed in giant insulated boxes with cold gel packs and delivered to the Miami airport. From there it was flown to St. Martin, where it was off-loaded on the runway—in the sun—and transferred to a private plane operated by an enterprising Anguillian named Benjamin Franklin, who flew it over to Anguilla. At that point paperwork slowed down the race, and often our baby lettuce and raspberries wilted in the heat. Customs inspected each box, matched it up with invoices, and separated, stapled, stamped, and initialed several colored forms indicating the duty owed. Little Joe, previously the electrician, now our trucker, loaded the boxes and drove them to the restaurant, at which point I'd make last-minute menu changes after discovering that something hadn't arrived.

It wasn't until our ice cream machine stopped running that I truly realized the costs of doing business on a tropical island. I called the store in Florida where I'd bought the machine, and because toll-free numbers don't work from Anguilla, it took a $90 phone call to determine that I needed a small rubber belt—only $3, they said.

"I'll just stick it in the mail and you'll have it in a few days," the man offered. I explained that the last package sent to me by mail still hadn't arrived and it had been six weeks. No, I said, I couldn't take chances with the mail, and I asked him to send it by Federal Express. Several days later I got a call that the box had arrived and was in the customs warehouse at the airport.

Bob drove to town immediately, hoping to get the part in time to still make at least one flavor of ice cream that night. The three o'clock scene at the airport resembled any other tourist destination when new arrivals are welcomed. Concierges displayed signs identifying which hotel they represented, porters with dollies offered to help with luggage, and taxi drivers lined up waiting for a fare. Unfortunately for us, customs was tied up for over an hour when American Eagle unleashed its thirty-something vacationers. Bob had no chance of clearing our little box until everyone had been shuttled through the system, so he chatted with taxi drivers and hoped he'd be out in time to get ready for work.

At four o'clock Bob was finally allowed into the customs office, where he was handed the invoice for the part ($3) plus the receipt for Federal Express ($85).

"Where's the package?" Bob asked. The officer nodded toward the warehouse.

"How much duty do I owe?"

"You gotta do an entry and pay at the treasury," the man explained.

Bob's frustration must have shown on his reddened face, because the man apologized for the procedure. He handed the invoice over to Bob, who then had to locate Tippy. Three days passed before we could pay the duty and were permitted to take our little rubber belt back to the restaurant. The $3 part cost us $215.

Part	3.00
Phone call	90.00
Federal Express	85.00
Tippy	15.00
Duty	22.00
Total	$215.00
	(PLUS EIGHT DAYS WITHOUT ICE CREAM)

During dinner Blanchard's turned into a hub of activity for more than the staff alone. Taxi drivers hung out in the kitchen, and I gave them samples of coconut cheesecake and Caesar salad while waiting for their customers to finish dining. They'd talk with our staff about politics or boat races or business in general. For me, it was like taking a night course in island life, illuminating fragments of Anguilla through these little snippets of conversation.

"Mel," they'd say, "you seen Vanessa's wedding Sunday?"

"Who's Vanessa?"

"You know, she Cynthia's husband's cousin. She work Cap Juluca. She drive the yellow jeep with number six-three-four-two. Mel, she have the biggest wedding yet here in Anguilla."

I had no idea who Cynthia was, much less her husband or her cousin, but I was curious to learn about the biggest wedding in island history. The fact that I was supposed to know everyone on the island, what they drove (including their license plate number), and where they worked was a constant challenge.

"Mel, she go Puerto Rico for her dress and everybody else's outfits in the whole wedding. Her cousin from St. Thomas come to make the cake, and they say it the biggest, most beautiful cake ever. People say there was four, maybe five hundred people there. The cars from church go for miles. I know you see it, Mel. They go right past your house. It was a breakfast wedding, so they passed early, and they was tootin' their horns all the way."

Everyone was disappointed that I had somehow missed the wedding, so Clinton changed the subject. "I ain' never wearin' a seat belt. Not me. You seen that car accident in North Hill? That guy was lucky he ain' had a seat belt on. They jus' make it so you can' get outta the car."

I started to explain about car safety, but nobody listened. Bob and I might be the only people in Anguilla to wear seat belts. Clinton actually was worried that I might be putting my life in danger with this practice and had tried to convince me to listen to reason.

It was a happy kitchen. Without question, Bug had the most tedious job in the restaurant. Most people would complain after hours of washing dishes. Not Bug. He stood bent over his sink of scalding water, telling funny stories to keep the rest of us in good humor.

Bug loved to mimic me, much to the delight of the rest of the staff. From behind the line I'd call, "Table six," indicating that a waiter should come pick up an order, and Bug would echo, "Table six, table six, *please* come get this food." If nobody came immediately, I'd yell again, "Table six." Mirroring my animated orders, Bug would place his soapy hands on his hips, stamp his foot, and yell in a still higher register, "Table six! Does anybody work here anymore? This food is getting cold. Table six. Now. Please!"

Clinton learned to dice, chop, puree, and julienne like a pro. He carefully saved the seeds from any vegetable and wrapped them in paper towels. Each night he would carry them home to plant in his garden the next day. As he worked, Clinton bounced to the rhythm in his head. One particularly hectic evening he sang quietly to himself, "He's got the whole world in his hands . . ." I joined in to lighten the mood of a crazy night, and within minutes the entire kitchen was rocking: "He's got the whole wide world in his hands . . ." Garrilin decorated desserts with a new flair, Shabby knocked the spatula on the grill to the rhythm, Bug blew soapsuds into the air, and Ozzie's body wiggled to the music without ever moving his feet. Had a stranger walked into the kitchen just then, they might have thought I had completely lost control. Nights like that were the best.

I stopped in the road just a hundred yards from the restaurant, waiting for our neighbor, Elbert, as he coaxed his herd of goats in front of my car. The lead goat—I assumed it was the patriarch—was out in front, dragging a black rope behind. A few stragglers wandered at the rear, and Elbert rounded them up, prodding with a stick.

Every morning he waved and smiled as he drove his herd of goats down to Meads Bay, where he tied the leader to a tree or sea grape. The rest of the herd—apparently unaware that they were not tied up as well—spent the day close by, foraging for food. Their ears were soft and floppy, and they flicked their short tails in play. The babies frolicked in and around the group, rediscovering their mother's milk when hungry.

The lead goat intrigued me, though. If untied, would he run off to explore the island, racing wildly up the road looking for adventure? I pictured the rest of the gang trotting along behind, heads down, embarrassed by the rebellion.

Elbert's herd safely crossed the road, and he waved goodbye as I continued toward the restaurant. Elbert's day was pretty open. His entire life was pretty open. I thought back to my years at Blanchard & Blanchard, recalling my calendar jam-packed with commitments. Sunday nights Bob and I would study the week ahead, wishing there were more hours in a day. Waiting for a herd of goats to cross the road would have stretched my patience to its limits, but now I was starting to look forward to stopping in the road in the quiet of early morning, waiting as Elbert and his goats, rope dragging behind, leisurely crossed to the other side.

Chapter 7

THERE ARE NO TURKEYS IN ANGUILLA.
We decided to fly them in from
Miami, even though air freight
would cost more than the turkeys
themselves. It was risky planning Thanksgiving dinner on a British
island in the Caribbean, but tourists and expatriates began calling
several weeks ahead, hoping we would observe the tradition. Ten
large frozen birds arrived by plane. We roasted and baked for days:
old-fashioned stuffing, sweet potatoes with maple syrup and rum,
cranberry sauce, pumpkin pies, apple pies, and a Caribbean version of cornbread with little bits of crushed pineapple.

Thanksgiving morning I turned on the TV in the kitchen at
nine o'clock. On NBC the Macy's parade was just starting, and it
was odd to be in Anguilla watching the floats go by my old building
on Central Park West. Bob, Marcus, and I watched the festivities as
we prepared dinner. Marcus was enthralled with the parade. He
stood at the sink, eyes glued to the TV, his huge high-top Nikes
untied as usual, hair braided into short tufts that stuck out in all
directions.

"What that one is?" he asked as each new float or balloon
appeared. He recognized some of the cartoon characters and identified them with great pride. "That Bullwinkle. That Superman.
Who that one be?"

Although Marcus had a hard time working and watching TV at the same time, we enjoyed pointing out to him the high points of the parade. I don't think he ever understood just how big the balloons were. Bullwinkle shifted in a gust of wind, and Marcus laughed as it popped an arm on a streetlight. He stopped what he was doing for a while, leaning and pulling on imaginary ropes as if he were guiding the giant balloons himself.

Marcus's lack of respect for anything mechanical was already legendary in our kitchen. If something didn't fit or was stuck, he just pushed or pounded harder until either it gave in or it broke. We had already replaced a sheared-off bolt on the juicer two days before—Marcus had broken the arm right off. As he watched the Ohio Fife and Drum Corps march down Central Park West, I heard a loud snap. He looked at me with big, ashamed eyes, holding the broken handle to the Cuisinart in one hand.

"Sorry, Mel. Sorry. I sorry," he said.

The heat in the kitchen was unbelievable, and I'd been cooking turkeys for what seemed like forever. Suddenly I needed to get outside. I decided to let Bob deal with Marcus, and I walked down the path to the beach and sat on the sand to collect my thoughts. My mind was racing. How many times had I shown Marcus how to remove the bowl from the Cuisinart? I had never seen someone so incapable of following instructions. My mind wandered and I missed Jesse. How could we have decided that he shouldn't fly home for the holiday?

Just as I was starting to feel really sorry for myself, Bob's voice came from behind. "Mel, there's a timer going off, and I don't know what it's for."

"Oh, no." I jumped up. "The pumpkin pies!"

We ran back to the kitchen and found Marcus taking the pies out of the oven.

"I think these done," he said.

"Thanks, Marcus."

"I sorry I mash up that machine," he said.

He reminded me of Jesse when he was small. "That's okay, Marcus. Just try to be a little more gentle with things."

"I fixed the juicer," Bob said. "I bet I can fix the Cuisinart too. Maybe a little superglue would do it?"

I went back to basting turkeys, and Marcus went back to watching the parade.

Thanksgiving brought a notable increase in the number of visitors on the island. The restaurant grew steadily busier. The increased pace was both exhilarating and profitable. At the end of the week we were exhausted, but we had a little money left over. There was a little more cash flowing in than out, and we could see a light at the end of the financial tunnel. We went for our walks on the beach with a growing sense of satisfaction.

"It would be cold in Vermont now," Bob said as he waded through the frothy turquoise water. We both let the image of Thanksgiving in Vermont sink in a little. The foliage would have made its spectacular showing in October, then been stripped to a pallid gray by a relentless rain, egged on by an arctic wind. Snow flurries and nightly frosts, wood smoke in the air, the last weekend for the hunters to bag their deer and secure a freezer of venison for winter. And here we were in bathing suits and suntan lotion, walking in eighty-degree water past browned, relaxing tourists.

Strolling on the beach had taken on a whole new character with the opening of the restaurant. We had become a topic of conversation among the many guests who found our lifestyle intriguing and even enviable. A pattern had quickly developed, which usually began with a wave on their part as we walked by in one direction, sometimes accompanied by "Great dinner last night" or "Look, it's the Blanchards." Bob and I would wave back and continue our amble toward the end of the beach. Now and then we'd stop when someone indicated they wanted to know more.

"We love your restaurant. Is this the chef?" they'd say, shaking my hand vigorously. Then they'd fire a line of questions: "Where are you from? How'd you choose Anguilla? Is it pronounced An-ghee-a or Ann-gwil-la? Were you in the restaurant business in Vermont? Oh, my God, *you're* Blanchard & Blanchard? We have your salad dressing in our refrigerator at home right now!"

And so it went. Our quiet beach walks had become *This Is Your Life.*

In early December the restaurant slowed back down to an average evening of thirty or forty dinners. The last of the turkey sandwiches had been polished off, and we began to brace ourselves for the onslaught of the Christmas season. Thomas had brought a fifty-pound bag of lobsters one afternoon, and I went in a little early to boil some water and get them ready for Shabby. I met Bug sitting in his car, listening to a cricket game blasting on the radio. He was patiently waiting to attack the mountain of pots and pans from the morning's prep work. He carried the heavy burlap bag of lobsters inside for me, placed a large stockpot under the faucet in the sink, and turned the water on. Nothing came out.

"Pipe ain' runnin'," Bug announced. "Water finish."

I stared at the sink faucet in disbelief. Five thousand gallons of water had been delivered only the day before—the bill was sitting right on my desk at home.

"Check the cistern, Bug," I said. "There's gotta be water in it. Maybe the pump isn't on. I'll call Bob." Bug trotted off to look down in the cistern with a flashlight.

"Go out back and see if the pump is running," Bob said.

"It's running," I told him.

Bug returned and said, "Cistern dry."

"How can this be?" I asked both Bob and Bug.

"I ain' know," Bug said apologetically, as if I were somehow blaming him. "Maybe cistern's gotta leak—I can fix it with Thoroseal."

"I'll be right there," Bob said, and hung up.

"What should we do?" I asked Bug. He eyed the mound of pots and pans to be washed and offered with a bright smile, "Leff we go outside an' look. Maybe if the cistern gotta leak, the ground be wet."

I followed Bug out the front door and around the corner of the restaurant to where the fill pipe enters the cistern. Bug looked around for signs of leakage.

"See, water there." He pointed toward the side of the building, where a large puddle had formed near the sea grape tree. He ran over and picked up the end of a garden hose that we used for watering the plants.

"Here the problem," he said, showing a mouthful of brilliant white teeth. "Somebody leff it running. Look there." Bug pointed to a small white patch on the stone path where a tourist, used to an endless supply of water, had apparently washed the sand from his or her feet and left the hose running. "Least you ain' got a crack cistern," he said, trying to console me. "That a bigger problem."

"Okay, we've got to hide these hoses, Bug, so nobody can find them again." I went to call Junior to refill the cistern, muttering to myself, "Two hundred dollars' worth of water on the ground so somebody could clean their feet." At least the plants would be happy for a few days.

Back in the kitchen, I addressed the new challenge of how to prepare for dinner with no water. I needed some of those dirty pots, but not immediately. Filling the steam table was the most urgent problem. One by one, I poured in four cases of Evian.

Bug came inside and dumped more Evian into the lobster pot, then more into another to boil water for the sink. The pile of Evian cases was disappearing fast. It was not going to be a profitable evening.

Bob drove into the parking lot in a cloud of dust and ran by the back door to check the pump, then dashed through the kitchen to shut off the circuit breaker and stop the pump from running. "I hope we didn't burn it up," he said. "It was really hot."

"Somebody washed their feet in the garden and drained the cistern," I said. "Bug has already hidden all the hoses so it won't happen again."

"This water thing is turning out to be as much as the rent," Bob said, and disappeared outside to check the pump again.

We used up all the bottled water for cooking and washing pots and pans, and there was none left to make coffee. The plumbing was not functioning, Bug moped around, unable to wash dishes, and the ice machine stopped making ice. Guests arrived at six-thirty, and we hoped that nobody had to use a bathroom. Junior, the water man, arrived at eight o'clock, just at our peak dinner hour. His truck, as it pumped the water into the cistern, sounded like a hundred motorcycles revving their engines, and our poor guests had to endure half an hour without any possibility of conversation. It was a rocky night, all in all.

The next day, as I was taking a tray of bread puddings out of the oven, I was startled by a voice from the back door in the kitchen, cheerfully greeting me with, "Good morning." I turned to see the silhouette of a man in a bathing suit standing in the doorway.

"Good morning," I returned. "Need some help?"

"No, I smell your cooking from the beach and came to see what you makin'. I John Hodge, but everyone call me Uncle Waddy. It is my family that owns this land with James."

"Oh, you're John Waddington Hodge," I said. "I saw your name on the lease. You're the executor of the land, right?"

"Yes, all this land on Meads Bay belong to my family. I James's great-uncle. Since I the oldest member of the clan, they appointed me executor. I make eighty-five years next week."

"You don't look eighty-five," I said, staring at his muscular body.

"I try to stay in shape," Uncle Waddy said with a little grin. "The secret is the sea. Every day for nearly eighty years I swim in the sea and I walk the length of Meads Bay. And I don't drink rum and I eat plenty of fish."

Uncle Waddy had grown old gracefully, with a dignity that I wished I could teach others back home. He was not a big man, but he carried himself with a stateliness that exuded self-esteem and confidence. He was full of stories about the old days in Anguilla and what life was like before tourists arrived. Fascinated by him and his tales, I encouraged him to visit my kitchen often; he loved playing the role of professor, and I relished being the student. He would usually leave with a bag of oranges after sharing some bit of island folklore.

Cornbread

With Uncle Waddy watching carefully, I continued making cornbread to serve that night. We talked about how to combat the problem of cornbread being dry and crumbly, and I promised him a piece when it was finished. Customers often requested this recipe, and I was always happy to oblige, if only to see their surprise when they heard the ingredients.

Cream 1 cup butter and ¾ cup sugar in a mixer. Add 4 eggs, beating well after each addition. With mixer on low speed, blend in 1½ cups creamed corn, ¼ cup crushed pineapple, 1 cup shredded Monterey Jack cheese, 1 cup flour, 1 cup cornmeal, 2 tablespoons baking powder, and 1 teaspoon salt. Pour into a buttered 9-inch-square cake pan and bake at 325° for about an hour, or until golden brown. Serves eight.

"Where do you get your cornmeal?" Uncle Waddy asked.

"Florida," I answered. "Why, would you like some?"

"Oh, no. I grow my own corn and take it to the Agriculture Department in The Valley, where they have a grinder to turn it into meal. I used to walk all the way to town carrying my corn, but now somebody usually give me a lift. "I hope you don' mind," he continued, "that I pick some sea-bean vines for my goats. Come." He motioned for me to follow him outside.

Two round, green bundles of the vines that grew wild on the beach lay on the ground, tied into neat bales by their own leggy shoots. Lavender flowers poked through the strands.

"I pick these out in front of your restaurant. I hope you don' mind," he repeated.

"Of course not. It is your land, you know. But how will you get them home?" I asked.

"I just live up the hill in Long Bay." And with that, he hoisted the two big bundles onto his shoulders and strode down the driveway.

I stared after him, astonished. Eighty-five years old, dressed only in a bathing suit, with the body of a thirty-year-old, and carrying two heavy bundles of greens for his goats. "Will you come to dinner on your birthday?" I called out. "Our treat."

Uncle Waddy stopped and turned with a wide smile. "I would be honored. It next Wednesday. I be here at seven o'clock." And off he went.

Maybe Anguilla is the fountain of youth, I thought as I returned to work.

The chatter in the kitchen each night continued to further my education in Anguillian culture. Heated arguments about a boat race or a cricket game would often get out of hand and I'd have to quiet everyone down, reminding them we had guests in the dining room. Bug was always in the middle of these disputes, and his high-pitched voice easily rose above the rest.

"Hey, Bob," he asked, "what go faster, a cruise ship or a speed-boat?"

Although he was anxious to get back to the busy dining room, Bob could see he had been appointed referee for a touchy issue. But before he could answer, Shabby said, "Bob, tell he what go faster. A cruise ship *must* go faster. Tell he."

Bob pondered the question briefly as Clinton, Lowell, and Miguel circled around, waiting for the verdict, leaving the diners to themselves. The debate escalated when it became clear that Bob had absolutely no idea which one went faster. The group argued about engine sizes, the weight of the boats, and which could get to Tortola first, a speedboat or a cruise ship. I reminded them that we had a full dining room, and everyone went back to work for a few minutes. Then Ozzie raised a new subject for discussion. "Mel," he said, "you think Saddam Hussein should be assassinated?"

I was sautéeing corn, steaming baby green beans, and stacking portobello mushrooms with spinach and shaved Parmesan, and wasn't sure I'd heard him correctly. "Saddam Hussein?" I asked.

"Yeah, Mel," Ozzie said. "He evil. He gotta go, right?"

"Mel, what you think about the new airport?" Clinton asked a few minutes later as he sprinkled coconut on a cheesecake. "Everybody in Anguilla have a different opinion on this one. What you think?"

Now here was a truly difficult subject, and I took time before answering. The government was considering building a new airport that would change the island forever. I had learned to tread lightly on political issues, and in fact I could see both sides of the debate. How grand it would be to bring in more tourists—more business for everyone. But the thought of jumbo jets roaring over our secluded beaches, disgorging hundreds of people onto this tiny island, cast a shadow upon my visions of tranquillity. Where would all those people stay? Would our exquisite dunes be bulldozed to make room for high-rise hotels?

Anguillians had watched St. Martin lose its innocence. Over twenty short years, the arrival of giant resorts and casinos combined with a poorly managed immigration department had made it a haven for unemployment, crime, and a population that had lost control of its own destiny. "Not in Anguilla," Joshua always told me. "Daughter, we will never let that happen here," he would say. "Never."

But Joshua was of the old school. There was also a generation of young souls torn between the conservatism of their parents and the lure of the outside world. Instilled with respect for the simple life in Anguilla, they were still drawn by the promise of more jobs and more money. Change had come quickly to Anguilla, and people were caught in the middle. Only twenty years before, most had not had the luxury of electricity and telephones. They had taken a giant leap through cultural time, and a new airport would be an irrevocable step again.

I finally came upon an answer. "I'm sure Anguilla will make the right decision."

We had a run on jerk shrimp that night, so I asked Shabby to get some more from the walk-in cooler. He just stared at me.

"What's the matter, Shabby? Are we out of shrimp?"

"No, but I can' get it. I got gas in my shoulder, and that'll make it worse."

"Gas in your shoulder? What are you talking about? All you have to do is get some shrimp," I said.

"I can' touch the cold shrimp after I be near the grill. Can' go from hot to cold. Not only my shoulder get gas, but the cold give me arthritis."

Health issues were forever under discussion in our kitchen, and how colds were caught was an especially fraught topic. Our theories about germs had no foundation, Bob and I were told, and the perils of sudden temperature changes were impossible to dispute. Cooking in any restaurant kitchen calls for frequent trips into the walk-in cooler, but in Anguilla this took some coaxing. When necessary, our staff dutifully went in, but not before placing a small towel on top of their head. This, they agreed, would ward off the flu.

One day, on our way to The Valley to do some errands, we heard a shriek from a fellow on a bicycle. *"Blanchard,"* he yelled as we drove by. Neither Bob nor I recognized him, but he was waving frantically to get us to stop. He had turned his bike around and was now chasing us down the road. When we pulled over, he bent into the car window and with a giant smile revealed a gold cap that had been carved into the shape of a star on his front tooth. He was a Rastafarian with thick, fuzzy locks of hair down to his waist. Out of breath from the chase, he said, "Good morning. My name I-Davis. I Clinton an' Shabby brother. They tell me all 'bout you. You come see my shell collection? I like you see it."

I-Davis gave us directions to his house, and we promised to visit later that day. After we bid I-Davis goodbye, Bob explained that he'd read somewhere that Rastas always put an *I* in front of their last name—something to do with their religion and positive energy. They believed it added strength and purity to a name. We arrived in what we started to call "Davisville," since Shabby, Clinton, and at least seven of the ten other Davis brothers and sisters had settled on the same piece of land. I-Davis gave us a hug as he welcomed us into his home, and sure enough, he gave us a tour of his collection. He and his wife had strung hundreds of sand dollars, olive shells, cockles, and pieces of conch shells with fishing line and hung them from sticks to make wind chimes. They swung musically from doorways and windows in all directions, making the house feel like some sort of sacred place. Thousands more shells were sorted in rows by shape and color all over the floor, and I-Davis told us stories about where he'd found them all. He loved the ones with purple and orange most, he explained, but some of the plain white ones made the prettiest sound.

Before we left, we were handed a pencil and asked to sign a rock wall in the living room to show we had visited. Names and messages covered the surface, and it was hard to find a bumpy little space to leave our mark upon I-Davis's stone guest book. He smiled brightly, showing his gold star once again, and insisted we choose a wind chime to take home as a gift.

On Sunday mornings in Anguilla families gathered in churchyards for the service. Little boys wore jackets, usually handed down from a long line of brothers and cousins, and girls were in pastel dresses, lacy socks cuffed at the ankle, and shiny black patent leather shoes, their hair braided with ribbons and bows to match their dresses. The big children held on to the littler ones and clutched a Bible under one arm. As they walked along the road to church, fathers often carried a tambourine along with their Bible, sometimes giving it a little warm-up shake along the way.

The music was the best part. Women in straw hats sang with voices that soared through the churches' open doors. Congregations belted out hymns of all kinds, some wild and frenzied, others soft and tender. Through the windows we could see the crowd sway back and forth, the whole building seeming to move to the rhythm. Congregants cooled themselves and their babies with makeshift paper fans.

We were listening to the music outside the pink church in South Hill when Garrilin and her six-year-old niece Roxana pulled into the yard. I complimented Roxana on her braids, which were finished at the ends with alternating silver and gold beads.

"Mel," Roxana said, "I went by Brenda yesterday to get my hair done. I got there eleven, I finish one. Mel, she plat sooo fast."

"Plat?"

Roxana giggled at my ignorance. "Braid, Mel. *Plat* mean 'braid.'"

"Two hours sounds like a long time to sit still to me," I said.

"No, two hour fast. Sometime it take five hour." Roxana held up five fingers to emphasize her point. "These a lotta braid, ya know."

Garrilin and Roxana urged us to join them inside, but we weren't dressed for the occasion. We listened to the music as it flowed like honey through the front door.

After his last finals, Jesse left Walla Walla at four A.M. on Horizon Air. He connected with a seven-thirty American flight to Dallas, then on to Miami, where he spent the night. The next morning he caught an early flight to San Juan and then the American Eagle to Anguilla. Christmas travel plans were a challenge, since it was high season in the Caribbean—Jesse was lucky to get any flights at all. Thirty-six hours after leaving school, he stepped off the plane, looking a little bedraggled and clearly in need of a haircut, but otherwise healthy and happy to be home.

We drove to the house under a barrage of stories about school and questions about life in Anguilla. Jesse asked about Clinton, Lowell, and Shabby—there was so much to catch up on. We talked for hours that day until it was time to go to work.

"Jesse reach?" Bug asked as soon as we walked in. "He marry yet?"

"He's here," Bob said. "He's coming in later and no, he's not married yet."

"We gonna be at the wedding when it come time, right?" he asked.

"Bug, Jesse doesn't even have a girlfriend," I said. "It's too soon to talk about a wedding."

"Jesse gettin' old. He need to give you some grandchildrens," Ozzie said.

"Jesse's still in school. I promise you that as soon as he decides to get married, you'll all come to the wedding."

Bug added one last thought. "We make gumbo for the wedding?"

"What?" I asked, not sure what he was getting at.

"That gumbo you make with that spicy sausage—I think Jesse would like that. We make a great big pot for he wedding."

Clinton explained to me that each night after dinner, Bug finished up whatever gumbo was left. I had no idea he was such a fan of that dish.

"Okay, Bug. We'll make gumbo for Jesse's wedding," I said.

"I see you was late getting Jesse at the airport," Garrilin said with disapproval.

"We got there before he cleared customs," I said. "How'd you know we were late?"

"I see the plane go over before your car pass through South Hill."

"You're kidding. You saw me driving to the airport?"

"I can see the road on Back Street from behind my house. I knew American Eagle was a little early, and I worry you be late."

Dear Betsy,

Moving to Anguilla is a little like having a second childhood— I learn something new every day. It's eye-opening to be a minority for the first time in my life. Skin color here seems to have little significance, though. There are only a handful of foreigners on the island, and every now and then someone refers to me as the "white lady," but it doesn't make me uncomfortable. In fact, sometimes, I feel like the whole island is watching out for me; people know my every move.

For me, the pulse of the island is in my kitchen. It's really the hub of our existence. Beyond earshot of the customers, it's where our staff talks about politics, love affairs, boat racing, and all sorts of topics they hear about on TV. They get more channels on TV here than we got in Vermont, so they're up on world events. CNN is as popular as wrestling and religion.

We had an early-morning sprinkle today, and the color of the water seemed to turn more green than blue. There's little change in

the weather in Anguilla, but life in the slow lane allows us time to
detect the subtleties. You just can't *be in a hurry here. Our staff,*
though, is the best surprise of all. It's like we have a whole new
family.

Love,
Mel

We went to Malliouhana for lunch that week and saw Leon Roydon, the owner, and his son, Nigel, in the lobby. "Brace yourselves," Leon said in his ever-so-proper British accent. "They are arriving for the holidays in only two short days. Are you ready for the rush?"

"I think we are," Bob said.

"Brilliant." And away he dashed.

"I don't know if we're *really* ready for this," I said faintly.

From the Malliouhana dining room, we could see a craggy point that juts out into the turquoise sea. That spot had become a special place for me—a place for private thoughts. I'd sit with the crabs as they scurried in and out of the crevices and holes. I didn't really go there to think about anything in particular—more just to reclaim a sense of calm. The rocks were sharp and uneven, but I could sit there for hours watching the water swoosh in and out of the caves under the cliff. I'd shared my deepest thoughts with the pelicans off that point.

We watched an old man standing barefoot on the weather-beaten rocks. He shook his net out to get the weights arranged in a circle; it looked like an old-fashioned hoop skirt. He cast out the net, spinning it like pizza dough, and it landed flat on top of a swell, immediately sinking from sight. Pulling on the rope, he hauled it in and emptied out dozens of tiny silver fish, flip-flopping onto the rocks like coins spilling out from a sack. The old man knelt down, scooped up the catch with his hands, and emptied them into a plastic pail full of seawater. Looking down from the terrace, we could see the fish dance and shimmer in the wet sunshine.

"He's probably been fishing from that point since long before this hotel was here," Bob said. "I'll bet high season won't really affect him too much."

"I wonder if those little fish are for bait or to eat."

Michel Rostang was in from Paris to change the Roydons' menu for the holidays. We tried his baby artichokes in lemon sauce and the newly added bouillabaisse. Local food in Anguilla is hearty—the original comfort food—but I'd be lying to say it's not a treat to have a three-star Michelin chef from Paris preparing our lunch now and then. On the way out the driveway, we passed the old man balancing the pail on his head. A couple carrying tennis rackets and dressed in crisp whites walked by the fisherman in the other direction, oblivious to the silvery fish inside the pail. They were making plans to play with the tennis pro the next day.

The weeks had flown by and we hadn't thought much about holiday shopping. Garrilin suggested we go to St. Martin and treat ourselves to a few gifts. What she neglected to say was that all nine thousand people who lived in Anguilla would be doing the same thing.

There was always a certain amount of activity at the ferry terminal, but the week before Christmas was something else entirely. Extra boats were running but still couldn't accommodate the crowds trying to get to St. Martin to buy Christmas presents. Incoming boats were filled with people lugging dozens of shopping bags and boxes—the one porter with his wheelbarrow could have had ten assistants and still not have kept up. Outgoing boats were jammed beyond capacity, and Jesse, Bob, and I sat on the roof of Frankie

Connor's boat waiting to make the crossing. Frankie was blasting a cassette inside, and we listened to Christmas carols through the speakers mounted precariously on the top deck. *"Feliz navidad, feliz navidad . . ."* And then: *"Let heaven and nature sing, let heaven and nature sing . . ."* The songs were all familiar but were played in a livelier tempo with a reggae beat. There were long interludes of steel drums and maracas adding pep to even the slowest of carols. An energetic version of "Joy to the World" was barely audible over the sound of the engines as we roared out of the harbor.

Most Anguillians preferred to shop in St. Martin on the Dutch side of the island, where stores had lower prices and more practical items. We couldn't bear the thought of sitting in traffic, so we chose to stay in Marigot to browse the French boutiques. The three of us split up so we could buy gifts, and though we kept bumping into each other, we managed to fill several shopping bags. Living in Anguilla and having St. Martin only a quick boat ride away seemed like the best of both worlds. We loved Marigot's bistros, patisseries, and shopping, but after a day of crowds and traffic, we were always relieved to step on the dock back in sleepy Anguilla. The *Lady Odessa* was tied up next to the ferry, its deck covered with pallets of water, soda, beer, and food. A load of red and white poinsettias covered the bow, and a new car straddled the middle of the deck.

We placed our wrapped packages up on the counter for customs to assess the duty. We had made a pact on the ferry that if they made us unwrap our gifts for inspection, we would not peek at what the others had bought. But the officer, a woman we'd seen countless times, smiled and said, "Happy Christmas," as she waved us through without payment. I made a mental note to bring her a cheesecake.

On the way home we spotted Christine from the shop in Long Bay, hitchhiking. Instead of sticking out her thumb for a lift, she was hiking up her skirt, revealing a generous amount of a very large thigh. As she got in the backseat Bob said, "Christine, you're showing off a lot of leg there."

"But Mr. Blanchard," she said, "don' you know that the best way for a lady to getta liff?"

"You never know who you might be tempting," I said.

"I guess I could handle mos' anyone. Nobody gonna mess with Christine."

The Sunday before Christmas we had an Anguillian version of an office party with the entire Blanchard's staff. We took all nine to a casual Italian restaurant on the beach called Trattoria Tramunto. Alan, the proprietor, had lived in Italy and was married to an Anguillian whose family owned the little restaurant. We feasted on pasta and lobster, tiramisu, and panna cotta. Rum punch and piña coladas replaced the traditional spiced cider and eggnog at holiday parties back home.

"This cake taste great," Bug said. "What it is again?"

"It's called tiramisu, Bug," I explained.

"I could eat this cake till my belly get so big it would tear-a-my-suit." Bug grinned.

After Bug polished off a second tiramisu, Alan passed around a concoction of fruit-flavored grappa, held up a glass for himself, and toasted us in Italian. *"Salute,"* he said.

Our glasses clinked and we all shouted, *"Salute."*

"Everybody happy?" I asked. "Clinton, you okay?"

"I here in a cool, Mel," he replied.

"We gonna do this every Christmas?" Miguel asked.

"Absolutely," Bob said. "Everyone enjoy, because tomorrow we get slammed. We have ninety-four reservations in the book for dinner, so get ready. The season is here."

"We ready," Bug said. "Leff them come."

"Salute," Ozzie cheered one more time.

"Salute!" we all repeated.

"Here's to Blanchard's," Lowell said. "We the best."

Chapter 8

ON DECEMBER 23 hotels filled to capacity, taxi drivers abandoned the domino tree, and our phone started to ring nonstop with people calling for reservations. Overnight the tourist population on the island tripled; it was an invasion of monumental proportion. Sleepy little Anguilla had awakened; in fact, it was in overdrive.

Several taxi drivers were in and out of Blanchard's ten times each night. Teddy shuttled customers continually between Cap Juluca and our restaurant and no longer had time for his usual Caesar salad at the bar. During the day he would stop by to use our gardening hose and give his new red van a quick wash on the way to pick up guests at the airport.

The change of season brought an entirely new kind of tourist. Gone were the curious budget-minded travelers—the people who read our menu with raised eyebrows, shared one dinner for two, and were outraged that we charged for bottled water. Hotel rates skyrocketed as Anguilla became a tropical paradise for movers and shakers from around the world. Private jets landed in St. Martin because our runway was too small. Tiny chartered planes would then shuttle people over to Anguilla. Taxi drivers loaded Louis Vuitton luggage into their cabs instead of the backpacks of low-season tourists. Spirits were high.

Our mellow mornings of kitchen prep became frantic tests of endurance. I answered the phone twelve times before I was able to finish cracking a dozen eggs. I needed exactly forty-five eggs for a batch of vanilla bean ice cream, but how to keep track with all the interruptions?

"Hi, this is Cindy at Cap Juluca. I need a table for six at eight o'clock tomorrow." I wiped off my hands and put the guest's name in the reservation book.

Thirty seconds later: "Hi, this is Heather from Carimar. I have a guest who wants a table for four at eight o'clock on New Year's Eve."

As soon as I hung up: "Good morning, it's Hermia from Frangipani Beach Club. One of our guests would like to dine with you on Thursday. It will be a table for two at eight."

"Quick, Bob," I called out. "Finish weighing this cream cheese and start browning the—" Before I could finish giving instructions, the phone rang again.

"Hi. It's Sylvene from Covecastles. I have guests who want to book five nights with you during their stay."

I had to teach Marcus to do more of the prep work so that Bob and I could take turns handling the phone. He learned how to dice red peppers into perfect, identical squares and how to grate lemon peel and ginger root. Often I had to juggle the reservation book while demonstrating culinary techniques such as how to gently fold egg whites into a bowl of chocolate. Thomas's daily lobster deliveries got bigger and bigger. His burlap bags, which had once weighed in at thirty pounds, were now up to seventy-five pounds. It took two people to lift them up and hang them from the scale.

At holiday time our little restaurant could have been set in New York. The bar was a sea of people who seemed to spend their days planning how many lobster cakes to order for the table and wondering how we made the chocolate coconut shells. Our menu, service, wine list, and entire reputation were suddenly under intense scrutiny. "Is your calamari fried? Because I only eat grilled calamari." "There's no cream in the chowder, right?" "Can I get this sauce on the side?" "You'll fillet the whole fish for me, won't you?" "Can you take the lobster out of the shell?" "I'm allergic to peanuts." "I'm allergic to butter." "I'm allergic to everything, what would you recommend?"

Bob and I were exhausted. The pressure, both in the kitchen and in the dining room, was intense. This was *definitely* no sleepy little beach bar.

The jet-setters of the world also had definite ideas about dinnertime: they collectively insisted on a table at precisely eight P.M. Even eight-fifteen would not do. And if we somehow convinced them to accept an eight-fifteen reservation, they'd show up at eight anyway. Luckily, they loved us. The word about Blanchard's spread quickly on the beaches, and as our popularity grew we were able to convince people to come a little earlier or a little later. It was, we explained, impossible to serve an entire island at one time.

Christmas Eve was our busiest night yet. We served almost a hundred dinners and finished work just before midnight. Bob, Jesse, and I fell asleep without our usual late-night snack. We were exhausted, and morning prep would come soon enough.

"Bob, I hear a noise," I said, shaking him from sleep only minutes after we had crawled into bed. "There's someone outside."

Bob sat up and listened. "If it's a prowler," he said, "he sure isn't trying very hard to be discreet." It sounded as though a huge crowd was forming in our front yard. I heard the rattle of someone climbing over the chain-link fence as a car engine shut off. The clamor intensified and seemed to be getting closer. Voices were all talking at once, metal clanked as if something had been dropped, and then a large, heavy object was dragged noisily across our porch.

"What should we do?" I asked Bob. "This is horrible. Someone's breaking into our house, and there's nothing we can do. Do you think they have guns?"

"Calm down," Bob whispered. "The door is locked, and I don't think they can get in very easily."

"Should we wake Jesse?"

"No, just stay put." Bob quietly prepared the lamp on his nightstand for defense. He pulled out the plug and unclipped the shade.

"We've been so stupid. It never even occurred to me that someone would break in here. I've always felt so safe and—"

"Shhh," Bob said. "What's that?" he asked, straining to hear more.

"It sounds like music. Do you think thieves here come with radios?"

"Shhh," he repeated. Clutching his lamp club, he left me alone in the bedroom while he sneaked out to investigate.

Without warning, he yelled, "Mel, quick, get out here and wake Jesse!" My heart pounded in my throat.

I dragged Jesse out of bed and we tiptoed into the living room, where Bob was unlocking the sliding glass door. I quickly counted twelve people—men, women, and children—lined up on our porch, all shuffling around and instructing each other to switch positions. Bob slid open the door, and at that moment the room filled with sounds of music like I had never heard before. There was an entire band out there, complete with keyboard and guitars. Children backed up the musicians with a rhythm section, tapping out the beat on Coke cans and scraping washboards with forks and spoons.

"We wish you a merry Christmas . . . we wish you a merry Christmas . . . we wish you a merry Christmas . . . and a happy New Year."

The black sky camouflaged the performers, but their silhouettes were brightened by gleaming white smiles. The songs were both familiar and new—"Silent Night" and "Joy to the World" followed by a song about baby Jesus with a reggae pulse that made the entire group swoop and rock to the syncopated beat. It was a heady twenty minutes before the leader signaled the others to stop and announced that they were the Church of God of Prophecy Serenaders. "Happy Christmas," he said, "and welcome to Anguilla."

The sun was already hot at eight o'clock on Christmas morning. All three of us giggled with delight that we could wear shorts on this winter holiday, and we reminisced without nostalgia about snowy fields and the smell of pine boughs on the mantel over a crackling fire. "Let's go on a picnic," I suggested. "We're in good shape in the kitchen for tonight, and we should celebrate the holiday at the beach."

Bob and Jesse jumped at the thought of escaping the phone for a few hours. Jesse gathered up beach towels and suntan lotion, and we went over to the restaurant to prepare our lunch. Bob picked a few fat green limes from our trees, and I rolled them around on the kitchen counter, pressing hard to release their juice for a pitcher of limeade. Jesse steamed a big christophine squash, an island variation of zucchini, and when it was cool he diced it into bite-sized chunks and mixed it with a little sour cream, a generous grinding of black pepper, and lots of fresh dill. Thomas had brought me his usual burlap bag the day before, and I made a salad of cold lobster and homemade Dijon mayonnaise.

Jesse begged for our family specialty, coconut cupcakes, so we delayed our picnic an hour longer to bake a fresh batch. The secret, I reminded him as we mixed and blended, was the almond extract. And, of course, plenty of coconut. We put coconut in the cake batter, coconut in the frosting, and sprinkled more coconut on top. We shared one as soon as they were done, and laughed at the thought of our customers seeing their chef on Christmas morning munching on cupcakes.

We decided to drive to idyllic, remote Captain's Bay. We were happy to find the bakery in town open on a holiday, and the smell of freshly baked bread was intoxicating. The woman said we had arrived just in time. They were closing in a few minutes, but luckily she had a fresh loaf for our sandwiches.

Feeling as if we were on vacation, I'd brought along a camera for the day. I found myself stopping and—as if seeing Anguilla for the first time—taking pictures of a blue-shuttered cottage, two baby goats cooling off in the shade of a car, and a man cleaning fish on a piece of plywood. We bumped along the dirt road to Captain's Bay and then lugged towels, books, a portable edition of Scrabble, two umbrellas, and all the food down to the deserted beach. There was not a soul or building in sight, and it was the busiest week of the year in Anguilla. There were plenty of beaches to go around.

Before lunch, we each grabbed a coconut cupcake and went off to explore the rocks on either end of the bay. They rose just thirty feet high, but at the top they afforded a view of the sea that went on forever. The water at the shore was the lightest of green; farther out it mingled with cobalt as puffy clouds cast their fleeting shadows. The slap of the waves at Captain's Bay seemed louder than on the western side of Anguilla. There was a wildness at this end of the island that was even more dramatic than I'd remembered.

Our lobster sandwiches were heavenly, and when lunch was over, Bob napped under an umbrella while Jesse and I played a game of Scrabble in the sun. By three we felt relaxed and ready for the busy night ahead at the restaurant. The answering machine, when we returned, had twenty-three new requests for reservations, and we were already full for the whole week. Bob spent an hour returning calls and taking names for a waiting list while I went to work baking rolls for dinner.

The dining room at Blanchard's over the holidays was filled with celebrities from around the globe; producers, directors, fashion icons, actors, models, politicians, and Wall Street gurus arrived daily. A hush fell over the room each time a superstar was shown to his or her table. Some were difficult to recognize in casual attire with no stylist or hairdresser for miles around, but they added an element of excitement to each evening.

On one particularly busy night a woman dining in the restaurant had told us she was writing an article on the villas of Anguilla. She was including a section about restaurants and asked Bob if she could take some pictures of him in the dining room. He didn't mind, but said it was imperative that she not bother any of the customers. She followed him around taking pictures and was very discreet until Bob reached a table in the corner. The woman pointed her camera directly in the customer's face, practically blinded him with the flash, and made a beeline back to her table.

"What the hell is going on here?" the gentleman demanded.

Bob apologized and explained about the article, saying that the woman was supposed to be taking pictures of him. The guest's wife became indignant and said, "We reserved under other names, but you really don't know who my husband is, do you?"

Once the gentleman introduced himself, Bob realized he had a serious problem on his hands. This was a major movie star, and Bob was terribly embarrassed not to have recognized him. He went back to the woman with the camera and asked for the film, which he then turned over to the celebrity. We never did see any mention of Blanchard's in any article about Anguilla's villas.

We hadn't given much thought to New Year's Eve, or Old Year's Day, as it is called in Anguilla, until concierges began calling with questions. Carimar Beach Club wanted to know if we had a fixed menu, Blue Waters asked about entertainment, and Covecastles was hoping for fireworks.

Leon Roydon called from Malliouhana, warning us about a particular guest who would be joining us for dinner on New Year's Eve. Dr. Gibson was one of his best customers and had never before ventured off the hotel property; he had apparently heard about our restaurant and was planning to give it a try.

"Please understand," Leon explained, "my only interest in calling you is to ensure my guest has a positive experience. His Anguilla visits have been very protected until now, and I don't want to take any chances. He's something of a gourmet and a wine buff, particularly fond of Montrachet, so I wanted you to be prepared. He also tends to dine with a large group, so the number in his party may grow; he loves to entertain. I'd suggest preparing a large table for the chap, just in case."

"Bob," I said after hanging up the phone, "this Gibson is a heavy hitter. We'd better not make any mistakes or I'm afraid we'll ruin our good relationship with Malliouhana."

Sure enough, Dr. Gibson's table grew and grew. The concierges called repeatedly. We felt as if we were preparing to serve dinner to the president of the United States.

"Hi, this is Patricia from Malliouhana. Could you make the Gibsons' table an eight instead of a six?"

"No problem," Bob said.

"Hi. Patricia again. Dr. Gibson wants to add two more."

"Melinda, it's Rosalind. Put down another two for Dr. Gibson."

"Hi, Bob, it's Agatha from Malliouhana. Dr. Gibson would like to increase his group to twenty-one people. Is that a problem?"

"Twenty-one?" Bob asked. "All at one table?"

"That's right. That's no problem, is it?"

Bob could hear from Agatha's voice that it *couldn't* be a problem. There was no choice. "It'll be a little tight, Agatha, but we'll get them in."

That night before dinner we had a staff meeting specifically to prepare for the Gibsons. Our largest table so far had been ten, so twenty-one discriminating guests from Malliouhana demanded our utmost attention. Their table must be ready on time, orders taken promptly, wineglasses kept full—every detail must be perfect. Lowell and Miguel assured us that they would be on their toes. When Bob said the large party might drink a case of red wine and a case of white, Bug couldn't see what all the fuss was about. "Leff them come," he said. "We got plenty wines in that room. They ain' gonna drink all."

Clinton and I were a little less confident. We could imagine the talk around the pool the next day. "We had the most horrible meal at that ghastly little place next door. Absolutely wretched. Oh, no, don't bother. Cancel your reservations."

At eight o'clock sharp Gibson and company marched in. Bob, Lowell, and Miguel helped the party get settled at the long table, the host at one end and his wife at the other. Bob and Dr. Gibson discussed the wine at length and chose a 1990 Chassagne Montrachet from Domaine Bernard Morey to start. Miguel ran to get several bottles and started to pour. It took almost five bottles to fill one round, and he started to worry we would run out. Choosing a red wine to serve with the main course took even more time. Dr. Gibson chose an '82 Calon-Segur, but another gentleman said he would prefer a Margaux. The discussion continued back and forth for fifteen minutes as Bob looked around the room nervously; the restaurant was completely full, and he couldn't break away to help the other guests.

We had made up a fixed menu for New Year's Eve, so Lowell didn't need to take any orders, but a woman in the group called him over for a favor. Dressed in what looked like an Armani gown, her hair pulled elegantly back into a jeweled clip, the woman complained of a tummyache.

"What I would really like," she said, "are some scrambled eggs."

Lowell was speechless. We had spent days preparing the menu for this special occasion, and now he had an order for scrambled eggs. "No problem," he assured the woman. "I'm sure the chef would be happy to oblige."

Lowell came rushing into the kitchen. It was time to send out the first course for the big table. "The only problem," he said in a very quiet voice, "is that we need an order of scrambled eggs."

"Scrambled eggs?" I screamed. "Are you out of your mind? Do you see what's going on back here? I don't even have a free burner on the stove."

Clinton could see the pressure was getting to me. "Mel," he said, "I make the eggs. Don' worry. Jus' show me what to do."

I talked Clinton through the egg ordeal as Shabby, Garrilin, and I sent out the rest of the orders. Space in the kitchen was at a premium that night. Crayfish was mounded on the grill, and dozens of plates covered every surface as we worked our way in assembly-line fashion through each of the six courses. Just before midnight Bob pulled the kitchen clock off the wall and carried it into the dining room for the countdown. Lowell, Miguel, and Alwyn passed out noisemakers and hats, and palm-tree confetti flew through the air. The Happy Hits played "Auld Lang Syne" with a calypso beat. I led the kitchen staff out to the bar to join the festivities, and everyone danced and toasted the new year.

"That went pretty okay," Miguel said as the last guest left. "They drank us out of the Chassagne Montrachet, though. Those people could drink some serious wine, man."

"Miguel," I said, "that was more than pretty okay. That was a great evening. Everything was perfect. We did it!"

"And we even serve a little breakfast in the middle," Clinton added.

Bug's three-bay sink had developed a small leak. It began as an intermittent drip but was becoming more persistent. He stood cheerfully in the new pond, as he called it, unaffected, and continued to wash his dishes, though his feet were a little soggy.

"I bringin' my bathin' suit to work tomorrow," Bug announced. He watched with delight as Bob and the rest of the waiters slid, skated, and sloshed past him. Carrying bowls of hot corn chowder on a *dry* floor takes practice; on a wet, slippery floor, it becomes acrobatic. "Shabby, you best bring in yo' lasso sticks tomorrow, 'cause I think we got lobsters to catch under this sink."

Several near collisions resulted in dinners having to be replated, as snapper slid and tuna shifted. I looked up for a split second from arranging raspberries around a chocolate birthday cake and saw Bob teetering on one foot, desperately trying to steady a tray of cappuccino. Just as he was about to tip over, Lowell came from the other direction with an armload of dishes. As they collided, conversation in the dining room came to a halt with the sound of breaking china and clattering silver. Bob and Lowell were both covered with cappuccino, though luckily neither was burned.

"Mel, you better buy some bibs if they can' keep theyselves clean," Bug chirped. "They lucky they ain' all mash up."

"I'll call Charles the plumber first thing tomorrow," Bob said.

Sunday morning Jesse, Bob, and I bounced up the road to Island Harbor to spend our day off at Scilly Cay. Jesse was determined to go back to school tanned, and we always loved a day on this teeny island. Scilly Cay is an outcropping of volcanic rock covered with sand and lush vegetation that sits in the center of the bay in Island Harbor.

We parked the Suzuki in the sand next to a row of beached fishing boats, their bright colors dazzling against the sapphire water. Two fishermen tinkered with an outboard motor lying on a lobster crate, its wooden slats covered in drying seaweed and barnacles from months of being submerged in the bay.

We sat down on the dock and waited for the motorboat that shuttles customers the few hundred yards out to Scilly Cay. Three young boys in their underwear were doing somersaults off the end of the pier, and with our arrival, their fun became a performance. They jumped high into the air, sometimes spinning head over heels and landing feetfirst, sometimes diving in headfirst. As each scrambled back up the ladder onto the pier, he'd glance our way to make sure we were paying attention. The littlest one, no more than five, tried hard to keep up. He needed help getting back up the ladder and often got a boost from an older boy; as soon as he was up, he plunged back into the water. They laughed and jumped, showing off for their audience, until the boat arrived to carry us off on vacation for a day.

Scilly Cay is only about the size of a big backyard. Covered in palm trees, bougainvillea, cactus, and scattered thatched roofs, it's as much an escape from Anguilla as Anguilla is from the rest of the world. The sand was hot, so we walked quickly to the tiny island's bar and ordered two lobsters and a grilled crayfish, and then stretched out on lounge chairs to bake in the sun. Actually, Jesse and I baked and Bob snoozed under an umbrella.

The sun began to work on my muscles, and I felt as if I didn't have a bone in my body. I stared at the puffy white clouds floating over us and watched a pelican swoop down in a kamikaze dive, then bounce back to the surface to devour its catch. The prehistoric-looking bird bobbed along on the waves, tipping back its large floppy beak to swallow. Then, in a burst of energy, it became airborne again, searching for dessert. Gliding effortlessly back downward, its wings tapped the water as it skimmed along the calm surface.

A small lizard poked its head around the edge of the low conch shell wall that kept the water from washing over Scilly Cay in a storm. It scurried under Jesse's chair, craning its neck from side to side, looking for insects or crumbs, and eventually made its way back into the cracks of the wall.

Along with a group of tourists, Jesse and I watched a man remove live lobsters from a wooden box anchored just offshore.

Enjoying the attention, the man held up the lobsters for everyone to see, and people snapped pictures as we all waited for lunch to be served.

"Aren't you from Blanchard's?" one woman asked.

"Yes," I said meekly, not knowing what she was about to say.

"We had a great meal at your place last night. That was the best tuna I've ever had. Honey," she called to her husband, "these are the people from Blanchard's."

Jesse and I enjoyed the feeling of minor celebrity as we answered dozens of questions about what it was like to live in paradise. It was starting to hit me that our restaurant was a success. *We* were telling visitors what it was like to live in Anguilla.

We joined Bob in a thatched hut for our lunch of grilled lobsters and crayfish surrounded by piles of fresh fruit and pasta salad. After lunch we napped in the sun, and by the time we drove home we felt as though we had been on a tropical holiday.

Blanchard's kitchen staff was never dull. I was charmed by Ozzie's ability to chop vegetables and dance at the same time, his gyrating movements emanating from his hips and spreading rhythmically out through every little muscle in his body. His internal metronome was subtler than Clinton's, who also sang as he moved. Ozzie's moves were more subliminal—they were just a part of his being, and his work improved noticeably when he was in motion.

Shabby loved his position at the grill but often said it was "too mucha heat." Even for someone with a frame like Superman and arms like an octopus, his was a grueling job. He'd stand as far back from the grill as he could and still reach the food with his extra-long tongs. But he solved the heat problem one day when he cut a piece of heavy cardboard in the shape of a shield and slid it up under his shirt. That ingenious extra barrier protected his chest from the fire; it became a prized possession and was carefully hidden for safekeeping each night.

Garrilin worked with me behind the line, decorating desserts, building salads, and keeping me fully informed on island news, scandalous or otherwise. She had a firm underpinning, as Bob's mother used to say, and her strong presence provided me with a welcomed sense of security. On Saturday nights she would sometimes come to work wearing green hair curlers neatly covered with a scarf in preparation for church the next day. She had moved to a new church recently, the pink one with a sign that read ONE STOP FOR ALL YOUR SPIRITUAL NEEDS, and wanted to look her best.

Bug had the worst job and the best attitude. He washed dishes nonstop in scalding water and told jokes the whole time, gnawing on empty lobster shells whenever he had a chance. When his soap bubbles climbed to eye level, he'd scoop up the excess with his arms, filling huge trash cans with suds. "You go in here now," he'd say in the kind of voice usually reserved for babies. "I have no room for you in the sink anymore. Go now. Go."

Austin the taxi driver lived just up the road from Blanchard's and was therefore a frequent visitor. The way taxis work in Anguilla is that whoever picks you up at the airport usually drives you around for the rest of the week. The drivers hand out stacks of business cards, and tourists just call anytime they need a ride during their stay. Austin was an entrepreneur extraordinaire and could juggle more customers in one night than seemed possible; he defied our theory that everyone in Anguilla moved on island time. All the drivers have cell phones, but Austin's rang continually. When he dropped off a guest for dinner, we'd invite him in for a drink at the bar. More often than not he'd take a couple of sips and rush off to get his next fare. Luckily his next fare often brought him right back to Blanchard's. Guests would tell us that on the way over to dinner, Austin gave them the history of how Bob and I came to Anguilla. It was his way of launching their evening with us. "He told us how you used to make salad dressings in Vermont," they'd say, "and that Blanchard's was written up as the best restaurant in the Caribbean. He's a big fan, you know."

Since Austin lived nearby, we'd also see him at the domino table outside Christine's shop in Long Bay. Christine's domino games would often go until four in the morning. She thrived on the excitement of those late nights of action, and the next day she would have stories to tell when I came into the shop.

"Oh, Mrs. Blanchard," she'd say—Christine never called me by my first name—"last night was a lulu. We play dominos till the wee hours," and then in a whisper, she'd add, "I sell plenty Heinekens too. What a night!"

One day she recalled for me the wild nights of her youth. "Mrs. Blanchard, when I was young—I was much smaller then, you know—I use to dance all night long. Even when I was a child, back when we still use pounds, shillings, an' pence, my mum would give me a coin to go to the shop. I'd keep the change and save up to go to the—well, these days you'd call it a disco."

"When did Anguilla stop using pounds, shillings, and pence?" I asked.

"Oh, I guess sometime 'round 1954 or 1955. I love to dance since I was a little girl," Christine went on, anxious to continue her story. "And when I was working in England, oh, how we'd rumble." Perhaps she could see I was having a hard time envisioning such a large person rumbling, so she stood up and demonstrated. Even in her sixties, Christine could shimmy and shake better than I—that was certain. "Mrs. Blanchard, I tell you. We'd be rockin' an' rollin'. I could rhumba, I could jive, I even waltz." Christine danced, and her three-year-old niece Kadeshya shadowed her every move. "She got the moves," Christine told me proudly. "Kadeshya got the moves."

Health inspections for restaurants in Anguilla were vastly different from those at home. When we started to build, we had asked about codes, regulations, and other hygiene-related requirements. We were told we needed a bathroom—that was it. Bob, Marcus, and I were prepping in the kitchen one morning when we heard a voice.

"Inside. Inside," a man called.

Bob poked his head around the back door, and a handsome young man holding a small ice cooler introduced himself. "Good morning. My name Oliver. I work for the Health Department."

Bob tensed, assuming we were in some sort of trouble. Our kitchen was all stainless steel and would certainly pass any inspection back home. But what if there was an obscure island rule we had missed? Would we fail some test?

Oliver came in through the kitchen door and continued his introduction. "I Lowell's cousin. I live right up in Long Bay. I just come to give you some fish."

"Fish?" I asked.

His cooler was about the size of a six-pack. He flipped open the lid, and inside were a dozen tiny fish swimming in a few cups of water.

"I come to put fish in your cistern. Where the cistern be?"

"Are you serious?" Bob asked. "You're putting fish in our water?"

"That's right," he said. "You won' have to worry anymore. These fish eat bacteria."

We hadn't been worried about our water before, though we never considered using cistern water for anything but cleaning. Our staff thought it silly, but we insisted on using bottled water for everything to do with food; we weren't about to take any chances.

Bob escorted Oliver to the dining room and lifted the cover camouflaged as part of the floor. I could hear their voices boom with an echo from the cavernous cistern below. Oliver scooped out three fish from the cooler and dropped them into the vastness.

"There," he said as he covered his cooler. "You all set for a while."

Three little fish now swam around in our 7,500-gallon cistern, protecting our water supply. No chemicals, no filters, just three little fish.

Chapter 9

DISASTER STRUCK ON JANUARY 15 AT 7:12 P.M. Our dining room was packed, and I had a full set of orders in front of me. Shabby's grill was covered with lobsters, veal chops, steaks, snapper, dorado, and shrimp. We were in full swing.

Without so much as a sputter, the main generator for the island shut down, plunging all of Anguilla into total blackness. My stomach flip-flopped as all my orders and the food on the ten-burner stove disappeared from sight. The orange glow from the grill and the blue flames on the stove were suddenly our only sources of light. As the exhaust fan in the hood coasted to a stop, the temperature rose rapidly, and thick smoke from the grill began to fill the room. Just as my eyes were adjusting to the eerie flame color of the kitchen, a curtain of smoke descended around us, and Shabby's muscular frame disappeared into the purple haze.

"Mel, I can' see," he said.

"Me either. Do we have a flashlight?" I remembered seeing an impressive display of flashlights and batteries at Anguilla Trading and wished I'd taken the hint.

Bob's voice came out of the smoke. "Is everybody okay in here?"

"Yeah, man. Irie. We jus' here in a cool," Clinton answered.

"We okay," came several other voices. Lowell and Miguel brought in candles from the dining room, and within minutes, through the flickering lights, I could make out a few forms moving through the smoke-filled inferno. Garrilin was attempting to assemble two Caesar salads, Ozzie was still dancing, and Clinton was humming some melody, keeping time by tapping on his worktable.

"Anybody have any idea what happened?" Bob asked. "Everything is dark outside, too. No streetlights anywhere."

"Gotta be Anglec," Clinton said. "Anglec been havin' trouble with the big generator. Current gonna come right back on, man. Don' worry. We better plug out the fridges. When the current come back on, she sometime have a surge an' it can mash everything up."

Lowell came in from the bar. "Current ain' comin' on for a while," he said. "I jus' call Anglec. They blew somethin' serious at the plant and they say it could be all night."

My mind wandered for a split second, remembering long-ago visits as a tourist to Anguilla. Power outages were never part of those vacations. All the hotels have big backup generators that turn on instantly during a blackout. The lights might flicker for a second or two, but that was it. No standby generator was going to kick on at Blanchard's, however, and I wasn't sure how I was going to turn out all these dinners in the dark.

"Where's Bug?" I asked, realizing he hadn't shown up for work yet. He was often late on Saturdays. Returning from his weekly trip south to St. Martin, he sometimes got deeply involved in a domino game at the ferry dock. "Anybody heard from Bug?" I repeated. "I need bowls washed!"

"Bug in St. Martin," Ozzie said. "I wash up some bowls for you, but I gotta have some water in the sink. Pump ain' work without current."

"Ozzie, come," Clinton said. "Bring a couple clean pots. We gonna get some water outta the hot-water heater." They disappeared out the back door with a flashlight, and I contemplated my stack of clean dishes, trying to estimate how long they would last.

The steady trade wind was helping to move a little of the smoke outside, but without the exhaust fan the temperature was easily 110 degrees. As Shabby and I tried to figure out which orders we had on the grill, I was aware that Bob was surrounding us with more candles. I grabbed a small flashlight, placed it firmly between my teeth, and began slowly arranging dinners on plates as they were done.

"Melinda, should I flip the steak above?" Shabby asked. "I can' see if it done." The two of us juggled orders as best we could, but the smoke was stinging our eyes. Ozzie washed dishes with very little water, and the waiters took orders and cleared tables in the dark. Clinton worked on his appetizers more by touch than by sight, and Garrilin groped in the dark for the cheesecake as dessert orders began to pile up.

The night seemed to last for days as we turned out dinner after dinner in the heat, smoke, and darkness. Meanwhile, Bob managed to appease most of the guests, even if their meals did take longer than expected. In fact, the customers loved the adventure. The dining room was even more romantic in the dark, with no music, no electric lights, just the sound of the sea and the flickering of candles. The first round of early guests left, making room for the more fashionable nine o'clock reservations. Only one table lingered over their cognac and coffee, oblivious to the fact that another party had been waiting almost an hour for their table.

"I'm sorry it's taking so long," Bob said to the hungry foursome waiting for their table to open up. But a very proper British gentleman in a navy blue blazer, white trousers, and a shiny new pair of Cole-Haans was losing his patience. "Precisely how much longer must we wait for our table?" he demanded.

Bob managed to convince the lingerers to let him buy them a round of drinks at the bar. Their table was cleared and quickly reset, and the foursome was ushered in at last. When Bob went over to take their order, he noticed an unusually large puddle developing next to their table. On extra-hot nights, the wine buckets dripped continually from condensation.

Before Bob had a chance to explain that without electricity we had no baked Brie bundles (they required an electric oven), the man announced they were ready to order.

"We'll start with four orders of baked Brie bundles," he said. Bob's face went white in the candlelight as he started once again to apologize, but the man's patience had reached its limit. He slapped his menu down on the table, pushed his chair back, and announced they were leaving. But as he stood to make his exit he stepped backward into the puddle of water. His well-shod feet slipped out from under him, and the gentleman fell flat on the floor. Bob stared in horror.

In utter silence the guests, the waiters, and poor Bob watched the man rise to his feet, his blazer dripping. But when he became aware that everyone in the restaurant was watching to see what he would do next, somehow his mood shifted. He removed his wet jacket, broke into a big smile, opened his arms wide, and said, "Ladies and gentlemen, there's no charge for the entertainment."

The entire restaurant burst into applause, with many guests standing to get a better view. As Bob's visions of lawsuits began to fade, he helped the man back into his chair, offering to pay for the dry cleaning. Patting himself dry with clean napkins, the gentleman ordered four Caesar salads to start, and lobsters for the table; Miguel poured a bottle of Dom Pérignon, on the house.

The table of four was the last to leave, and after they thanked us for "a truly unforgettable evening," taxi man Teddy took them back to their hotel. Our entire crew collapsed into dining room chairs with a collective heavy sigh. We sat staring at the full moon as exhaustion swept over us. "I wonder what the temperature is in the walk-in cooler," I mumbled, and Bob got up to check.

I looked at the kitchen staff through my sore and swollen eyelids; together we had managed to turn out ninety-two dinners in the dark. "Nobody can say to us, 'If you can't stand the heat, get out of the kitchen,'" I said.

"The temperature in the walk-in is fifty degrees," said Bob. "I'm going to St. Martin tomorrow to buy a generator. Clinton says you can get one for twenty-five hundred dollars." Suddenly a generator seemed like the most wonderful machine ever invented, and I agreed that he should take the night's proceeds and be on the first ferry to St. Martin in the morning.

Ba-boom, ba-ba-boom, ba-boom, ba-ba-boom—it was the familiar sound of an approaching car outfitted with giant woofers. *Ba-boom, ba-ba-boom* came louder and louder; then headlights and a cloud of dust appeared. It was Bug, only seven hours late.

"Bug, where have you been?" I asked.

"I stuck in St. Martin," he said with a grin.

It was hard to get too angry with Bug. He had, after all, come to work at eleven-thirty at night to attack a mountain of dirty dishes by candlelight.

Water was no problem for Bug, who not only had come to work but had come prepared. From his car he produced a five-gallon pail on a rope, which he proceeded to lower into the cistern and pull back up full of water. "We ain' need no pump," he said.

We boiled buckets of water on the stove so Bug could clean up. "This more fun in the dark," Bug said in his crazy falsetto.

Uncle Waddy's morning visits had become a regular part of our day, and I looked forward to seeing his smiling face as we traded recipes for cornbread, johnnycakes, and chowder. He always came with his rolls of sea bean, the large, purple flowers wrapped up in the long vines, having gathered them on the beach for his goats. Though he never asked, Bob usually loaded the greens into our car and drove Uncle Waddy and his bush, as he called it, up the hill to his house. He insisted the exercise was good for him, but at eighty-five years old, he also never refused the ride.

As he had told me, Uncle Waddy walked the length of Meads Bay every day. He marched up and down the beach, swinging his arms high in the air and taking long strides, as if he were a man half his age. But over a few months his visits became a little less frequent. We saw him sitting on his porch one day and stopped by to say hi. We could tell from his soft voice that he wasn't feeling his usual energetic self. He refused to see a doctor, arguing that several neighbors had gone to the hospital and never come home again.

Uncle Waddy's health deteriorated quickly. His eighty-five years suddenly caught up with him, and each day he looked years older. He came into the kitchen one morning and, after refusing his customary fresh orange juice, announced he was going to the hospital. We never saw him again.

The funeral was held in the historic Methodist church in South Hill, and it looked as if the entire island had come to pay tribute to John Waddington Hodge. The church was built from stone in 1878. A survivor of hurricanes and a revolution, it had Gothic arched windows that opened to the breeze drifting up from the harbor below. Standing in the churchyard, we were afforded one of the most spectacular views in Anguilla: Sparkling Road Bay was filled with fishing boats and sailing yachts, and beyond we could see Sandy Island, its tiny tuft of palm trees sticking up in the center.

Bob and I stood in the doorway along with the rest of the crowd that couldn't squeeze inside. We peered in and spotted Lowell and his family, Elbert the goat herder, James, Bennie, and many other familiar faces. Everyone sat quietly waiting for the service to begin; the only sound was the swooshing of paper fans moving back and forth across hot, sad faces.

A car with the license plate CM pulled up in the yard, and the crowd parted to make way for the Chief Minister and his entourage, who filed into the reserved pew in the front row. The Chief, as he is referred to, is an elected official and, along with his executive council, administers the legislation of the government. Once they were seated, the minister began the eulogy.

We listened as Uncle Waddy's life was recounted. We heard about his courageous role during the Anguilla Revolution. He was credited for improving education on the island as well, and the youth of Anguilla were urged to follow Uncle Waddy's example of exercise, diet, and healthy living if they wanted to live to be eighty-five.

A neighbor from Long Bay played guitar and sang hymns with two other men, and tears rolled down my cheeks as I remembered Uncle Waddy's bundles of sea-bean vines lying next to my kitchen door. We joined the procession of cars, led by Ozzie driving the old white hearse, to the cemetery in West End. John Waddington Hodge was put to rest overlooking Meads Bay, where he had walked, swum, and gathered vines for nearly eighty years.

Back in the kitchen, I stared at the empty doorway. A younger generation was replacing the Uncle Waddys of the island, and I felt sad that some of the traditions of old Anguilla had just been buried at Meads Bay.

I hadn't seen Joshua and Evelyn for several weeks, and losing Uncle Waddy inspired me to pay a visit to Rey Hill. In a pensive mood, I drove extra slowly, taking in the smoky breeze from a smoldering coal keel where someone was making charcoal along the way. I breathed deeply, savoring the old ways still remaining in Anguilla. Two boys were working on a boat in their yard. An older man, perhaps the boys' grandfather, sat in the shade of a flamboyant tree, watching. The art of boatbuilding was being passed on to a new generation. In South Hill a man wearing a faded T-shirt and a New York Mets baseball cap pushed two white pails in a rusty wheelbarrow through the bush. Presumably he was hauling water from the government pipe nearby. His house must not have had a cistern.

Farther along I passed a little wooden cottage with a huge pile of wire fish pots in the yard. Only a very few of these wooden houses had survived Hurricane Donna in 1960. An old-fashioned vernacular of wooden shingles and bright shutters had given way to the practicality of flat concrete homes that could withstand a severe storm.

I turned into the labyrinth of roads that led to Joshua's house and passed a group of schoolchildren walking home. Two older girls were holding the hands of little ones who couldn't have been more than three or so. They had to take two steps for every one of the big girls in order to keep up. I found Joshua and Evelyn sitting in their living room, listening to a radio that looked as though it was from the 1940s. It sat on the bookshelves between two porcelain dolphin figurines. A framed picture of Evelyn standing under a palm tree hung on the wall next to the radio. We had taken the picture five years earlier and sent it to them for Christmas.

Evelyn eyed me up and down and said, "You comin' nice."

I just smiled.

"You comin' real nice," she said again, hoping for more of a reaction.

"It's nice to see you," I said, knowing it wasn't quite the right answer.

Joshua helped me out. "She mean you put on a few pounds. You look good."

"I don't think it's nice. I feel fat," I said as I patted hips that were a little plumper than I would have liked.

"No, you ain' fat. You healthy."

Had I been visiting my own grandmother, I'd be getting advice on weight loss. She'd tell me of the latest diets she'd heard about on TV and list my options: high protein, low protein, high carb, low carb, ignore calories, or count calories, with, of course, all of the diets promising I would never be hungry again. If worse came to worst, I could always go to a spa and hide out until I was presentable again.

Evelyn, I was sure, had never heard of a spa and would never consider going to one even if she had. Why would anyone spend money to be skinny?

We talked for a while about Uncle Waddy and about traditions lost and times gone by. Evelyn explained that in the old days, when times were less prosperous for Anguilla, you hardly ever saw heavy people. Sometimes fish was the only thing to eat, since long droughts were common, and the already meager crops would die. "It hard to get big with only fish to eat," she said.

Driving to The Valley was a daily challenge made infinitely more interesting by the various obstacles encountered along the way. There were animals, speed bumps, tourists forgetting to keep left, and, just like everywhere else in the world, a younger generation of hot-rodders.

Rawldy, on the other hand, drove too slowly. Top speed for Rawldy was 15 mph, and his rattletrap station wagon could often be found at the head of a long line of cars. Rawldy was Anguilla's own traveling salesman. He drove around with a selection of hand-crafted brooms made of gnarly sticks and palm fronds tied to his roof rack. From the back of his car he offered mangoes, sweet potatoes, bananas, christophines, coconuts, and papayas.

Prospective customers would hail Rawldy, and he'd stop in the middle of the road to discuss a potential sale. With his tailgate open, entire neighborhoods would gather around his car to squeeze mangoes or inspect brooms for weight and balance. Meanwhile traffic piled up behind him. Sometimes cars would inch around, but usually everyone just waited.

If we came to a slow crawl in an endless line of cars, or if traffic was stopped entirely, Rawldy was usually at the front of the line. *Island time,* we'd remind ourselves.

Bob and I settled into the leisurely pace, breathing deeper and walking slower. Always in shorts and sandals, we pictured friends up north coping with sleet and slush. Accustomed to the bright blue sky and mornings of intense yellow sunlight, we even began to find a welcome relief in the occasional rain. Tourists, on the other hand, had not come for rain. A morning drizzle was tolerated in good spirits by most—after all, what's so bad about spending a morning on the balcony reading a good book? A little respite before an afternoon of sun could easily be accepted.

An entire day of rain was pushing it, though, and two consecutive days brought out the cranky side of visitors. "What's with the weather?" they'd ask Bob in the dining room each night. "Does it always rain in Anguilla? We went to St. Barts last year and had perfect weather." He'd explain that St. Barts was only fifteen miles away and usually had the same weather as we did, and actually, it was even a little rainier there because of that island's mountains. He assured them that if it was raining in Anguilla, it was most likely raining in St. Barts as well.

Far worse than the occasional shower, however, were Anguilla's infamous Christmas winds. Anguilla's weather is usually constant, with an average temperature of eighty degrees and annual rainfall of thirty-five inches. It's the most northerly of the Leeward Islands, with a gentle trade wind blowing from the east. But just as Provence is visited by the cold, relentless wind of the mistral and California has its Santa Anas, Anguilla was occasionally plagued by the Christmas winds, which sometimes lingered into January. The trade winds, usually from the east, would shift around to the west, pick up speed, and turn into a gale. Glasses and flowers blew off tables in the dining room, and we would have to lock all the shutters, closing out the gardens and fountains, making the restaurant feel cramped and claustrophobic. Rain pounded against the building in cold gusts and seeped through the louvers, soaking tablecloths and seat cushions on the western side. Customers were hostile. Cancellations and no-shows were rampant, and tempers were short among the soggy souls who did turn up.

After a week of Christmas winds, the entire island sank into a melancholy funk. The open-air restaurants closed, taxi drivers had few fares, and disappointed guests were forced to stay in their rooms.

Even the Blanchard's kitchen crew sulked. Bug came to work in a wool hat. "Too mucha water," he grumbled. "I gonna build an ark if this keep up."

But ten days after the winds began, they blew themselves away abruptly one night during dinner. As we cautiously opened the shutters the mood in the restaurant turned cheerful. The next morning dawned crystal clear, the sun started to dry the island out, and a wave of contentment swept over our thirty-five square miles of paradise. Tourists went back to lolling on the beach and told horror stories about the weather to naive new arrivals. Anguilla returned to normal, and Bug put aside his boatbuilding plans.

Crisp Thai Snapper

One of our best-selling items on the menu turned out to be the crispy crusted snapper with a Thai citrus sauce. Luckily, it was also one of the easiest dishes to prepare, so anyone in the kitchen could help as orders came in.

For the snapper, just spread a thin layer of coarse-grained mustard on each fillet. Then press a layer of shredded (uncooked) Idaho potato firmly on top of the mustard. Sauté in a little olive oil, potato side up, for about two minutes. Turn over carefully and cook until potato is crispy and brown.

The sauce is just as easy. For four servings, whisk together 2 tablespoons fresh lemon juice with ¼ cup honey until the honey dissolves. Add ¼ cup soy sauce, 2 teaspoons minced ginger, ½ teaspoon minced garlic, and mix well. Whisking constantly, add ½ cup vegetable oil in a slow, steady stream until well blended.

Conversation in the kitchen one night centered on the news of the first cruise ship to arrive in Anguilla. "She a new brand boat," Shabby said, glowing with excitement. "From Germany. She gonna leave Santo Domingo and come every other Sunday. We all gonna have to learn German 'cause next year we be full of German tourists. Once these people see how beautiful it is here, they'll go home and tell all their friends 'bout Anguilla."

The taxi men who came through the kitchen that night were ecstatic about the new ship. I gave Nell a Caesar salad and Teddy a piece of cheesecake while they made their case. No more hanging out under a tree waiting for business, they said. They were ready to provide island tours for the masses. A few even debated ordering larger vans to accommodate the anticipated hordes of people. Merchants were going to set up temporary stalls for T-shirts and gifts, and the beach bars in Sandy Ground prepared special lunch menus in German.

Twelve hundred people arriving on this tiny rock was big news indeed, and though many islanders saw it as a real breakthrough for business, there were skeptics as well. "Who will clean up their litter on the beach?" people asked. "Whose bathrooms will they use?"

But to me, the most important question raised was "What about all the tourists who come to Anguilla to get away from cruise ships and crowds?" The debate intensified, and we heard the pros and cons repeated all over the island. Everyone had an opinion.

The first big Sunday arrived, and we joined the crowd of locals perched on the cliff overlooking the sleepy harbor of Sandy Ground. There it was—a white monster of a boat that appeared to be half the length of the entire bay.

"It's huge," I whispered to Bob. "It's like an invasion."

"Mel," he said, "you can't deny the people here their right to expand their economy. Think of what this could do for the taxi drivers alone."

"But I'm worried about the tourists who love that there are so few people here; they'll stop coming. It'll make Anguilla more like St. Martin."

I caught bits and pieces of conversations around me in the crowd as everyone eyed the giant vessel. Some looked on with admiration, others sounded apprehensive. We decided to drive down the hill into Sandy Ground to get a firsthand look. A banner hung from posts on the beach: WILLKOMMEN AUF ANGUILLA.

But where were the twelve hundred tourists spewing onto the beach, and why were the taxi drivers still just hanging around? Only a few cruise passengers chose to come ashore, and they were examining the T-shirts for sale; other than that, not much was going on.

Over the next few weeks local enthusiasm for the German cruise ship faded. Bob and I felt bad that hopes had been dashed and plans for German lessons were no longer in the offing. Secretly, though, we were relieved. The cruise ship experiment ended after the initial trial run, and Anguilla, for the time being at least, remained a quiet hideaway.

Our lives had settled into an Anguillian rhythm during the day. Each morning on the way to the restaurant Bob and I waved to Elbert the goat herder. We put in about four hours of prep work in the kitchen along with Marcus, who always arrived a little late. Marcus had no concept of time and no structure in his life except for the few hours a day he worked with us. We'd given up trying to make him come on time, and since he continued to break most pieces of equipment he touched, his duties had been restricted to shucking corn, peeling and chopping potatoes and carrots, and washing pots and pans. Sometimes Marcus was so late that we were just finishing our work as he arrived. Rather than wait for him to do his job, we left him there to lock up when he finished.

After cooking each morning, Bob would drop me off at home to do my ordering, pay bills, and add up the receipts from the night before. I juggled phone calls from London, New York, and Düsseldorf, taking dinner reservations from people I'd never met. They'd either heard about Blanchard's from customers who had just returned home or read about us in the articles that were starting to appear in various publications.

Bob would head for The Valley in search of the inevitable missing ingredient. I'd send him on a mission to find tomatoes or perhaps some cream. If a boat had just come in, the undertaking was relatively easy—two or three stops and he might have what we needed for that night's menu. More often than not we would either do without or make a quick trip to St. Martin.

Lunch became the high point of our day as we rotated our way through all the restaurants on the island. Sitting at the beach bar at Cap Juluca with a swordfish sandwich topped with grilled onions and local hot sauce, or at Uncle Ernie's eating grilled chicken and ribs, we felt as if we were on vacation for an hour or two each day. Uncle Ernie's was just the sort of place we'd had in mind when we first thought about opening a restaurant on Anguilla: two Weber grills, three tables in the sand shaded by Heineken umbrellas, and chicken, ribs, or fish with fries for $5. Ernie served lunch only and had an easy life. I often wondered how different our lives would have been had our rent allowed us to have a simpler business. We'd probably be bored.

An afternoon nap became an essential part of our routine if we were to make it through dinner without yawning. We'd sleep from about two to four, and then our alarm clock would remind us it was time to confirm all the reservations that had been left on the answering machine. By five o'clock, we were back at the restaurant, getting ready for another curtain call.

Every Saturday Roxana's parents earned some extra money by setting up a tent by North Hill Road and serving lunch to passersby. Vi, Roxana's mother, and several of her friends from church spent two days preparing bull-foot soup, salt fish, conch stew, johnnycakes, and sweet-potato dumplings; her husband, Bernard, organized the tables and chairs, grills, and ice coolers.

I consider myself an adventurous eater, but it took some coaxing from Garrilin and little Roxana before I sampled the bull-foot soup. The two of them laughed when I grimaced and told them all I could imagine were giant brown bulls with hooves the size of footballs. But I joined them at the tent one Saturday specifically to try the sweet-potato dumplings. Roxana rubbed her tummy and said, "Mel, you gonna love these. Everybody in Anguilla love these."

As Garrilin brought our dumplings to the table, she confessed, "Mel, you seen these leaves before."

I couldn't imagine what she meant.

"See, the potato wrap with sea grape leaves. Bernard and Roxana pick these from in front of Blanchard's. They *your* leaves."

"That's great," I said. "We have lots more they can have." I looked at the green bundles. They were bigger than I'd expected—about six inches long and almost three inches around.

"These are huge. Are we each really eating a whole one?" I asked Garrilin.

"They big, yes. Each one weigh a pound. But you gonna love it, man."

"Tell me how they're made," I said.

"We take two, maybe three leaves, dependin' on size, and roll them around the filling. Our sweet potato not like yours, you know. It white inside. Anyway, then we chop up the boil potato with spice and butter and nutmeg. If the potato ain' sweet enough, we add a little sugar."

"What kind of spice?" I asked.

"You know. Spice. We grind up those little brown sticks—they look like bark."

"You mean cinnamon?"

"Yeah, man. I forget you call it cinnamon. We jus' call it spice."

Roxana interrupted, "Garrilin, you forget to boil the leaves. Mommy boil the leaves before she roll 'em."

"Oh, yeah." Garrilin stood corrected. The sea grape leaves were too stiff right off the tree, so they had to be boiled to make them pliable, she explained.

"Then," she continued, "we take strips of cloth—usually from ol' sacks a flour—an' we tie the leaves 'round the potato so they hold when they cook in the water. That all we do."

I carefully unwrapped my dumpling, hating to pull apart such a perfect package. Three big leaves unfolded like a flower, revealing the sweet, steaming log inside. The spice, as Garrilin had called it, made the white potato brown, and it was smooth as silk on the outside with a few tiny ridges formed by the edges of the leaves.

Had I not known it was a potato filling, I'm not sure I would have guessed. I'm a big fan of cinnamon, so I loved the flavor, and the texture was like a firm bread pudding—another one of my favorites.

While I was eating, Garrilin went back to the food table under the tent and brought back more things for me to try.

"Here, Mel," she said. "This pigeon pea soup. You see the peas dryin' out in people's yards or on cisterns—anywhere they have space. We dry the pods in the sun and use 'em in rice or soup. Everyone in Anguilla eat peas in somethin' most every day."

I had eaten rice and peas at Cora Lee's often and was familiar with the fact that what were called peas here would be beans back home. Tiny brown flecks, similar to lentils, floated in a broth with carrots, onions, and celery. There were dumplings in the soup as well, these made from flour, cornmeal, and water, and shaped into two-inch torpedoes that reminded me of matzoh balls.

"Where's Mac today?" I asked.

"I dunno wha' keepin' he back. He say he meet us here. Musta got a puncture in he tire."

Then came the moment of truth. Garrilin placed a bowl in front of me. She and Roxana fell silent. There was no way I could get out of giving it a try. "It's just the name I don't like," I explained. "I wish I didn't know what was in it."

"Try it," Roxana urged.

I've never been able to refuse the pleas of a six-year-old with big black eyes, her long lashes fluttering a little flirtatiously. In the end, the bull-foot soup was quite good—a bit like beef and barley, but instead of the barley, it had more of the same flour dumplings as the pigeon pea soup. There were red and green peppers, lots of onions, and a few pieces of the dreaded bull foot itself. It was very good, I admitted, but the name would probably still keep me from ordering it too often.

At work that night Garrilin announced in the kitchen, "Mel eat like we today."

Bug said, "She comin'. She comin'."

Chapter 10

Marcus lived with his uncle Julius, a fisherman from West End whose lackadaisical lifestyle served as a sharp contrast to the atmosphere at Blanchard's. Because he was the only member of our staff who worked in the morning, Marcus wasn't as much a part of the Blanchard family as the others. Bob and I liked him, though, and felt something of a parental responsibility toward him in spite of his less-than-perfect performance as an employee. He walked with a playful bounce in his step and always seemed to be smiling. No job was too menial for Marcus, and in fact he often volunteered to do additional mopping or scrubbing when he saw the need. His enthusiasm made up for the broken equipment and his lateness.

On more than one occasion we stopped by the restaurant while Marcus was still cleaning up and found several of his friends in the kitchen watching him work. We felt a little uncomfortable about our kitchen being used as a gathering place and asked Marcus to meet his friends when he was done.

"I ain' got no trans," Marcus said. "They jus' here to give me a liff."

There is a code of silence that exists in every workplace when it comes to turning in another employee, but in Anguilla, telling the boss that a co-worker is doing something wrong is almost a violation of national honor. Informants can be permanently ostracized.

So when one of our staff came to us to talk about Marcus, we recognized the risk he was taking.

He arrived at our house early one Sunday morning and made us promise not to tell Marcus—or anyone else—that he had come. After Bob and I solemnly swore ourselves to secrecy, he took a deep breath and blurted out his news.

"Marcus dealin' drugs from the kitchen." He paused, waiting for a reaction, but we were dumbfounded. "You gotta get ridda he," we were cautioned. "He a bad dude, an' if the police catches him dealin' drugs at Blanchard's, you in trouble too. One a he friends a big dealer. Marcus work for he."

"Damn that Marcus," Bob said. "I can't believe he would do this to us. Do you think the rest of the staff knows about this?"

"Everybody know 'cept you." He looked at us apologetically, as if he had just insulted us. "He gonna bring the whole place down if you ain' get ridda he."

"Look," I said. "First of all, I want to tell you how grateful we are that you came here to tell us about Marcus. I know how difficult it must have been for you to make that decision, and it means so much to us that you did."

"You's good people, and Blanchard's is too important to the rest of we. I had to say somethin'."

"We'll let him go tomorrow morning, and we will not mention your name to anyone," I promised.

"Poor Marcus," Bob said.

"Poor Marcus, nuttin'." Our informant was disgusted. "He a bad dude." With that he got up to leave, and as we thanked him again for coming forward, he repeated, "Marcus a bad dude."

He drove away, and I immediately said, "Bob, we have to get some advice on how to handle this. I know we have to let him go, but what if we fire him and he complains to the labor department? We don't really have any proof, and we could end up in big trouble. I think we should call Bennie and see what he thinks."

"Oh, God, I hadn't thought of that. Just what we need. We try to fire a drug dealer, and the labor department comes down on us because we can't prove it."

I caught Bennie at home just as he was leaving for church. He knew I wouldn't be calling on Sunday morning unless it was important, so he insisted I give him a full report. "It's very easy," Bennie said when I finished, relishing his role as our advisor. "You do have to fire the boy, but you must notify the labor department before he has a chance to go in and make a formal complaint. Write a letter to him explaining why you are letting him go. Tell him you cannot tolerate any chance of drug activity at your place of business, and therefore you are not giving him the usual required notice. Send a copy to the labor department, asking them to keep it on file. That's all you need to do to protect yourself."

Relieved, I thanked Bennie and wrote the letter. The next morning we waited for Marcus to arrive at the restaurant. I felt as if I were about to kick my own son out of the house, yet I knew he had to go. I kept repeating our employee's words to bolster my courage: "He'll bring the whole place down." There was no question that if the police found any drug activity at Blanchard's, we would be blamed. It was also a little scary not knowing how deeply Marcus was involved. Firing a drug dealer could have further ramifications. What if Marcus decided to get even? His unsavory friends could be dangerous.

At ten-thirty, Marcus wandered in with his usual bounce and a cheery "Good morning."

I looked at Bob, knowing I couldn't say the words. "Marcus," Bob said, "we're going to have to let you go. You've been dealing drugs from here, and we can't allow that."

Marcus's expression told me he was shocked that we had found out. He knew how much we cared about him, and tried to defend himself. "I ain' been dealin' no drugs."

"Yes, you have," Bob continued.

I felt like crying. Marcus looked like a scared little boy, and I wanted to hug him and tell him we were there to help. I knew that was impossible, though. Not in Anguilla. Our work permits could be canceled at any time, and we just couldn't risk getting involved.

"We also know one of your friends is a big-time dealer," Bob said.

Marcus dropped his head and said, "Please, Bob, I wan' this job."

"I'm sorry," Bob answered, "but you've jeopardized the whole restaurant, and we have no choice. I just want to say a couple of things, and I want you to listen very carefully." Bob spoke slowly, choosing his words cautiously. "Melinda and I both care about you, Marcus, and we feel very bad about this. I think you are headed down the wrong road, and someday you will get caught." He paused, either to let that sink in or to figure out what to say next. "I know you go to St. Martin a lot, Marcus, and if you get caught over there, you'll end up in the underground prison in Guadeloupe. That's where they send drug dealers; you'll never see daylight again. Do you understand that?"

I handed Marcus the letter of termination as a formality. I knew he couldn't read it, but Bennie said it was important.

"You ain' gonna turn me in, are you?" Marcus asked.

"No," Bob said, "but I want you to think about what I've said, okay?"

And with that, Marcus turned and walked down the road. I could still remember him mimicking and laughing at the cartoon characters in the Thanksgiving Day parade. He was just a child.

It was two weeks before the local election and our kitchen buzzed with political banter. Every five years each of the seven districts on the island voted for their representative to the House of Assembly. England provides Anguilla with a British governor, but from what I gathered from the political debates among Blanchard's staff, locally elected officials are the ones who really have the power.

Campaigns here are simple. There are no investigations into past indiscretions and no rules about divesting oneself of conflicting interests. Politics in such a small community understandably revolves around people more than issues. Constituents vote for the people they are closest to, the people they trust. And with only a handful of surnames dominating the phone book, many times the vote goes to a family member. This is not to say elections are unfair or even predictable; like anywhere else in the world, voters select officials they feel will make the right decisions. It's just that in tiny Anguilla, the choices are closer to home.

After the election, the new members of the House of Assembly decide who is most qualified to fill the various positions within the local government. They appoint a chief minister, a minister of finance, a minister of public works, a minister of education, and others. The governor, sent by Her Majesty the queen, works in conjunction with the local officials and shares in running the government.

Night after night, kitchen cleanup was completed in record time so that our staff could get to a political rally. Ozzie was the smallest of our crew, but when it came to politics, his presence filled the room. "Mel, Eddie talkin' tonight," he said animatedly. "He the first man who get school bus to go Sandy Ground, ya know. Eddie Baird, he the man." Ozzie's usual dance routines turned into brilliant impersonations of the various candidates. He strode around the kitchen, chest puffed up and feet turned out, mimicking the opposition.

"Yeah," Bug would argue. "But David the man who gonna keep Anguilla goin' the right direction. He the man we need. He think bigger than school buses."

"You ain' got children in Sandy Ground," Ozzie retorted. "We ain' wan' our kids walkin' up that long hill to go school."

Blanchard's kitchen reflected the political divisions of Anguilla, albeit in the friendliest of fashions. Bug cheerfully disagreed with Ozzie and Garrilin with Lowell. They all cared deeply about the future of Anguilla, and their passion was sometimes deafening. As with so many kitchen discussions, I had to remind them we had customers just around the corner.

Posters were stapled to telephone poles, flyers were distributed at local shops, and billboards on elaborate wooden stands were erected along the main road. Nobody was making campaign buttons, but I thought it would have been a good business to start. Everyone seemed to wear a T-shirt promoting his or her preferred candidate, and the local radio station continually broadcasted political speeches and commentaries.

Politics permeated every facet of local life, yet our staff knew better than to lobby Bob and me. We listened to the debates but said not a word. We had friends representing all parties in the race and wanted to keep them as friends.

At six o'clock on the night before the elections Blanchard's was busy with its usual predinner activities. The dining room was being set, Shabby was filleting fish, and Garrilin was washing greens for salad. I went into the walk-in cooler to take a quick inventory, and by the time I came out, everyone was gone. Ozzie had deserted his station; Bug's sink was filled with suds and ready to go, but there was no Bug. I ran to the dining room and found it empty as well. Just as I was starting to get nervous that I'd missed some emergency, Bob came into the bar, motioning for me to come outside.

There they all were in the parking area, a jumble of excitement. "What's going on?" I asked Miguel.

"Motorcade" was all he said.

"Mel," Lowell explained, "this a motorcade for the opposition. These the people who *ain'* in power and who *wanna* be in power."

"But I don't see any cars," I said.

"They comin'," Ozzie said. "They jus' pass though South Hill and they comin' Meads Bay now." How he knew their exact location, I hadn't a clue. But as our entire clan stood by the road I could feel the tension mount, and in a few minutes I heard horns tooting in the distance. As the cars rounded the corner by the salt pond, our staff burst into loud cheers and jeers, depending on whose side they were on.

I don't know how many vehicles were in the motorcade, but it went on for miles and miles down the road. Hundreds of people were piled into the back of pickups, dump trucks, and jeeps; even a backhoe had a slew of hangers-on. By the time they were directly in front of Blanchard's, the chorus of tooting horns was blaring. I saw dozens of familiar faces, and everyone waved frantically as they passed.

Fifteen minutes later the horns were fading in the distance, and we all filed back into the restaurant to prepare for dinner. We were behind schedule and had to work extra fast to make up for lost time.

A few minutes later Garrilin looked at me and grinned. "Here we go again." Before I knew it, the entire gang was back outside. I followed, knowing there was no hope of getting anyone to focus on dinner with motorcade number two now approaching.

"This the other side now," Lowell said. "These be the people *in* power and they wanna *stay* in power." Each party had a symbol that they used for the campaign: the hand, the clock, the bird, and the tree. This motorcade clearly had a large contingent from the tree party, because people were energetically waving huge branches out of car windows and trucks.

The motorcade was almost past when our first guests arrived for dinner. We weren't quite ready and explained about the big day coming up. Bob bought them a glass of wine and stalled them with a few stories. It was an exhilarating evening in the kitchen. The polls would open the next morning at seven, and everyone was fired up and ready for the count.

The voting took place in schools and under tents in each district around the island. People lined up to make their mark and drop their paper into the ballot box. A candidate can sometimes win by only a few votes, so the count was done carefully and in public, to avoid any mistakes. On election night everyone showed up early for work. They couldn't bear the thought of being apart when the results started coming in. The TV in the kitchen was tuned to the local station, where the counting of the ballots was being televised, and Ozzie's car radio was tuned to Radio Anguilla as it reported the tally. Bug and Ozzie took turns running to the parking lot to hear the latest commentary.

Each and every ballot was pulled out of a box and read aloud while someone held it up for verification in front of the TV camera. The live telecast continued throughout dinner, and more than once I heard Clinton chime in to the rhythm of the count:

OSBOURNE FLEMING . . . THE HAND
RONALD WEBSTER . . . THE HAT
OSBOURNE FLEMING . . . THE HAND
OSBOURNE FLEMING . . . THE HAND
RONALD WEBSTER . . . THE HAT

Then, counting another district:

FRANKLIN CONNOR . . . THE BIRD
HUBERT HUGHES . . . THE TREE
HUBERT HUGHES . . . THE TREE
HUBERT HUGHES . . . THE TREE
FRANKLIN CONNOR . . . THE BIRD

And on it went for hours, seven districts, sixteen candidates. It was hypnotic—so much so that Clinton and Shabby would mimic aloud the counting process for weeks to come. It was as though they had fallen into a trance. When the results were finalized that night, half our staff was cheering and the other half was silent. It was the first time we'd ever seen Bug without a smile.

We figured that was the end of elections for five years. We figured wrong. That night everyone again was out by the road, cheering and jeering. The winners were driving the entire length of the island in one last colossal motorcade, thanking their constituents for their victory. I reckoned elections were really over now and I had five years to figure out how to make campaign buttons.

The traditional food for Easter is salt fish, and Roxana wanted to make sure I sampled her mother's recipe. She, Garrilin, and I met under the Saturday food tent where I'd tasted the bull-foot soup. One of the women from the church heaped a mound of what looked like yellow shreds onto our plates; we pulled out bottles of water and soda from a cooler, and before I picked up my fork, Garrilin wanted to tell me what I was about to eat.

"The fish ain' from here, ya know. It imported from up by all you. Up there in the States. It codfish that be dried, and it keep forever—that why we like it. It come too salty, though, so we boil it in water with some sugar to sweeten it up. The sugar dissolve the salt—you know 'bout that?"

I had no time to answer before Roxana chimed in, "Mommy cook it twice. After she cook it in the water an' sugar, then we all help to remove the bones. Mel, there a lotta bones in that fish, ya know."

I took my first bite and wished they had used even more sugar. Garrilin and Roxana were eating steadily, obviously not at all bothered by the salt.

"Mel, here some ginger beer to wash it down," Roxana said, handing me a cup. I'd tasted ginger beer before and knew it was strong. It's made from fresh ginger soaked in water with just a little sugar, vanilla extract, and a drop of lime juice.

"So anyway," Garrilin continued, "after all the bones outta the fish, we chip it up and cook it in a little oil with celery, peppers, onion, garlic, and a little curry, and let it stew to mix all the flavors.

Mel, every house in Anguilla cook salt fish for Easter. It a local . . . what that word you use?" She thought for a moment. "It a real *delicacy*. That the word I try to think of." *Delicacy* wasn't the word that came to my mind. I was happy to have a johnnycake on the side, to help cut the salt.

Easter Monday is an official holiday in Anguilla, set aside for the national sport of boat racing. The tradition developed a hundred years ago, when ships came down from Nova Scotia to the Caribbean laden with lumber and salt cod and sailed back north with rum, sugar, molasses, and cotton from more prosperous islands such as Antigua and Barbados. Anguilla, the northernmost of the Leeward Islands, was their final stop, where they'd top off their cargo with salt from the ponds before leaving the West Indies.

The schooners from Nova Scotia were faster, lighter, and easier to sail than the European boats that were also picking up goods from the region. Several industrious Anguillians replicated this schooner design and built their own fleet to transport cargo throughout the Caribbean.

Since work on Anguilla was always limited, people looked for additional income off island. Sugar companies from Santo Domingo set up a recruiting station in Marigot on St. Martin, and on the first or second day of every year hundreds of Anguillians, along with people from surrounding islands, piled aboard the sleek cargo schooners to go cut cane on the rich sugar plantations.

Sails would fill the harbor, and the schooners would all weigh anchor for the four-day journey to Santo Domingo. Competition was inevitable as captains and crew sailed off into the sunset. Even more passionate still was the race back home, when the men returned to Anguilla after months away. Hundreds of families would wait on the beach, cheering as the sails appeared one by one around the point at Sandy Ground. The speed of each schooner became public record, and the competition became even fiercer. Boat racing as a spectator sport in Anguilla was born.

The love of racing spread, and it is said that every day was a race day in Anguilla, with the local fishing boats chasing each other back home after a day at sea. By the 1970s, however, fishing boats were fitted with outboard motors and were no longer fun to race, so people started to build boats specifically for that purpose. Today Anguilla's racing boats still resemble the old fishing boats—the largest are twenty-eight feet long—and are completely open, with masts that soar up to fifty feet into the air.

Bob and I had listened to boat talk in the kitchen for months and were eager to witness our first Easter Monday race. The skill-fully handcrafted wooden vessels gathered that morning at Sandy Ground; some sailed in from Island Harbor, while others were hauled overland by trailer. We walked up and down the beach admiring each boat as the crews assembled the rigging. The huge sails were spread out on the sand; ropes were threaded through rows of grommets and then lashed around the mast. Once ready to launch, logs were placed under each boat, and a dozen hot, grunting men rolled and skidded the boats along the sand and into the sea.

We spotted Shabby pushing a bright yellow boat named *Stinger*. His massive shoulders were propelling the boat toward the water in forceful jolts; the rest of the men were helping, but when Shabby leaned into it, the Stinger really moved. Bob went over and offered his assistance, and Shabby said, "Yeah, man, grab hold. Okay, now push." The heavy wooden boat skidded a few feet. "Push," Shabby called out, and it moved again.

I sat down on the hot sand to enjoy the action. I counted four-teen boats up and down the beach and watched as hundreds of people gathered round for the race. The smell of fresh paint from the boats mingled with that of barbecued chicken and ribs from the dozen or so grills set up on the beach. A steady thumping beat boomed from Johnno's Beach Bar, where a group of people milled about, hips swaying and heads bobbing, many with a Heineken in one hand and a grilled chicken leg in the other.

Stinger floated off the beach, and Bob came back to tell me he'd seen Lowell's boat. "It's called *Light and Peace*," he said. "It's a beauty—shiny gray with a yellow stripe at the top."

Lowell saw us coming and waved from the boat. He was sitting on the gunwale along with seven other men, all wearing life preservers with the boat's name printed on the back.

"We goin' out to give 'er a try," Lowell yelled, using his hand as a megaphone to make himself heard over the crowd. As the big sail swung around, all eight men quickly ducked, the boom narrowly missing their heads. The sail filled with wind, and *Light and Peace* skimmed away from shore with her crew leaning far out over the side.

Lowell's captain maneuvered around the sailboats and yachts anchored in the bay, then tacked back and forth, testing the wind, before returning to shore. The crew jumped off and waded up to the beach. Lowell grabbed a shovel and began filling a nylon bag with beach sand. "She need more ballast," he said. "She too light." The men carried the sandbag out into the water and handed it up into the boat, where the captain placed it in the bottom along with the lead weights, rocks, and other sandbags.

"Why do you need ballast?" Bob asked. "Doesn't the keel have lead in the bottom?"

"No, man," Lowell said. "All the boats got live ballast so we can haul 'em up on shore when we done. They be too heavy if we couldn't take the weight out. Besides, on the way back, we sometimes throw some of the sand overboard to adjust for the wind. I gotta go. We startin' at eleven o'clock." He waded out to *Light and Peace*, pulled himself up over the gunwale, and took his place with the crew.

All fourteen boats were now in the water, sails unfurled, and the crowd on the beach was gathered at the water's edge for the start. Mr. Cool, the island's refrigeration authority and owner of one of the racing boats, was in charge. He marched up and down the beach with the start gun, asking if all boats were ready. Once satisfied that they were, he raised his pistol in the air and fired. The race was on.

A roar came up from the crowd as the boats pulled away in a rainbow of color. Bob and I watched as they got smaller and smaller, and soon all we could see were fourteen little white triangles, all tilted the same way, all headed west.

I stood with my feet in the water, wondering what it would have felt like a hundred years ago if Bob had been on one of those boats going to cut cane for six months in Santo Domingo. *I don't suppose they had suntan lotion back then,* I mused, picturing him fried to a crisp in the cane fields.

"I'm hungry," Bob said. "Let's go have some ribs."

We wandered back toward the grills. One ambitious operation had erected a series of tentlike structures, with two-by-fours sticking up out of the sand covered with blue tarps; plastic tables and chairs were set up underneath. The tarps overhead snapped in the wind as we ate and listened to people speculate about which boat would win. After lunch the boats were far from sight, and the crowd on the beach dispersed to form a caravan of cars that climbed slowly up the hill from Sandy Ground. Curious, we followed.

The procession continued west, tracking the race boats and stopping periodically at viewing points along the road. We, along with hundreds of others, spent the entire afternoon following the race by road. Nobody's property was private during a boat race in Anguilla. We stood on people's cisterns, on hotel balconies, in the back of pickup trucks, and even climbed onto someone's roof for a better vantage point. Everyone pointed and guessed who was in the lead.

"*De Chan,* she up fron'," I heard someone say.

"No, man," replied another spectator. "She headed too far south. Hear me now. *Light and Peace,* she gonna win this race."

From so far away, the boats looked the same to me, but everyone else could identify them all. They rounded the western tip of Anguilla and then sailed nearly the length of the island, around a buoy, and back again. The Anguillian police boat monitored the race, making sure everyone sailed around the buoy, and at least a dozen more fishing boats, loaded with cheering fans, followed along for support.

It was four o'clock by the time *De Chan* came into view at Sandy Ground, followed by *De Wizard* and then *Bluebird*. Nell the taxi driver owned *Bluebird* and had been at Blanchard's the night before, boasting about his new sail from St. Thomas. Alwyn sailed on *De Wizard,* and we were excited to see one of our staff place in the top three. But *Light and Peace* had fallen back, and *Stinger* was nowhere in sight.

The crowd had returned to Sandy Ground to cheer for their boats as they came in. Bets were collected, and arguments broke out over the amount of ballast a boat did or didn't have, whether a particular tack had been a good decision, or if a new sail was needed before the next race.

That night the excitement continued in the kitchen.

"We woulda won, ya know," Shabby said. "But our boom bent as we came by Blowing Point."

"Shabby, you always think you gonna win," Bug said. "That boat ain' nothin' compared to *Bluebird*. Our new sail is the best in Anguilla."

"What happened to you, Lowell?" Ozzie asked.

"*Light and Peace* the best boat, ya know," Lowell answered. "She just go a little too far south, that all."

Alwyn's boat, *De Wizard,* apparently hadn't placed for a long time, so he was glowing. Everyone debated whose boat was in the best position to do well in the August Carnival races. These were the biggest of the year, with a week of qualifiers leading up to the Champion of Champions. Shabby said he and his brothers, along with a few other guys from Blowing Point, were thinking of building a new boat for Carnival.

"I'd love to help build it," Bob volunteered. "Do you think anyone would mind? Actually, what I'd really like to do is go out in a race too."

"No problem," Shabby said. "You know how to sail?"

"No, but you can use me for ballast." Bob smiled.

"You can' beat *Bluebird*," Bug jumped in.

"Aya, Lawd," Shabby said to nobody in particular. "Bug think he gonna beat us in August. He ain' gonna win."

That night I fell asleep listening to Bob talk about boats. It reminded me of when our lives in Vermont revolved around ski racing and I spent countless days freezing at the bottom of a mountain watching Jesse compete. Sitting at the finish line on the beach in Anguilla had opened up a whole new world of competition.

After Easter the island slowed down even more, and Bob took the opportunity to fly north to visit his father in Vermont. He was going to stop in Miami on the way back and buy a pickup truck to ship down. Our little red Suzuki had served us well but was having transmission problems, and we needed a replacement.

He'd been gone for two days when the break-in occurred. I came home from work around ten-thirty and noticed the sliding glass door looked crooked as I went up the steps to the porch. I opened the front door but backed right out again after glimpsing the mess in the living room. My desk had been ransacked, drawers were open, and papers were strewn across the floor.

The staff was still cleaning up at the restaurant, so I raced back to tell them what had happened. My mind replayed the people who had visited the house recently. Did someone know Bob was away? Had they been watching me? I knew I couldn't sleep there that night. Maybe I would never sleep there again. I wanted Bob.

Shabby, Clinton, Lowell, Bug, Ozzie, Alwyn, Miguel, and Garrilin were gathered in my yard in a matter of minutes. As Ozzie called the police for me, the whole crew began to investigate the evidence. The police arrived forty-five minutes later, and when they did, they ordered my staff to leave. They couldn't have so many people at the crime scene, they said. I insisted I wasn't staying there without my staff, and I explained that my husband was off island and they were there only for my support. Once the officers realized I was serious, they pulled out their fingerprint kit and went to work.

The break-in was a little crime, nothing serious. Anguilla has almost no crime whatsoever, and I knew that this incident was probably just some kids fooling around. Oh, there are crimes of passion in Anguilla—lovers gone astray, husbands not behaving. But crimes affecting strangers are essentially unheard of. Not much was missing, but without Bob I was uneasy. When he heard the news, of course, he wanted to skip Miami and come straight home, but we agreed it wouldn't do much good at that point. We also really needed a truck and couldn't find one in Anguilla. Any-one with a pickup that ran was not interested in selling. Miami was our only shot.

I spent the night at Malliouhana, and the next day Clinton and Lowell replaced the sliders with secure doors on hinges. "You safe now, Mel," Clinton assured me. "Nobody gonna bother you again. I talk to Bennie, and he comin' down to see you. He angry, man. He gonna teach whoever did this a lesson."

Bennie arrived now in the role of my guardian angel. "Anguilla has no crime, and we need to keep it that way," he roared. He began work on a secret weapon, pounding hundreds of nails furiously through a sheet of plywood. He turned the wood upside-down and placed it nail points facing up, inside our patio fence where the intruder had climbed into the yard. "If he come here again, he gonna get two feet full of nails. I already alerted the hospital," he said. "If anybody show up with nail holes in his feet, we got 'em."

After that, Bennie escorted me home from work every night and then sat in the shadows, watching my house. Determined to catch the thief, he spent his evenings parked in the bushes, waiting. In the end, it was the police who nabbed the culprits, and sure enough, they turned out to be more pranksters than criminals.

They were sent to jail until a trial could be held by a judge who travels throughout the British Caribbean territories.

Bob found, bought, and set up delivery of a great little Nissan pickup in Miami and returned on the afternoon American Eagle flight carrying a gift for Bennie. We drove from the airport directly to Blowing Point. Bennie was backing out of his driveway but pulled in again when he saw us coming.

"Bennie," Bob said, "we can't thank you enough for all you did while I was away."

"No problem. You would have done the same for my wife if the situation was reversed."

"We brought you a little gift," I said, handing over the box. Bennie tore into the package like a little kid; smiling, he handed the wrapping paper to Janet, his wife, for safekeeping. He admired the handsome briefcase, running his hand over the soft Coach leather.

"You really made Melinda feel safe," Bob said. "She wouldn't have gone back to the house if you hadn't been keeping an eye on her. Do you know the guys who did it?"

"Not really," Bennie said. "I know their families. Rest assured, though, they'll be locked up for a long time. Anguilla doesn't take this sort of thing lightly. We need to make an example out of this."

We agreed, said goodbye, and left Bennie holding his briefcase next to Janet, who was trying to smooth out the crumpled wrapping paper.

"Let's look for a different place to live," I said on the way back to the house. "There has to be someplace nicer—and now I can't walk into the living room without seeing everything strewn all over the floor."

"We'll put the word out that we're looking," Bob agreed. "Maybe one of the staff knows of something."

The restaurant seemed painfully slow after the intensity of the holiday season, and when Frankie Connor called from his ferry one night to book a table of sixteen, we all were thrilled. Bug even did a little jig in front of his sink, singing, "Sixteen people comin', yes, yes, yes. Plenty people fo' true."

Frankie's voice had been cool on the phone, but I could tell he was excited about something. "Where are these people coming from?" I asked him.

"You know they been shootin' a movie on St. Martin, right?" Frankie asked.

"Yeah."

"Well, this is who's doing it." He paused, hoping I would catch on, but finally whispered, "It Sandra Bullock and the film crew. And she want lobsters on the beach. Can you set up a big table right on the sand?"

"No problem. How soon will you be here?"

"I just leaving Marigot now," Frankie answered. "You got plenty of lobster?"

"We've got plenty," I said. "See you in half an hour or so."

We sprang into action. "Lowell and Miguel, you get the tables lined up and leveled on the beach," I said. "Let's put them as close to the water as possible.

"Ozzie," I continued, "you go up to Christine's and get twenty-five of those little brown paper bags that she uses for candy. We'll put sand in the bottom and candles inside. They'll look great on the beach all around the table."

Shabby cleaned sixteen lobsters, each of them weighing a hefty two pounds. Alwyn lugged chairs down our path to the beach, and I arranged flowers for the table.

"Who Sandra Bullet be, anyhow?" Bug asked.

"Sandra *Bullock*, Bug. You know her," Clinton said. "She was in *Speed*, that movie 'bout the bus that were outta control. Now they makin' the sequel over in St. Martin 'bout a boat outta control."

"I ain' seen it," Bug said. "What else she be in?"

"Bug," I said, "did you ever see the movie called *While You Were Sleeping*? It's where the guy is in a coma after getting hit by a train, and then the woman falls in love with the man's brother."

"Yeah, man. I see that. I cry long tears when I see that movie," he said. "That the lady who want the lobster on the beach?"

"Yeah, Bug," Shabby said. "You wanna see 'er?"

"Yeah, man. Maybe I can help carry out the plates."

Frankie arrived on schedule to a beach setting that was itself like a scene in a movie. The white tablecloths ruffled gently in the breeze, candles flickered from the little bags scattered on the sand, and the crystal clear sky was jammed with twinkling stars. The diners had lobsters and good wine, and waves lapped only three feet away. As Bob poured them some rum at the end of the evening, he looked up and saw Bug motioning him feverishly from the edge of our path. Wearing his blue apron and yellow rubber gloves, he asked Bob in a whisper, "Which one she be? Which one Sandra Bullet be?"

Chapter 11

WE'D GONE FROM
serving almost a hundred
dinners a night all the way down to
twenty or twenty-five if we were lucky. Time slowed down, and we
returned to the unhurried pace that had lured us here in the first
place. One particularly slow evening Shabby asked to speak with
Bob and me privately. Outside, behind the kitchen, Shabby's bulk
all of a sudden seemed smaller. He sat on a wobbly step stool and
hung his head low.

"I gotta leave," he said meekly.

"Leave where?" I asked.

"Blanchard's."

"You're leaving us? Why? Is something wrong? I thought you
liked it here." Questions tumbled out from us before he could
answer.

"You know I loves it at Blanchard's," Shabby finally said. "You
people come to me like family. But I gotta spend more time at
home. I work construction all day, rush to the house, take a shower,
and then I here till midnight. I gotta see my wife an' kids more. My
two little girls, man, they gettin' so big, an' I always at work."

Bob almost cried, remembering lassoing for lobsters with
Shabby when we'd first arrived. He could still see him in his black
wet suit gliding like a giant fish along the bottom of the sea. For me,

the kitchen wouldn't be the same. We'd worked side by side and now knew each other's moves without thinking. Shabby had perfected the job as grill cook and was a vital part of our success. His size-fourteen shoes would be hard to fill.

The next morning I called Lowell and asked how we should go about finding a replacement for Shabby. Lowell understood completely that a job at Blanchard's was not an ordinary position. We were a small, tight group and didn't want a newcomer who would rock our equilibrium. We needed someone willing to learn our way of doing things on the grill but also eager to become part of the team.

Lowell told me to sit tight. "Don' make a move," he said. "I find someone right away. I don' wan' you puttin' an ad on the radio. If the word get out on the street, Blanchard's would have people line up down the road for a job. Lemme do it my way."

One hour later Lowell pulled up in front of our house and tooted his horn. "Mel. Bob. Come," he yelled.

We walked out on the balcony, and Lowell introduced a young man. The two of them were beaming. "Melinda and Bob Blanchard, meet Huegel Hughes. He wanna be our new grill cook."

"That was fast," I said.

"I tell you it wouln' be hard. Hughes here work Malliouhana, but he like the idea a workin' somewhere small. He aks me 'bout a job a few months ago, so I go find him as soon as you call."

"Huegel," I started, "what is your job now?"

Lowell answered. "You can call him Hughes. He name Huegel, but we all call him Hughes. He work in the kitchen Malliouhana four years—since he sixteen. Up there they do everything, so he know how run the grill."

Hughes was a skinny, shy young man with an irresistible twinkle in his big eyes. His hair was tied in a dozen short braids sticking out in all directions. "I would like to work Blanchard's," he said. "Tonight's my night off Malliouhana. Could I come watch and see what it like?"

I was impressed already. He wasn't going to jump in blindly. "Sure, why not? Come by around five so you can see what Shabby does before dinner as well."

"My hair a problem?" Hughes asked.

"No," Bob said. "Why?"

"Some people think 'cause I plat my hair that I use drugs, but that ain' true. I ain' no Rasta."

Lowell nodded at me as if to say, *Would I bring you someone who would cause trouble?*

Hughes came to observe for the night, and just about everyone on our staff knew him; it was as if he'd been in the kitchen from the beginning. He was a worker too. Shabby showed him what to do, and he went right to it. His idea of observing was a lot more active than I'd expected. Shabby approved of Hughes, said he would be a good replacement, and agreed to stay the two weeks until he could begin work.

Shabby's last night was slow. With only twenty dinners to serve, we had extra time on our hands in the kitchen, and he asked me if he could make some pap for everyone.

"Pap?"

"Corn pap," he said. "You ain' try it yet?"

"I've never even heard of it, but I like the name. Pap."

Clinton said, "Mel, pap like hot cereal. We does eat it in the morning, but it good anytime. Leave Shabby make you some."

Shabby gathered together cornmeal, milk, sugar, butter, and cinnamon and simmered it all in a big pot on the stove. He spooned the mixture into bowls and put out some brown sugar for people to sprinkle on top. It was heavy, warm, and sweet—like a sugared polenta. It was comforting. I gave Shabby a big, tearful hug, Bob shook his hand, and everyone watched from the back door as he drove away—but not before I made him promise to come back for a visit and make us more pap.

At six o'clock one morning we were awakened by a tooting horn, rather than our usual reliable rooster. Whoever was outside was insistent, and the honking continued until we opened the door. It was Lowell with urgent information.

"I got big news. Big news," he called from his jeep.

"Are you and Stacy getting married?" I asked.

"No, man. This different kind a news. But it big."

Bob doesn't focus well without coffee, so he just sat down on the front steps. "Lowell," I urged, "what's the news?"

"Follow me" was all he said.

"Now? In the car? Do you know what time it is?" Bob asked.

"Yeah, man. Follow me. I got somethin' to show you."

Bob and I trailed the jeep over the dirt road to Long Bay village, past Christine's shop, then by Lowell's house, where his mother was hanging clothes. She hailed us with a cheerful "Good morning." The road curved around several bends, and palm trees lined the edges as it dropped down toward the sea. Lowell pulled over alongside some men working on an unfinished building. He saw me looking at the spectacular view and said, "It yours if you wannit."

"Mine?"

"Bob and Melinda Blanchard, meet my cousin's husband, Charles Richardson. He name really Cricket, though."

We shook hands, speechless. "You like this house?" Cricket asked. "There are three floors, each with its own apartment. Lowell say you might be interested in renting."

We were stunned. Lowell hadn't even hinted at what he was up to. Cricket's apartment building was perched twenty-five feet above Long Bay with an uninterrupted view of the water—so close that we could hear even the smallest waves break against the shore.

"Well, yes," Bob said finally. "Could we look around?"

Lowell and Cricket gave us a tour, and our house with a view of the Shell station was history. The apartment was smaller, but our balcony overlooked one of the most beautiful bays in the Caribbean. Lowell knew we loved Anguilla but had been so disappointed with our living situation. He'd been planning this for a while, waiting until construction on the building was almost finished.

The move changed our life. We became official members of the Long Bay community and were within walking distance of Christine's shop and Blanchard's. We bought lounge chairs for the balcony, and as the sun rose behind me each morning, I'd sit outside, watching the water change from green to blue and back again. An occasional cruise ship would pass on its way to or from St. Martin, and a handful of small sailboats glided by from time to time. We could see picturesque little Sandy Island and, farther out, Anguilla's two uninhabited cays, Prickly Pear and Dog Island—which always made me smile as I pictured Jerry Gumbs turning down Castro's offer to buy it. Other than that, there was nothing but blues and greens out to the horizon.

At night, after work, we'd go outside and gaze at the stars over the water. I wished I knew the names, but the Big Dipper and Orion's belt were the only constellations I could ever remember. Still, I loved seeing the very same stars in Anguilla that were twinkling back home in Vermont. *How can two such different worlds be so connected?* I'd wonder. *How can this balmy, blue-green water be part of the same icy ocean that crashes against the Maine coast?*

We could follow a footpath down to the sea. Long Bay was heavenly. The beach was almost a mile long, and we rarely saw another soul on it. At sunset the sand turned a pale shade of coral. There was a rocky point at one end, ideal for long hours of contemplation, and the water was always warm and gentle.

I loved coming and going along the palm-lined road, because of the view, but also because I got to pass by Lowell's house. His sister Angela was always happy to see us. "Good night, good night," she'd say, poking her head out a window as we'd drive home. "Okay, okay," Lowell's mother called out to us every morning. There were always nieces and nephews playing around their house. Just like Joshua and Evelyn's, the family extended over three generations, and the children barely differentiated among parents, aunts, uncles, grandfathers, and grandmothers. Family was family.

When I had time on Sunday afternoons, I'd often take Roxana out to the local ice cream parlor in The Valley. Owned and operated by an Anguillian couple that had lived in Italy for a while, it served over twenty flavors of homemade gelato. One Sunday I went to North Hill to pick up Roxana at her uncle Mac's house, and nobody was inside. I wandered out back to see if maybe they were hanging clothes on the line and found Mac's mother fanning herself from the heat that was pouring out of her old stone oven.

"I makin' potato puddin', Mel," she said. "Come."

The oven was ancient. Made mostly of rocks, it had an arch of bricks at the top that sloped upward in the front, allowing the smoke to roll out and away. The cooking level was waist high, with a thick, hot bed of ashes and coals on the bottom; extra bags of local charcoal were leaning on a table nearby, ready for refueling.

"I sells puddin' to the bakeries," she explained as she slid a large flat pan of the brown mixture onto the coals. "Roxana waitin' fo' you over there." She pointed past a pomegranate tree in the yard to where Roxana was playing with a new puppy.

As I walked over she jumped up and gave me a hug. "Ready for ice cream?" I asked. "I waitin' on you," she said. "Garrilin comin' with us; that okay?"

Every time I saw Roxana her hair was styled differently. That day it was parted into a dozen or so squares, each one centered by a long braid tied off with a different color plastic bead. On our way to the ice cream shop Roxana discussed the flavors she would order. When we finally got there, Garrilin had coconut and cream, I had guava, and Roxana, being the smallest, had kiwi, chocolate, vanilla, and lime. We talked mostly about school, and Roxana pulled out from her pocket her latest report card. She showed me a list of A's, and then grabbed it back when I started to read the teacher's comments.

"Mel, I ain' think you wanna see that," she said.

I stuck out my bottom lip in a pout, and she slid it back across the table reluctantly. I read it out loud. "'Roxana is an excellent student, but she chat too much in the classroom.' Good work on the A's," I said.

"Thanks, Mel." She sighed, relieved that I hadn't scolded her about the chatting.

Roxana asked if we could drive around a little before going home, so we turned east past The Valley, and Garrilin and Roxana shared the role of tour guide.

"See that place there?" Garrilin said as we passed a little shack on the outskirts of town. "Them wild in there. They got girls dancin' with their titties out." Roxana covered her mouth, pretending to be shocked.

"That St. Barts over there, ya know," Roxana said, pointing out past St. Martin.

"An' this furniture shop belong to Mac uncle," Garrilin continued.

We circled the island, the two of them taking turns filling me in on who did what, with whom, and where. The smells changed every mile along the way: intoxicating clusters of fragrant agatha, the aroma of banana bread drifting from an open window, a smoky coal keel, the scent of fresh lime from a recently pruned tree, and the pungent curry from the Roti Hut. We passed a house in East End village where a little girl about Roxana's age was swirling a purple Hula-Hoop around her waist. Two other children sat on the front steps watching and waiting for a turn.

The vegetation changed noticeably in the east. The white cedars, neem trees, and palms of the western end of the island disappeared. Instead, we saw hundreds of frangipani trees with their long, skinny leaves and white flowers at the end of each branch. There were cacti everywhere, and Garrilin helped me identify the different kinds.

As we entered Garrilin's village of North Hill again, she and Roxana pointed out two new benches that the neighborhood had chipped in to buy for the little park along the main road. They were painted yellow and white to match the telephone poles and trash barrels in the village. By the time we returned to Garrilin's house, Mac was just pulling into the yard.

"You all set for the big weddin'?" Mac asked me. "The guy call me yesterday and said he having the party at Blanchard's. He ask me if I could line up all the taxis."

"You mean for those people from Washington, D.C.?" I asked.

"Yeah, what the guy's name again?"

"H. P. Goldfield. He called me this morning, and I told him we'd work on a price. He wants to squeeze seventy-five people into our little restaurant. That's pretty tight for us."

"Mel," Mac said, "this is May. We gotta do the business while we can. Give the man a good price. We need people like he in Anguilla—especially in May."

"I'll call him first thing in the morning," I promised. Roxana gave me a squeeze goodbye, and I told her to have Uncle Mac bring her down for another drink at the restaurant. She loved Blanchard's frozen banana cabanas, and if we weren't too busy, she'd help Bob deliver checks to the tables. The guests adored her.

As soon as I got home Bob and I discussed H. P. Goldfield's wedding. Actually, it was the rehearsal dinner he wanted to have at Blanchard's. Mac was right. We were crazy to pass up an opportunity to do a private party for seventy-five people, even if it would be a little crowded. I came up with several menu options and called that night to discuss it further.

"Please call me H.P.," he insisted. "Melinda, don't worry about the space. We can set up tables in the bar, and it will be just fine. The most important thing is the food." He paused. "And, of course, the wine. My old roommate from college is a wine buyer at Christie's, and I'd like him to talk with Bob about the choices, if that's okay."

"No problem," I said. "What do you think about the menu? Shall I fax you pricing for the various options?"

"That's fine, but it's not so much the price I'm concerned about as the quality of the whole party. I've got important people from the White House coming down, and all the partners in my law firm here in Washington. Everything has to be perfect." He continued, "I have some friends who say you're going to be the next Martha Stewart. You did a special dinner party for them last month. And they said Bob's wine list is fantastic. I'm forty-five, and this is my first and only wedding; that's why I *need* you to make this work."

"As long as you don't mind a few tables in the bar, everything should be fine," I said. "Here's our home number just in case you have questions along the way and we're not at the restaurant."

At eight the next morning the phone rang at home. "H.P. here. How's everything down there in paradise? Listen, I have a little problem. My fiancée says I'm making a mistake not inviting certain people to the rehearsal dinner. After all," he said, "they're coming a long way for the wedding. What would it take to add another twenty people?"

"Another twenty people! H.P., our restaurant has sixty seats. We can't possibly fit in ninety-five. It just won't work."

"I knew you'd say that, but I had an idea. Why can't we rent extra tables and put them outside?"

"Because this is Anguilla," I explained. "We don't have a place to rent tables, chairs, or anything else for that matter. I'd really like to help, but I think you'd be much happier at a bigger restaurant. Why don't you call one of the hotels? They have much more space."

"You're kidding. You really won't do this? I can't believe it. We were counting on you."

I bowed out as gracefully as possible and gave H.P. the names of several people to speak with who might be better equipped to handle a large group. I wished him luck and said we hoped to see him when he arrived on the island. We knew it was the right thing to do, but we had some feeling of regret at passing up the business.

Three days later, eight o'clock in the morning again, the phone rang. "H.P. here. Listen, I know this is an unusual request, but I came up with another idea. First of all, we've decided to invite everyone who's coming to the wedding to join us at the rehearsal dinner. It's the right thing to do. How can we ask people to fly to Anguilla and then leave them out of such an important event? We still have a few weeks to go, so why don't we rent a big tent, tables, chairs, and whatever else you need, and we can set everything up on the beach in front of Blanchard's? There *must* be a rental company somewhere that would ship everything to Anguilla by boat."

Bob caught bits and pieces of the conversation and couldn't believe I was even considering such an option. He kept shaking his head and telling me to hang up the phone.

"How many people are you up to now?" I asked.

"Two hundred," H.P. whispered. I didn't dare repeat the number, afraid that Bob would grab the phone out of my hand. "Okay," I said. "Let me look into it."

I liked H.P. He was a real charmer—but sincere. He said he understood our situation but refused to take no for an answer. I told Bob to calm down and let me make some calls.

"Do you think we can handle a wedding for two hundred people?" Bob asked. "Lawyers and politicians from Washington?"

"Yeah. I think with some guidance and a lot of organization we could pull it off. I'd really love to do it."

With less effort than I'd anticipated, I located two brand-new white tents in St. Martin and a place that rented china, silver, glasses, tables, and chairs. Bob and I brought the staff together for a meeting and announced that we had committed to do a rehearsal dinner for two hundred people.

"It ain' no problem. Leff them come," said Bug. "Blanchard's can do anything."

Miguel was excited but a little worried. "You think we gonna need some extra help?" he asked.

"We've already asked Wayne and Jackie from Cap Juluca to wait tables, and we've lined up two extra bartenders and a couple of people to help in the kitchen."

"That cool," Miguel said. "We gonna be okay."

H.P. agreed to a fixed menu and chose items from our regular selections. His friend from Christie's called Bob, and they settled on Veuve Clicquot as we passed hors d'oeuvres, and Kistler chardonnay and Heitz cabernet with dinner. He added a 1950 rum from Martinique and Monte Cristo cigars to end the evening.

About two weeks before the wedding, our phone rang again at eight in the morning. "H.P. here. How are things progressing?"

"Everything is going smoothly," I said. "I think you'll be very happy."

"That's great. I just have another *little* favor to ask." There was silence on both ends. He finally continued. "I'm having trouble with the wedding reception. I've been working with a hotel on the island and just don't feel confident that it's going to be what we want. I think the problem is that the manager spent fifteen years organizing banquets in Las Vegas. He told me the chairs will be avocado green vinyl with a gold frame—more like a convention center than a wedding, don't you think? He said the lobster would have to be frozen, and it sounds like baked potato is about as interesting as the menu gets, and they insist it's unheard of to make the rum punch with fresh juice. Melinda, please, can you help me out here?"

Planning a wedding anywhere is a big job; planning a wedding of this magnitude in Anguilla was a huge challenge. But now H.P. had put us in charge of the entire weekend.

We had a staff meeting to announce the new plan, and everyone took it on without missing a beat.

Ozzie said, "Mel, me and Lowell, we get the tents and stuff from the port. No problem."

"Miguel," I said, "we've got two hundred white plastic chairs arriving next Wednesday on Tropical Shipping. Can you get them in your pickup?"

"Cool," Miguel answered.

"I talk to my friends about the music," Ozzie said. "Don' worry. We get Happy Hits for the first night and Dumpa's Steel Band for the next. It gonna be cool."

Bug knew we'd need things from St. Martin and said, "I goin' south on Saturday. Gimme a list a whatever ya need over there."

I reviewed the menu and explained that the reception would be more casual than the rehearsal dinner—barbecued free-range chicken and lobster.

Garrilin raised her hand with a question. "Wha free-range chicken is?"

Bob described the merits of birds that haven't been penned up or fed chemically treated grain and hormones.

Garrilin said, "We call them kinda birds yard fowl. They's all over Anguilla." She paused for a minute. "I don' think they wha you lookin' for, though. Our birds kinda scrawny."

Supplies began arriving daily, by boat and air. Since every single thing was imported, we had to anticipate each detail. If anything was forgotten, there would be no running to a local store at the last minute. H.P. told us what kind of flowers his bride preferred, and as she requested, we used as many local blossoms as possible. White frangipani and pink bougainvillea were the most readily available, and we worked with a local florist to fly in baby white roses as well. We collected sea grape leaves and more bougainvillea to decorate the hors d'oeuvre platters, and draped sea-bean vines over the top of the huppah and down the sides. H.P. was flying in his own rabbi, and we arranged for a local minister to be present as well, since for the ceremony to be legal in Anguilla, an off-island rabbi alone was not enough. We even bought extra gas for the generator just in case the power failed during dinner.

Three days before the event I received a phone call from our food supplier in Miami. "I have bad news, Mel," he said. "The plane with your food is in Puerto Rico."

"What exactly are you saying?" I asked.

"Well, if you want to know the whole story—"

I couldn't tell if panic was in order. "Joel," I interrupted impatiently, "what's going on?"

"The plane left Miami and landed on schedule a few hours ago in St. Martin. But the officials there wouldn't let your food be off-loaded."

"Why on earth not?"

"It turns out there were horses on the plane. I don't know exactly what happened, but the pilot was told he couldn't unload anything—something about immigration and papers for the horses, I think. So he flew to Puerto Rico."

"Joel, I have free-range chickens, smoked salmon, oysters, baby squash, and tons of fresh herbs on that plane; and two hundred people are arriving in forty-eight hours expecting us to provide a storybook wedding on the beach. I need that food today or I won't be able to pull it off. Plus, what about the ice? There's no way everything will stay cold enough."

"I'm afraid the food can't get there until tomorrow afternoon," he said.

Bug and Ozzie were standing next to me and could see I needed help. "Tell he to get a next plane," Bug said. "There be plenty planes in Puerto Rico."

Ozzie motioned for me to give him the phone. "Hi. This Ozzie. We gotta have that food. You ain' gotta next plane you could send? These weddin' people important, ya know." With that, he passed me back the phone.

Garrilin piped up and said, "Mel, all our vegetables swibbly. Tell 'em we needs new ones. These all swibble up. Looka these tomatoes. They got more wrinkles than my grandmother."

"Hi, Joel, it's me again. As you can see, we're *all* a little upset here. What about the idea of another plane? Is that possible?"

"Let me make some calls," he said.

For $1,800 we chartered a private plane small enough to land directly in Anguilla that afternoon. When the shipment arrived at the restaurant, it became clear that several items had gotten "lost" in Puerto Rico. Fifteen cases of raspberries, eight cases of plum tomatoes, and all the smoked salmon had vanished, never to be seen again.

The next day Lowell called Bob from Blowing Point, where he and Ozzie were picking up the tents and other rented items. "Bob," he said, "we gotta problem."

"What now?" Bob asked.

"Customs say everything gotta go in the warehouse till we do special paperwork, unless we wanna pay duty on it all."

"Lowell, we can't pay a twenty-five percent duty on things we're just going to return to St. Martin in a couple of days."

"I know. That what I *tell* he. He say we gotta do somethin' call an export entry if we wanna skip payin' duty. I tell he that we must have this stuff now or the whole weddin' gonna get mess up, but he won' leave us go with the stuff."

"Lowell, do whatever you have to do, for God's sake, but don't let them put everything in the warehouse. We'll never get it out in time! Find out who can do an export entry immediately, and just tell him you'll be right back."

"Okay, boss. No problem."

Lowell went to Christine's shop, knowing that the girls there worked on entries all the time. They managed to finish our paperwork in record time, and in two hours Lowell arrived at the restaurant with all our rental equipment.

"From now on," he announced, "we gotta use the girls at Christine's to do *all* our entries. They quick, man."

Ozzie squeezed eight cases of oranges for the rum punch, Bug made a quick trip to St. Martin for Monte Cristo cigars, and Bob organized a crew to build a dance platform under the tents. In the kitchen, Clinton, Hughes, and I worked on the food. We marinated the chicken in giant tubs of pineapple juice with rum and spices, cleaned two hundred pounds of lobsters, and tied countless bunches of herbs with satin ribbon to decorate the platters.

The morning before the rehearsal dinner, a man came to the back door of the kitchen. "Hi, I'm Craig Fuller, the best man," he said. "I've chartered a boat for the weekend and wondered if you could cater lunch for twenty. I'd like to take some of H.P.'s friends out for a sail every day."

Ozzie spoke up. "No problem. We take care a everything." I was standing next to Ozzie and had to grin at his unshakable enthusiasm. Bob thought we had lost our minds, but we were on a roll and couldn't say no. We spent a few minutes discussing menus that would stand up to a day at sea.

Banana Bread

Craig's wife asked if I could include banana bread for a snack each morning, and I was glad I'd experimented with various recipes several months before. Banana bread has always been a favorite of mine, but sometimes it's too sweet, with not enough flavor. My final recipe had a substantial amount of lemon juice, which made a big difference.

Preheat oven to 350°. Butter either one large or two small loaf pans and dust with flour. Using a mixer with a paddle attachment, cream 1⅓ cups room-temperature butter with 2 cups sugar until light and fluffy. In a separate bowl, whisk together 4 cups flour, 2 teaspoons baking soda, and 2 teaspoons salt. Beat 4 eggs into the butter mixture, one at a time, scraping the sides of the bowl after each addition. On low speed, blend in 6 mashed bananas and ¾ cup fresh lemon juice. Still on low speed, add the flour mixture and mix until just blended. To avoid overmixing, I like to do the final blending by hand with a rubber spatula. Pour into the prepared pan and bake for about an hour. A knife inserted in the middle of the loaf should come out clean when the bread is done.

I promised Craig Fuller that lunch would be ready, banana bread included, each morning at nine. "Bug," I yelled, now in a panic. "You need to go back to St. Martin. If you hurry, you can make the ten o'clock boat. We need two really big coolers and some things from the party store in Marigot." I gave him a list that included plastic cutlery, glasses, and plates.

"I gone to come back," he said on his way out the door.

"Bug," I called as he pulled out of the driveway, "no dominos today at the port. Okay?"

What started out as a private dinner for seventy-five people had turned into a gala weekend for two hundred. The night of the rehearsal dinner, twenty taxis lined up at Blanchard's, the Happy Hits shook their maracas, and Miguel and Alwyn poured almost five cases of champagne. Hughes grilled sixty racks of lamb perfectly and Garrilin decorated two hundred plates of chocolate fudge torte for dessert. The following afternoon at five-thirty, H.P. and his bride walked down an aisle created by rows of fragrant torches along the beach.

After the vows were exchanged, Lowell, Miguel, and Wayne were ready and waiting with more champagne. Lobsters and chickens were heaped on the outdoor grills, and for a moment I wondered what I would have served if the food had spoiled in Puerto Rico while immigration figured out what to do with an airplane full of horses. H.P. had no idea how close we came to serving him salt fish and pap.

Everyone danced to the steel band until long after midnight. As we were leaving, Bug announced, "Someday I gonna have Blanchard's do *my* weddin'."

Chapter 12

IN EARLY JULY SHABBY HAD invited Bob to help build the new boat in Blowing Point. Bob's skill as a carpenter coupled with his collection of tools made him a valuable asset to an Anguillian boatbuilding crew. After loading his table saw and various toolboxes into the back of the truck, he followed the directions Shabby had given him and pulled in next to a little building called Generation Bar, where the new boat was going to be built. A group of men were congregated in the shade of a big mahogany tree, and two of them were engaged in a heated argument. As Bob got out of the truck he tried hard to grasp what they were saying.

"No, man, we ain' gonna do it that way," the first man shouted.

"I done race these boats more years than you," said the second man as he downed the remainder of a Heineken. As Bob saw the man reach into a cooler for another one, tossing the empty off into the bushes, he wondered how they could drink beer at nine in the morning. All the men were barefoot except one, who wore a pair of rubber thongs. The ground under the big tree was strewn with nails, empty paint cans, gobs of epoxy, and bits of wood from years of boatbuilding. Off to one side, two hammers and a rusty hand saw lay on the ground next to a big stack of pine boards.

Shabby came over to meet Bob and peered into the back of the truck at the tools.

"What are they arguing about?" Bob asked, still trying to pick up on the conversation.

"They tryin' to decide how to shape the hull," said Shabby. "Errol say it should be like *Stinger*, but Chix say he wannit like *Bluebird*. Errol the captain a this boat," Shabby explained, "an' Chix his brother." Chix was the one drinking beer, and Bob recognized him from the Easter Monday boat race.

"You go ahead, build it like *Stinger*," Chix yelled. "You ain' gonna win nothin'."

"Chix been captain on lotta boats," Shabby said to Bob. "This Errol's first boat, and we all the crew. Chix kinda mad cause he ain' the captain."

Now it was clear: Chix was jealous and had come over to cause trouble.

"Once they decide on the hull, do you have a set of plans for the boat?" Bob asked.

"Kee Kee gonna design it," Shabby answered proudly. "He the best when it come to workin' with wood."

The argument continued. "Okay, I ain' gonna help then," shrieked Chix as he polished off his beer and flung the empty bottle into a group of squawking chickens. He picked up his cooler, tossed it in the back of his car, and made a dramatic departure, blue smoke coming off the tires.

"Okay, guys, the man with the tools here," Errol announced, looking at Bob. As they unloaded the table saw and toolboxes Shabby introduced the men to Bob, and they all bumped fists—the classic Anguillian handshake. Bob felt he had just joined the Blowing Point Yacht Club.

"Leff we go," Errol said once everything was out of the truck. "Rigby, you watch the tools." Rigby was asleep on the ground, and Errol went over and poked him with his foot. Rigby rolled over, opened his eyes, and stared up at Errol.

"You watch the tools," Errol repeated to Rigby, who rolled back on his side, closing his eyes. Several of the men climbed into the back of Bob's truck, but there were a few who hadn't moved yet. They remained on the ground with Rigby, sprawled out under the tree, apparently uninterested in the project but willing to help watch the tools. Errol and another carload of men followed.

"Where are we going?" Bob asked Shabby, who had climbed into the front seat with him.

"Goin' to *Stinger* so Kee Kee can shape the hull. Turn above," he instructed, pointing to a dirt path through the sea grape. Bob maneuvered over the deep ruts, finding that the path came out at a beach east of the ferry terminal.

"See, *Stinger* there." Shabby pointed to a boat lying on its side at the far end of the beach. When Bob pulled up, the men climbed out of the truck and wandered over to where the glossy yellow *Stinger* lay on the sand. Kee Kee led the group, holding six pieces of rusted steel rod each about eight feet long, the kind used for reinforcing concrete. Sam and Kee Kee began at the bow and bent the first piece of rod to fit the gentle curve of *Stinger*. They held it against the hull, bent it a little more, held it against the boat again, and readjusted the curve again and again until it matched *Stinger* exactly. Satisfied with the first rod, they moved down the hull about four feet, and bent another rod to duplicate the shape at that point. Bob realized they were going to use six simple pieces of rusty steel to form the graceful curve of the new boat.

After about an hour of bending, adjusting, and discussing whether it should be a little trimmer here and a little wider there, everyone piled back into the truck. Bob glanced in his rearview mirror at Kee Kee, who was proudly clutching his new patterns for the boat.

Nothing had changed under the tree. Rigby was still asleep, and Bob's tools were right where they'd been unloaded. Errol ran an extension cord from inside his bar over to the table saw.

"Leff we rip this pine," he said to Bob, who got out his tape measure and leveled the saw as best he could in the dirt.

"What's the pine for?" Bob asked.

"We nail it over the ribs that Kee Kee gonna make outta that plywood over there. It like the skin a the boat. We gotta rip these boards down to two or three inches so that we can bend 'em around the frame."

"So," Bob said, "do you want them two inches wide or three inches wide?"

"Don' matter. Somewhere in there."

Bob set his saw for two and a half inches, realizing that Anguillian boatbuilding was not a precise science. While Bob ripped the pine boards into long, skinny strips, Kee Kee traced the bent rods onto the plywood. After each shape was drawn, another man cut it out with Bob's jigsaw. Sam and Errol mixed epoxy and glued the plywood shapes together, doubling them up for strength.

By the end of the day, Bob had ripped the entire pile of pine boards into strips, and the others had cut and laid out the ribs in order. The result looked like a huge fish skeleton splayed out on the ground.

"Gotta lay down the keel now," Errol announced the next day, and three men carried a long, heavy timber over to where the ribs had been placed. They set the timber on two cement blocks and put a level on it. Bob wondered briefly how they would have done this without his tools. They shimmed one end of the timber up a little until Errol was satisfied it was level. "There," he said. "Keel ready for the ribs."

Sam and Errol applied epoxy to the bottom of each rib and stuck them onto the keel, clamping them in place. Three long strips of pine were glued and nailed across the ribs, stretched lengthwise from bow to stern. One was nailed at the top, one in the middle, and one more toward the bottom.

As the men bent the pine over the ribs, the lines of the boat were suddenly defined. At the end of the second day everyone stood back as Kee Kee and Errol walked around the frame, checking to see if they liked the shape.

"Yeah, man," Kee Kee said. "She look sweet. Tomorrow we plank 'er."

It took two days to plank her; several men had made a rudder, and two more had shaped and fitted strips of wood to the top of each side to make the gunwales. Next was "epoxy day." The thick, gluey mixture was troweled over the entire outside of the boat, along with fiberglass cloth, filling in all the cracks between the pieces of pine, sealing the wood and forming a waterproof skin. Then came sanding day, and by midafternoon the boat was smooth and shiny and ready for paint.

In less than two weeks these men had built a twenty-eight-foot sailboat with nothing more than six pieces of bent, rusty steel rod for patterns.

By the end of the second week the boat had been finished with several coats of glossy light green paint. The group christened it *De Tree* in honor of the mahogany tree under which it was built, and they painted the name proudly on each side.

"Now we jus' need a sail," Errol said, looking hopefully at Bob. "We could put 'Blanchard's Restaurant' on it," he offered, "as a little advertising."

"How much is a sail?" Bob asked.

"Maybe two thousand U.S. dollars," Sam said.

"Okay," Bob said, "where do we get it?"

"St. Martin," Errol answered. "They make them in the Sail Loft in Cole Bay."

"How do I tell them what size and shape you want?"

"Get a piece of paper. I draw it," Errol said.

Bob found an envelope and a pen in his glove compartment, and Errol proceeded to draw the sail. He drew a triangle and put the measurements on two sides, labeling one "boom" and one "mast." He studied the simple sketch as if it were a set of blueprints and then handed it over to Bob, saying, "Give this to the man at the Sail Loft. Tell him we wants it tight, tight, tight."

Bob realized at this point that he was in charge of *getting* the sail as well as paying for it. "Jus' tell the man to cut it tight for an Anguilla racing boat," Errol added. "Sometimes they cuts 'em too loose."

The next day Bob took the ferry to St. Martin to order the sail. After the owner of the Sail Loft turned Errol's measurements into a scale drawing, Bob gave him a check for $2,400.

Back in Anguilla, Bob pulled off the road at the Generation Bar and got out next to *De Tree,* where a large herd of goats had gathered in the shade of the boat. They watched placidly as Bob walked past the boat and around the back of the bar looking for Errol. He found him sitting on a stump cleaning a fish.

"Hey, Errol, how you doing?"

"Okay, Blanchard," he answered. "Y'alright? How the sail?" he asked without looking up from his fish.

"He's hoping to have it done the day before the first race."

"Cool," Errol answered.

"Don't we need to try the boat out before the race?" Bob asked.

"Yeah, man. We gonna do that. I got a practice sail from the *Stinger.* We gonna launch her Sunday down Sandy Ground."

"Great. Can I come help?" Bob replied.

"Yeah, man. You part a the crew now," Errol said as he tossed a fish head into a big pot. Bob felt he had just moved a little closer toward being accepted into Anguillian life.

Several of the goats had moved over to the shade of Bob's truck, and as he walked around to get in, they jumped up and trotted back over to the boat.

It seemed to be a day of goats. That night at the restaurant two babies wandered into the bar as if holding a seven o'clock reservation. Wobbly-legged, they looked as if they were only hours old, though their mother was nowhere in sight. Bob and Miguel stared in disbelief as the two tottered past the bar and into the dining room, made a left down the hall, and walked directly into the kitchen.

Without hesitation Bug said, "Hi, baby goats. You come to wash dishes with me?"

Attention in the kitchen temporarily shifted from dinner to our little visitors. I asked Ozzie to check with the neighbors to see if anyone knew whom they belonged to, but he predicted nobody would claim them. "Too mucha goats in Anguilla," he said. "Nobody gonna know who goats these is."

The two little newborns, one black and one brown, proceeded around the pickup counter and made a beeline for my legs. They nuzzled warmly against my ankles and stayed there all night, not seeming to mind that I moved back and forth as dinner orders came and went. Garrilin and I worked side by side, and she spent the evening trying to feed them milk from a spoon.

An American friend who had a house on the island said she'd look after the two kids until their owner was located. A week later we gave up the search, and she formally announced that she had adopted the babies. Their names were Blackie and Star. Those two little goats lucked into the good life when they wandered into our bar. Rather than forage for food in the bush like most goats in Anguilla, they were nursed from a bottle, and each had its own lounge chair by the pool. Blackie and Star had landed in the lap of luxury.

Sunday morning Bob was at Sandy Ground by nine for *De Tree*'s practice sail. He walked up the beach and spotted Errol and five or six of the crew wrestling with a flapping bright yellow sail on the beach. The practice sail was rolled out on the sand with a mast that looked like a telephone pole lying next to it.

A rope was tied to an eyebolt at the top of the mast. Errol threaded it through a grommet in the sail and wound it around the mast, through another grommet, and again around the mast, the whole time barking orders at the crew.

"Blanchard, haul on that rope," he said. "We ain' want no slack in the line."

Bob obediently pulled on the rope, keeping it tight, working it along behind Errol, until they reached the bottom of the sail. Then it was tied securely around the mast.

"Okay, boys, roll it up now," Errol ordered, and the sail was rolled and tied against the mast.

"Now the boat," Errol said, and everyone headed toward *De Tree,* which had been trailered to the edge of the beach. Several two-by-fours under each side propped it up from underneath. Gleaming in the sun, the light green boat still smelled of fresh paint.

Rigby and several more of the crew arrived, and everyone now circled the boat. Errol dragged over two roller logs, and with much grunting, *De Tree* was skidded, rolled, shoved, and pushed toward the water.

"Rusky," Errol yelled. "Keep the rollers movin'."

"I movin' them, Uncle," Rusky said as he ran around, moving the logs along under the boat.

After half an hour of concentrated effort, *De Tree* finally hit the water. As a small wave came up the shore it floated off the last log and was officially launched. Bob felt like cheering and applauding, perhaps christening its bow with champagne, but everyone else simply prepared for the next step, having done this many times before.

They carried the huge mast out into the water and passed it up into the boat. "How are we going to stand that thing up?" Bob asked doubtfully.

"We gonna hoist it up," Errol answered, as though this was self-evident.

The boat was now facing in toward the beach and rocking gently. One end of the forty-foot telephone pole mast, which weighed close to two hundred pounds, lay across the bow, while the other end rested on the shoulders of three men standing on the sand. A rope came off each side of the mast about one-third of the way from the top, while a third rope was tied around the very top of the mast. Errol and three other men held the end of that rope and stood in the stern of the boat.

"Ready, men?" Errol asked. "Okay, pull." He and his three men pulled on their rope, and the mast inched off the shoulders of the three men on the beach. "Pull," he yelled again, and the huge timber rose a little further in the air. "Pull on ya rope, Rigby," he yelled. Bob saw now the two side ropes were acting as guylines to keep the mast going up straight.

"When she's up," Errol yelled, "Blanchard, you an' Rigby gotta hold it from tipping over on top a we."

Bob suddenly felt responsible for the lives of the three men in the boat. What if the mast tipped over and crushed them? He dug his feet into the sand and clenched his teeth, preparing for disaster.

Once the mast stood fully upright, Errol tied it in place with an inch-thick rope and announced the mast was up. Bob waded out into the water and climbed over the gunwale to see how this huge pole was attached inside.

The mast didn't really look attached to Bob. It sat in a hole that had been chiseled into a wooden block on the bottom of the boat. A heavy plank, resembling a bench, spanned the boat from side to side and had a notch for the mast to go into; the mast was tied around the plank, which helped keep it going straight up and down. Bob pictured the rope breaking and the mast tipping over onto the crew, killing everyone in its path. Errol assured him this was the way it was done and told him not to be concerned. "It cool, Blanchard. No problem."

The boom was now being passed up into the boat from the men onshore, and Errol began to attach it to the mast. It had a steel fitting on one end, which slid into another steel fitting on the mast, allowing it to swing from side to side. The sail was then unfurled and lashed to the boom. *De Tree* was now a sailboat.

The sail swung back and forth in the wind, and Bob ducked as the boom narrowly missed his head. The men carried large, heavy rocks, pieces of lead, and sandbags out into the waist-high water, passing them up to Errol, who carefully placed each load in the bottom of the boat.

As soon as the ballast was arranged to Errol's satisfaction, he announced, "She ready, boys. Now less see how she sails." The rest of the crew piled into the boat, and Errol skillfully turned it around, hauled in on the sail, and got under way.

As the breeze filled the sail, *De Tree* tipped away from the wind, and the crew leaned far out over the other side in counterbalance. Bob hung on and leaned out with the rest of the men. Errol sat in the stern of the boat with one arm draped casually over the tiller. With his big, bare foot, he held the rope taut between the mainsail and a cleat on the bottom of the boat. As *De Tree* clipped along, heading out toward the open sea, Bob watched the shoreline of Anguilla get smaller and smaller, and he wondered how far out Errol would go before turning around. As if Errol had read his mind, he announced, "Get ready, boys, we comin' about." He pushed the tiller and as the huge sail slackened, *De Tree* turned. Errol pulled on the rope, hauling the boom in, and as the boat turned the long boom swung over the crew.

All thirteen men ducked as the boom passed over their heads. Suddenly the whole crew scrambled to the other side of the boat, and without stopping to wonder why, Bob moved with the rest of them. As the wind filled the sail again *De Tree* picked up speed in a new direction, but still headed out to sea. The crew once again leaned out over the side of the boat.

Bob had never been in a sailboat before and was fascinated by how fast the heavy boat could go. It was also surprisingly quiet. The only sounds, other than the men bellowing out commands, were the creaking of the ropes, the wind swooshing into the sail, and the splashing water. As the wind pushed on the giant sail the boat tipped so far over that the lower gunwale skimmed the tops of the waves. Water cascaded into the boat; salt spray covered the crew and added to the water already in the bottom.

"Rusky, bail," Errol ordered, and Rusky, at fourteen the youngest member of the crew, slid off the gunwale, grabbed a plastic bucket, and started throwing pails of water over the side. Bob hung on for dear life as he watched Rusky methodically fill his pail and toss the water back into the sea. It was a losing battle, as more and more water came over the side of the boat. As the bow crashed through the waves great splashes of water continued to soak the crew.

"Come up to the wind, Errol. Come up to the wind," Sam yelled. Sam seemed to be the navigator, and because he was the oldest man aboard, he commanded a certain respect from the rest of the crew.

"Yeah, bring her up to the wind," said Rigby.

Bob wasn't sure what "come up to the wind" meant, but he watched as Errol pulled on the rope and tightened up the mainsail. He also moved the tiller slightly, and Bob felt *De Tree* tip further onto its side. Now the lower gunwale was practically submerged, and as more and more water came into the boat, a second man jumped down next to Rusky and started to bail frantically.

"She sailin' now," said Errol with a big grin.

It was definitely sailing now, Bob thought as they crashed through the waves and water continued to fill the bottom of the boat. "I just hope she isn't *sinking* now," he muttered to himself, eyeing the two men bailing furiously.

"Bring 'er up to the wind," said Sam, and Errol pulled once more on the mainsail and adjusted the tiller.

"Sandbags," yelled Errol. Rusky stopped bailing and grabbed one of the bags of sand in the bottom of the boat. The bag outweighed Rusky by a hundred pounds, and he grunted as he rolled it up toward the crew's feet. He slid back down in the bottom, grabbed a second bag of sand, and rolled it up next to the first. He continued until he had five bags lined up by the crew's feet, helping counterbalance the boat.

"Okay, bail," Errol yelled at Rusky, who promptly stopped moving sandbags and went back to bailing.

Bob continued to balance his upper body out over the water, glancing from time to time at the shoreline, which looked very far away. The swells were getting bigger as *De Tree* headed out to sea. Bob's arms were aching from hanging on to the gunwale.

"We goin' clear down to Tortola?" Rigby asked. Apparently Bob wasn't the only one wondering how far in this direction they were to continue.

"Les bring 'er about," Sam said.

"Sandbags, Rusky," Errol commanded, and Rusky rolled the sandbags back down into the center of the boat. Each bag settled on top of the rocks and irons, which were lying in about a foot of water.

"Ready, boys? We comin' about," Errol said.

It took several hours and multiple crisscrossings to get back into Sandy Ground's protected harbor. Until that day, Bob's image of sailing had always been very romantic. It involved a captain sitting comfortably at the wheel, pipe in his mouth, passengers and crew sprawled on deck, as a sleek, smooth craft glided quietly over the water. *De Tree* did not fit that image. Its interior was completely unfinished, with no floor and no seats; Bob had a difficult time just keeping his balance on the steep sides of the slippery boat. After leaning backward out over the water for hours, braced against the gunwale, his back and his bottom throbbed in pain. By the time he climbed out of the boat and staggered up onto the beach, he was exhausted. His arms and legs ached, and he was sunburned and hungry.

He sat down on the sand and watched as the crew began to dismantle the sail and unload the ballast. They dumped the sandbags over the side and passed the heavy boulders and pieces of iron out of the boat and carried them up onto the beach. After removing the boom, they lowered the mast and carried it up onto shore. They positioned three logs under the keel, and, again with grunts and groans, they pushed, skidded, and rolled the heavy boat up onto the sand. Using two-by-fours, they propped it up at the edge of the beach, where it would remain until the first race.

"Only a week to Carnival," Errol said. "First race be Sunday, but it more a practice run. The big ones be on August Monday and August Thursday. I'd be puttin' some money on *De Tree*, Blanchard. She gonna have some sweet finishes."

"I'll be here," Bob said.

"Later," Errol said as he climbed into his old jeep.

Bob and I walked to the restaurant one morning following a small band of mourning doves alongside the road. Their heads bobbed back and forth at lightning speed, and it was the first time we'd noticed that they had a little hint of rose on their brown heads. We stopped with them for a minute as they circled around an older man stooped in his yard. He was filling a bottle with motor oil, using a rolled-up sea grape leaf as a funnel. The doves cooed good morning and continued with us down the road. As we passed the salt pond one of the birds stopped to check out a big crab at the edge of the water. I glanced over long enough to see its purple stripes but was distracted at the sight of Lowell and Clinton squinting up at the tall coconut tree in our parking lot.

"Man, we got a lotta coconuts," Lowell said. "You guys drink the milk?"

"I've never had it," Bob answered.

"There's a kid up the road name Skipper," Lowell said. "He climb trees real good. You wan' me to bring him down an' get those coconuts?"

"You go for Skipper," Clinton said. "We all wait here."

Five minutes later Lowell returned with Skipper. "Wait till you see this guy go up that tree," Clinton said. "He the best."

Skipper hopped out of the jeep and kicked off his shoes at the base of the tree. He was a wiry kid, about eighteen years old, and Clinton was right. He could really climb trees. Within thirty seconds Skipper had shimmied up the trunk and was hanging on by his legs, which were wrapped around the tree. Both hands were free, and he began dropping coconuts onto the ground. Once he'd picked it clean, he called out from his perch, which must have been at least twenty-five feet high, "I comin' down."

"Watch this," Lowell said as we all kept our eyes on Skipper. He turned himself upside-down and proceeded to slide down the tree headfirst. At the bottom he put his hands to the ground, let go with his legs, somersaulted over onto his feet, and landed with utter nonchalance. Clinton began chopping off the ends of the smooth green coconut shells with a machete. He handed one over to Bob and me and said, "Drink." We looked at the thin milky liquid inside.

"You first," Bob said.

I watched Skipper, who was draining a coconut, and it reminded me of going to Trader Vic's in New York as a child. My mom and I would share a ridiculously large tropical drink with straws sticking out of an imitation coconut shell. *I could use one of those long straws now,* I thought.

I lifted the coconut to my mouth, tipped it up, and took a sip. It tasted like sweet water. I passed it to Bob.

"You like it?" Clinton asked.

"It's not bad," I said. "I think I'd like it better if it was cold."

Bob and I finished ours, and Lowell, Clinton, and Skipper divided up the rest. They were going to take them home to grate the meat for coconut cake. Those little bags of shredded coconut I've always bought in the store all of a sudden seemed precious as I pictured the labor of thousands of Skippers harvesting coconut trees all over the world.

Anguilla's entry into the space age was the topic of conversation later that night in the kitchen. Everyone was discussing the unlikely subject of rocket ships and launch pads. News of an entrepreneurial Texan planning to lease Sombrero Island and turn it into the next Cape Canaveral was the subject of the latest in-house debate. Owned by Anguilla and only thirty-five miles away, Sombrero is surrounded by some of the richest fishing waters in the area and has nothing on it but a lighthouse and a large colony of booby birds. Anguilla fisherman have set their pots out by Sombrero for years and consider it to be a sort of wildlife refuge. No buildings, no tourists, no development whatsoever.

But now the natural rhythm of the island was being threatened by a Texan who thought he'd found a launch site far from anyone who would care he was there. Anguilla itself, he must have thought, was a small island in the middle of nowhere. Sombrero was just a desolate island that earned Anguilla no income and would be a perfect place for his rockets.

"You ever been Sombrero, Mel?" Hughes asked.

"No."

"I hear this guy gonna cover it up with concrete for he rocket ships," Bug warned. "If you wants to see Sombrero, you better go soon."

My mind filled instantly with images of *Apollo 13* streaking to the moon with a blaze of fire behind it and a thunderous roar shaking the ground below. I shuddered at the thought of visitors to Anguilla lying on the beach with a good book and a rum punch and then, *bang,* they look up in the sky and see a rocket blasting off over their heads. Ozzie explained that the Texan was only planning to launch one rocket a month and that the government would earn many thousands of dollars from the project. Still, what if on that one day a travel writer from the *New York Times* happened to be sunning on peaceful Anguilla?

The debate continued throughout the evening and I was careful to steer clear of questions. "They ain' gonna lettum launch rockets from here," someone said. "Oh, yeah," answered another. "They gonna launch the rockets an' Anguilla gonna have more money than ever before. You'll see."

Apparently the decision to rent Sombrero to the Texan was not finalized, and he was meeting more resistance than anticipated. International environmental groups were fighting to protect the booby birds, and local fishermen were fighting to safeguard their source of income. The future of little Sombrero Island made headlines from Los Angeles to London, and my guess was that the dispute would continue for quite some time. Cape Canaveral right here in Anguilla . . . that would take some adjustment.

"Local ice cream. Get your local ice cream, for true." We heard the loudspeaker from the road booming through the kitchen door. Talk of Sombrero and rocket ships was forgotten, and Ozzie began taking orders for ice cream from the staff. The owners of the ice cream parlor in town had a vehicle resembling a golf cart with a house over the top that they used to visit various villages and scoop ice cream. On Saturday nights they came to the west end, and Blanchard's was always one of their stops.

Ozzie and Garrilin distributed cups filled with every flavor: guava, passion fruit, coconut, kiwi, banana, and rum. We continued serving dinners while eating the ice cream, and I tried hard to pick up on the next conversation that had started. I was getting better at understanding the local patois, but at times it was still a foreign language to me. I caught bits and pieces about a man who was apprehended at the airport with $450,000 taped to his body under a wet suit. I heard something about drugs and smuggling and a private flight to St. Kitts. It was a touchy subject—and not something I thought I should know more about. I didn't ask any questions.

July 31 was our last night for the season. We were shutting down for August and September, along with many of the hotels, since it was peak hurricane season. We served only a few dinners that night and spent the evening emptying and scrubbing refrigerators and giving away the remaining food to the staff. We packed up the linens in plastic bags and cleared the dining room of all the candleholders and wine buckets. We carried the potted palms outside, where they would get some light and rain during our two-month vacation.

"We gonna miss all you," Bug said to Bob.

"We're gonna miss you too," Bob said. "But we'll be around for another week. Jesse's coming down tomorrow so we can all be here for Carnival. I wouldn't leave before the boat races, you know. *De Tree* is gonna win." Bob knew his prediction would spark a boat race debate, and he grinned as it began.

"No, man," Lowell jumped in. "*Light and Peace* gonna win this year."

Bug's voice was louder, and he said, "*Light and Peace,* nothing. *Bluebird* the boat to beat. Can't touch *Bluebird.*"

"*De Wizard* sailin' sweet, ya know," Alwyn countered. "We be lookin' over our shoulders at all you."

Everyone was yelling at once, and they were speaking so fast and so loud that Bob and I could barely follow what they were saying. We smiled at each other, enjoying the last kitchen squabble of the season.

It was hard to believe we'd lived in Anguilla a whole year. I thought back to building the restaurant with the Davis brothers, the opening the previous fall, Thanksgiving, then the high season. I looked at Clinton, who had gone from being a mason to a dishwasher to a prep cook and was now my sous chef. He had no idea how proud I was of him. And Lowell, who was Bob's right hand, had moved up from being a waiter to practically running the dining room. He had a key to the restaurant and would be responsible for checking on it regularly while we were up in Vermont visiting friends and family. I watched Miguel polishing a wineglass. His knowledge of wine had expanded immensely over the year; he could talk confidently about everything from puligny montrachet to zinfandel.

Hughes grilled leftover steaks, lobster, and fish, and we all feasted while the boat race discussion continued. Bob opened several bottles of champagne and poured it into plastic cups.

By midnight Blanchard's was scrubbed and empty. The refrigerators were unplugged and propped open. The gas was shut off along with the ice machine, and only the coolers in the wine cellar continued to run. We said goodbye to everyone and watched as our crew drove away, backseats loaded with leftover cheese, milk, butter, lemons, oranges, and lettuce.

I changed the message on the answering machine to say we'd be closed until October, and then Bob shut off the lights. We locked the door and walked down the winding path to the beach. The full moon lit the waves, and we stood for several minutes quietly listening to the soft sound of the surf.

"You loves Anguilla?" Bob asked, recalling Joshua's familiar question.

"I loves Anguilla," I said, and we turned to go home.

Part Three

Chapter 13

JESSE LANDED ON THE AFTERNOON American Eagle flight, and we drove home, anxious to show him our new apartment. After he dropped his bags and got a quick tour, he changed into shorts and we walked down to the beach.

"This is amazing," he said. "No more gas station and no more traffic in front of the house. And look at this beach!"

We walked along the edge of the water, following three sandpipers that darted up and down in front of the waves. Their sticklike legs moved in a blur as they raced down behind a receding wave, then scampered back up ahead of another. At the end of the beach we sat on some rocks and watched two pelicans circling and diving for fish.

"Tomorrow is the Sunday warm-up race," Bob told Jesse. "I'm going out in *De Tree*."

"Mom told me you've turned into quite a sailor."

Bob said, "I'm the only foreigner in a boat, and it's kind of an honor to be included. The boat feels like it's going to tip over half the time, and it's hard to hang on, but I love it."

"August Monday is the first big race for Carnival," I explained to Jesse. "You and I are going out in Lowell's motorboat and we'll follow the race. And I thought we'd go to J'ouvert Morning, too."

"What's J'ouvert Morning?" he asked.

"It's the official opening of Carnival. It starts at four A.M., and there are bands and people dance in the streets in town. Ozzie and Hughes said we shouldn't miss it."

We walked back up the beach and spent the rest of the afternoon reading on our balcony. It reminded us of the old days when we were tourists. The restaurant was closed, and we were once again relaxing in paradise. We walked up to Malliouhana to enjoy a rum punch and watch the sunset. The bar at Malliouhana is one of the most elegant and relaxing places on earth. Extra-deep, cushiony couches are built in and around the white stucco arches and columns. Lots of batik throw pillows make it even more comfortable. Tall mahogany shutters, hinged at the top, are propped outward, letting the sea breeze blow through. The bar opens wide onto a terra-cotta terrace perched on the edge of a cliff, with the sea directly below. We sat on the terrace under a fat palm tree that looked like a big pineapple, and ordered our rum punches. They were a muddy pink, from Mt. Gay and assorted freshly squeezed juices, and arrived in extra-tall skinny glasses. The sun poked through a hole in the orange clouds on the horizon, and a stream of yellow shot down and danced on the sea. We walked home on the beach as the colors faded into the evening.

Talk around the island shifted to calypso and boat racing. Word was out that three new boats were getting their final coats of paint and were almost ready for August Monday. "New brand boat in Island Harbor," Clinton had said. "Mr. Cool say she gonna be *fast*. She built by the same guy that build *UFO*. You know *UFO*. She that Island Harbor boat. Can' beat *UFO*. She tearin' up the island."

That night we went to Bandorama, a competition of local musical groups, which took place in an outdoor amphitheater called Landsome Bowl. During Carnival there is a different show there every night. The main street in town was decorated with a rainbow of lights strung overhead. They crisscrossed the road from telephone poles to rooftops, forming a multicolored canopy of bulbs almost a mile long. The lights turned down a side street and led directly to Landsome Bowl. A huge crowd was gathered outside, and food vans, grills, and tents were everywhere, as people wandered around eating johnnycakes, sweet-potato dumplings, and grilled chicken and ribs.

We could hear the thumping of bass pounding from inside the arena while we waited in line to pay our admission fee. We entered the arena, stepping over a goat sleeping alongside the crowd. He didn't even know we were there. The music was so loud, I could feel it vibrating in my chest. *Everyone will be deaf tomorrow,* I thought.

Landsome Bowl during Carnival is not unlike a fairground in Vermont. Carnival Village, as it is called, has an outdoor stage with benches, and the perimeter is lined with vendors selling food, drinks, Carnival T-shirts, popcorn, and souvenirs. Cora Lee had a new cotton candy machine, and a swarm of kids was lined up in front of her booth.

When we arrived, four teenagers were performing onstage. Walls of giant speakers blasted out the music, and the crowd swayed and rocked to the beat. The stage was framed by shimmering silver tinsel that was bathed in the colors of a multitude of blinking Christmas lights. One of the musicians played a keyboard, another thumped on a bass guitar, and the other two belted out a song at the top of their lungs. They wailed out something about young love or true love, but I couldn't for the life of me understand the words.

We walked around, checking out the various vendors. "I'm hungry," Jesse said. "Let's get some ribs."

We got in line in front of a grill and stood behind a large woman in a very tight red dress who was wiggling to the music. Just like Ozzie in the kitchen, she could move every part of her body and still keep her feet firmly planted on the ground. Her hips moved like liquid as she danced in place—the rhythm penetrated right through her. We bought two orders of ribs and a johnnycake and continued walking around, eating from the tinfoil used to wrap the food. Bob saw Rigby talking with a group of men, and Jesse and I followed as he went over to say hello.

"Happy Carnival," Rigby said.

"Ready for the race tomorrow?" Bob asked.

"Yeah, man. *De Tree* sailin' sweet. Errol put on the new sail from St. Martin today, so we gonna fly."

"You sailin'?" one of Rigby's friends asked Bob.

Rigby answered. "Blanchard a sailor, man. He cool."

"See you tomorrow morning," Bob said happily.

"Later," Rigby replied.

We knew that Lowell, Miguel, Ozzie, and Hughes had rented a booth and were selling drinks in the village, so we set out to find them in the crowd. We spotted Miguel playing dominos and found the rest of the gang inside their booth, surrounded by beer, soda, malt, and coolers of ice. Hughes had untied his usual braids and his hair was gathered into a giant puffball on top of his head. I commented on his new look, and he laughed. "Yeah, man," he said. "I needed a new style for Carnival." Bug was standing next to the domino table, waiting to get into the game, a Heineken in one hand and a chicken leg in the other.

We watched the dominos for a while and listened to the music. A new band was onstage doing some kind of rap thing. The sound of the dominos slamming on the table was completely drowned out by the band.

I walked over to the benches and looked up and down at the crowd. There were so many people, and for a split second it occurred to me that there wasn't another white person in sight. Just then I saw an arm waving at me from down in the front row. It was Garrilin. When she stood up out of the sea of people to say hi, I noticed that her hair was curled into ringlets and piled on top of her head and she was all dressed up. I wasn't used to seeing her in anything but her Blanchard's chef's coat, and she looked beautiful.

"Where Jesse and Bob?" she asked.

"Over there with the guys." I pointed to the booth with our staff. "You look gorgeous." The music was so loud, we had to scream to make each other hear. "What time do you think we need to go to J'ouvert Morning to see everything?" I asked.

"They does tramp from four, but you can reach for six."

"We won't miss anything if we go at six?"

"No, sweetheart." Garrilin smiled. "Six, they really movin'."

"Will you be at the boat race tomorrow?" I asked.

"No, I ain' trouble with no boat races. I gonna sleep tomorrow an' go church. I goin' back to my seat before somebody grab it. You have fun. Later."

The music was beginning to make my head throb, and I was hoping Bob and Jesse would be ready to go home. I found them leaning against the booth, Heinekens in hand, watching Bug, who had gotten into the domino game.

"I have to get away from this music," I yelled into Bob's ear. We said goodbye to the boys and made our way back to the car, where the thumping finally started to fade.

"My ears are ringing," Jesse said.

"Hughes said we should come back for the big calypso night," Bob said in the car. "There's a guy from Trinidad called the Mighty Bomber who's supposed to be really great. He comes with a saxophone player and a trombone and sings old-time calypso. He wasn't sure what night it was, but it should be in the paper."

"Do you think we could ask them to turn down the volume?" I said.

Jesse and I stayed home for the Sunday practice race. The boats sailed right past our balcony, and we watched through binoculars as *Light and Peace* came into view at around two o'clock. We could see Lowell among the crew and waved and cheered him on. Next came *De Chan* and then *Bluebird*. I counted eleven boats before *De Tree* came around the cliff from the east. It was dead last.

"Dad's not going to be happy," Jesse said.

An hour later *Bluebird* came back into view from the other direction, with *Stinger* right behind. They both passed close to shore, only a few hundred feet from our balcony. We spotted a boat far out, taking a completely different route, and through the binoculars I could recognize the pale green paint of *De Tree*.

"What are they doing out there?" Jesse asked. "You think the captain knows how to sail?"

"Dad says he does, but I can't imagine why they're so far away from everyone else." We watched as *De Tree* came about and began a new tack. The rest of the boats passed, some in close and others halfway between *De Tree* and the shore. Pretty soon they were all out of sight again, and we had to wait for the results.

Bob came home at five-thirty, wet, sandy, sore, and tired.

"We got fourth place," he said. "We moved from last up to fourth. We had a bad start because a big yacht got in our way going out of Sandy Ground. Errol wanted to turn around and demand a restart, but he decided to keep going. Boy, she really sailed on the way back."

"Why were you almost out at Prickly Pear?" Jesse asked.

"Errol said he wanted to 'try a little ting,' as he called it. I think it's what put us ahead of all the other boats. He also said we didn't have quite enough ballast for the size of the new sail and we'd fix that tomorrow. I'm ready for bed." Bob flopped down on the couch and closed his eyes.

"It's only five-thirty," I said.

"I'll just close my eyes for a minute," he said. He was sound asleep for the night in no time.

The alarm went off at five A.M., and we piled into the truck for J'ouvert Morning. Bob was sore but didn't want to miss anything.

We drove into town and parked alongside the road at the end of a row of cars that stretched half a mile. We could hear the music down the road, and a crowd of people jammed the main street that runs by the post office.

As we walked closer to the music we saw the band. They were playing from a makeshift stage set up on a flatbed trailer that was inching its way along the street. A generator on top provided power for the amplifiers and the ten-foot-high wall of speakers. A tarp was set up to shade the performers as well as a second-story platform for the lead singer. Thousands of people were dancing in front, behind, and all around the truck, following its path around town. It reminded me of the Norwich Fair in Vermont, where the hometown band rides down the Main Street parade on the back of a farm truck.

"So this is tramping," I said, looking at the crowd moving to the beat. I recognized concierges, taxi drivers, waiters, fishermen, and people from just about every part of the island. Some were wearing costumes, and several younger guys had covered their nearly naked bodies with shiny green paint. Almost everyone in the procession was carrying tall purple-and-green fluorescent cups filled with some concoction—rum, I guessed.

The music was deafening, and we moved down the street to where another truck was creeping along with yet another crowd of people tramping and dancing around it. We spent about an hour greeting friends and getting the feel of the morning but decided that J'ouvert Morning was probably a once-in-a-lifetime experience for us.

Ozzie teased us. "You's jus' old folks," he said.

We drove Bob to Sandy Ground at nine o'clock so he could help rig *De Tree*. Jesse and I spent the morning talking about college and catching up on each other's lives. He had decided to major in studio art and was no longer considering changing schools. I was relieved to know that he could survive a crisis even if we were thousands of miles apart. We drove back to the race at eleven-thirty, taking the scenic route that overlooks the harbor. I pulled over near a group of people gathering to watch the race from high up on the cliff. Boat race chatter was in full swing, and the Mt. Gay and Heineken were flowing.

Jesse and I walked up and down the beach tasting conch chowder, barbecued chicken, and piña coladas. I had never seen so much activity on the beach before. Dozens of booths had been set up, and smoke from a multitude of grills filled the air. The beach was so crammed with people, it was hard to get through. Johnno's had a band playing, and the familiar thud of the bass pounded through the crowd. The freshly lacquered boats rocked in the bay, the sun reflecting their bright colors in the clear water.

Sails, folded into stuffed bags, were lined up along the beach. A group of excited kids were doing back flips off the wharf, and the shore was lined with motor yachts from St. Martin here to see the race. *De Tree* was out practicing, along with a few of the other new boats, so Jesse and I wandered around looking for Lowell.

The Davis boys were gathered under a blue plastic tarp, and I-Davis bounded out to greet us. "Irie, Blanchards," he said, the gold star on his front tooth gleaming. "*De Tree* gonna win today." His dreadlocks hung all the way down to his waist. He was wearing a faded tie-dyed T-shirt, khaki shorts, and big black work boots. "Come in the cool shade," he said, and we followed him under the tarp where Clinton, Rocky, Kee Kee, and little brother Steve sat in plastic chairs.

After chatting with the Davises for a while, Jesse and I went in search of Lowell. We were excited about going out on his motorboat and didn't want to miss our chance.

"Jah live," I-Davis said, bidding us farewell. "One love."

"See you later," I said.

"Cool," Kee Kee and Clinton said at the same time.

We found Hughes, along with Ozzie, Sweenda, and their two-year-old daughter, sitting on the beach waiting for Lowell to bring his boat closer to shore. Jesse and I joined them on the sand and watched a little boy, maybe six years old, throw a Coke can into the sea. He pulled it back in repeatedly, using a string he'd attached to the pop-top. It was twenty minutes before Lowell returned with the boat, and the Coke can game continued the whole time—I got the feeling he would be entertained for days.

We all waded out to the boat, climbed up over the side, and helped pass in a cooler with drinks and several life preservers. Lowell's older brother Glen, the customs officer, was also on board. Lowell pulled up the anchor, and we cruised slowly out of the harbor to watch the racing boats practice. By two o'clock all fifteen boats were lined up along the beach, ready to go. The crowd roared, the music thumped, and Mr. Cool fired the start gun. The boats set off crisply in the fresh wind, and the race west was uneventful. The wind was from behind, and there was no tacking or maneuvering. All the boats cruised along in a big pack until they made their first turn.

Lowell's motorboat was called *Baby G*—named after his brothers' two new baby girls. Jesse and I, along with everyone else, bumped along as the little orange boat rose and fell with the waves. The water splashed over the sides and felt warm and agreeable. We couldn't move around much, since *Baby G* was crowded and we had to hang on to something most of the time. The sun reflected off the water in a million directions, and we covered ourselves often with suntan lotion, hoping Bob had remembered to do the same. As we passed Sandy Island a school of dolphins appeared and swam alongside *Baby G* for a while, following the race like the rest of us. The perspective of the island from the water was totally different from what we saw on land. We saw our apartment above Long Bay, then Malliouhana, Carimar Beach Club, and Blanchard's. The restaurant looked very small compared to the hotels, and it was odd to think how our entire life in Anguilla revolved around that little building. I thought of the thousands of happy customers who had dined with us over the past year, their candlelit evening a treasured memory of a perfect vacation.

We passed Meads Bay and Barnes Bay and soon rounded the western tip of the island. A tiny outcropping of rock formed its own island, called Anguillita, marking the end of Anguilla, with open sea stretching out for miles beyond it.

De Tree was somewhere in the middle, but as they approached the turning pin Glen began to yell.

"Watch *De Tree* now," he shouted. "She gonna make a move. Watch 'er now."

Sure enough, all the other boats swung around to the south, making a big arc around the floating pin. *De Tree* was headed straight for the pin. It passed three other boats, narrowly missed *Stinger*, made a dramatic turn, and reset its course, headed north. *Bluebird* and *Light and Peace* had been in the lead, but *De Tree* cut them off and was now out in front.

Glen and Lowell yelled at the captain of *Light and Peace*. "How you could let he cut you off? That Errol wicked, you know. Up the road," they shouted. "Up the road."

As we followed the boats closely, Lowell passed around some sugar apples he had brought along for a snack. They were funny-looking fruits, really—like little green pinecones. Inside, though, they were sweet and soft, almost like a melon. I spit the seeds out into the water and watched the colors of ocean life swirl beneath us. A school of jellyfish swam under the boat. They were milky white, almost clear, and about the size of small saucers. They opened and closed rhythmically, passing quickly out of sight.

Inside *De Tree*, Bob was still shaking from the near miss with *Stinger*. The crew had scrambled to the other side during the move, and everyone was yelling all at once.

"Jib. Jib. Jib," Errol screamed. "Haul the jib, boys." Shabby and Rigby tightened the jib sail until Errol yelled, "Good jib."

"Come up to the wind, Cap," Sam called. "Pinch the mainsail. Pinch the sheet."

Errol and Sam tightened the rope a little on the mainsail, and *De Tree* came up onto its side until the gunwale skimmed the water.

They continued toward the north, away from the rest of the pack. Clearly Errol had his own game plan. After about ten minutes *De Tree* came about and took a new tack toward the east.

"*De Tree* above everybody," Glen said. "She done cross everybody."

We followed along next to *Light and Peace,* since Glen and Lowell were supporters, and Jesse and I enjoyed the sunshine and sea spray. Other motorboats zoomed around us, hailing us as they passed. James came up close with about a dozen people in his fishing boat, all waving Heinekens and cheering before speeding away. Miguel waved from another speedboat, and Thomas flew by in his lobster boat.

By the time we got back to Sandy Ground, *Bluebird* and *De Tree* were neck and neck, vying for first place. Each boat gracefully tacked back and forth around the throng of anchored sailboats, speedboats, and fishing boats. *Bluebird* passed the finish buoy one boat length ahead of *De Tree,* and a roar came up from the crowd. *De Tree* had grabbed a respectable second place for its first August Monday race.

We spotted Bug on the beach dancing and waving a Heineken in the air. He was singing, "Can' touch *Bluebird. Bluebird* the boat to beat."

The race for third place was a heated one. *Eagle* and *UFO* were tacking back and forth, narrowly missing each other each time they crossed. *Eagle* was ahead by one boat length, but *UFO* was closing in. As the two boats passed, both crews yelled, "Hard lee, hard lee," and instead of changing their tack to avoid a collision, it became a game of chicken. Neither boat would give way. *UFO* was headed straight for the starboard side of *Eagle.*

Lowell, Glen, Ozzie, and Hughes were screaming and shaking fists along with hundreds of people onshore. The *UFO*'s bow struck *Eagle* broadside, and the heavy rocks, sandbags, and lead in the bottom sank her almost immediately. Within minutes *Eagle* came to rest on the sandy bottom, her mast sticking up about halfway out of the water. *UFO* continued past the finish line, taking third place.

Eagle's crew was shuttled ashore by the police boat, and everyone argued on the beach for almost an hour. I'm not sure if *UFO* was eventually disqualified or not, but apparently this sort of thing happens from time to time, and nobody took it too seriously.

"How are they going to get *Eagle* up?" Bob asked Errol.

"See them divers?" he said, pointing to a group of men swimming out to the sunken boat. "Once they take out the ballast, she jus' float back up. Then they take off 'er mast an' bail 'er out. Don' worry, man. She be ready for the race tomorrow."

That night we returned to Carnival Village to see the Mighty Bomber, the grand old entertainer from Trinidad. We stood with Lowell, Miguel, Hughes, and Ozzie by their booth, listening to the calypso until midnight. His performance was much more our style than the loud, pounding bands we had heard earlier. Surprisingly, the young people in the crowd enjoyed him as well. The Bomber, as everyone called him, wore a light gray suit with a hankie stylishly flared out of his pocket. He had on a white top-hat rakishly tipped to one side. He told the audience that he'd been entertaining since the fifties, and I had a feeling his act hadn't changed much since then. "Va va va voom," he'd sing, and the crowd swooned. Clinton joined us midway through the show and said, "Mel, this the real thing, ya know. He the best."

On our last night before leaving the island for vacation, we went to visit Jerry Gumbs. We hadn't seen him as much as we'd hoped throughout the year and wanted to make sure we said goodbye. I wanted to have the image of his long white beard, round brown belly, and big smile firmly embedded in my mind in Vermont.

"Jerry," Bob said, "I didn't see you at the boat races. I went out in *De Tree*."

"Haven't you noticed I'm an old man?" he said with a smile. "I used to go to every race, but not now."

Bob told him about getting second place and about the new boats from various villages. We drank Ting and sat around the old card table on Jerry's veranda.

"Jerry," Jesse said, "have you ever heard of little fruits called canaipes? They grow in big bunches and have a tart jellylike inside. We had them once in Barbados, and I wondered if they grow here."

"Ginips. We call them ginips in Anguilla. You like ginips?" Jerry asked in his resonant bass. "You got some time?" he continued, not waiting for an answer.

"Sure," Bob said.

In a matter of minutes we were driving toward The Valley with Jerry, who was taking us to his favorite ginip tree. He led us to Crocus Hill, which at 212 feet above sea level is the highest point in Anguilla, yet still barely visible from the sea. Jerry pointed out his childhood home and told us how Crocus Hill had once been the center of town. We'd always thought Jerry had been born and raised in Blowing Point—he seemed to have been there for centuries. Fifty years ago, he said, the post office, clinic, government building, and courthouse were all located in Crocus Hill village. It was the hub of the island before The Valley.

Looking around that night, Crocus Hill village was barely discernible—only a few scattered houses, all with spectacular views of the island and beyond. We could see the northern landmarks, Sandy Island, Prickly Pear Cay, and Dog Island, as well as the lights of St. Martin to the south.

"Pull in here," Jerry said at the crest of the hill. He directed us into the driveway of a house where he assured us no one would be home. We followed him to the backyard, and he pointed to a giant tree with dozens of branches weighted down by bunches of little green ginips. The fruit was all out of reach—someone had already cleaned off the lower branches. Jerry gave Bob and Jesse the okay to climb, and while the sun plunged like a blazing ball into the sea, they maneuvered arms and legs over and around the thick branches of the tree. Jerry and I stood on the ground, the evening breeze rustling the coconut palms around us on the hill. We filled a cardboard box with ginips as Bob and Jesse flung down bunches of the cherry-sized fruit from above our heads.

I looked up at the silhouette of the ginip tree and watched the stars pop out one by one. Anguilla never really experiences dusk as we know it. When the sun goes down, the sky is dark within half an hour. A sliver of moon was growing brighter in the north, and I felt as if time stood still up on Crocus Hill. I knew that had I been there picking ginips under the moon a century before, nothing around me would have been different.

Eating ginips takes time. You can't be fussy about peeling the skin. It's best to just pop the whole thing in your mouth at once, break the thick skin with your teeth, and suck out the tart jelly inside. Then you spit out the skin and the seed inside. Bob had little patience for it, but Jerry, Jesse, and I bit, sucked, and spat happily the whole way home.

On the way back to Blowing Point Jerry entertained us with his stories of Castro and the Anguilla Revolution. He remembered nostalgically the speech he had made at the UN in 1967. Back at Rendezvous Bay, Jerry settled into his tattered lounge chair, and before we said goodbye he recited, word for word, his favorite poem. His deep voice was captivating, and he paused for dramatic effect each time he came to the line "This too shall pass." We drove home to pack, comforted by the thought that Jerry would be sitting in his lounge chair when we returned in October.

The next morning we were up at five-thirty to catch the eight o'clock American Eagle flight. Our apartment was in order, our suitcases were loaded in the truck, and we walked out onto our balcony for a final gaze at the sea. The sun was just peeking over the hill behind us, and the clouds over the water were yellow on the top and a bluish gray on the bottom.

I leaned on the railing and took a long, deep breath of the cool morning air. The sound of the waves below would seem far away in Vermont. I tried to plant the view, the breeze, and the gentle, repetitive swoosh of the surf firmly in my mind; we closed the door and drove away.

At the top of the hill above our apartment I glanced over my shoulder for one last glimpse of the turquoise water beyond. We passed Lowell's house and waved goodbye to his mother, who was standing on her porch in her housedress. We drove by Christine's shop on the left, and as we eased over the speed bump in front of Bernice's, I could almost smell the barbecue.

The next barbecued chicken we would have would be at a fair in Vermont. I wondered if the pace in Vermont would seem fast to me now. Had I become so much a part of this new life—this gentle Caribbean life—that even Vermont would seem harried to me now?

Garrilin, Roxana, and Mac were waiting for us at the airport to say goodbye. We unloaded the luggage, parked the truck in the lot, slid the keys under the mat for Lowell, and checked in at the counter. As we said goodbye and paid our "non-belonger's" departure tax, I thought, *I can't think of a place I belong to more than Anguilla.*

Chapter 14

LOWELL'S CALL CAME ON SUNDAY, September 3, at three in the afternoon. "Mel," he said with no preamble, "you see the Weather Channel?" I could hear panic in his voice.

"No," I answered. "Why? What's going on?"

"Man, this is the big one. I ain' never see nothin' like this *ever*. Hurricane Luis, man. He headed straight for us. Luis gonna mash us up, man. I gonna get the rest a the guys and bar up the restaurant. We ain' got much time."

"I'll go turn on the TV," I said, and handed the phone to Bob.

"Hey, Bob," Lowell said in a hurry. "This storm ain' makin' no joke. I jus' wanted to tell you we already buy plywood from Anguilla Trading an' we barrin' up all the shutters and doors at the restaurant. Me an' Clinton roundin' up the rest a the guys."

"I'm coming down," Bob said. "Let me see how soon I can get a flight. You put on the plywood, and I'll call you as soon as I know my schedule."

Jesse had already returned to school, and Bob and I were staying at Pat's house in Vermont. I turned on the Weather Channel, and sure enough, all they were talking about was Hurricane Luis.

And the white line showing its projected path went straight through Anguilla and St. Martin.

SEPTEMBER 3—3 P.M. TROPICAL UPDATE
LOCATION: 54.90 W   17.40 N
SUSTAINED WINDS 135 MPH
GUSTS UP TO 145 MPH
CATEGORY 4 HURRICANE
MOVING 12 MPH WNW
500 MILES FROM ANGUILLA/ST. MARTIN
PREDICTED LANDFALL: 40 HOURS

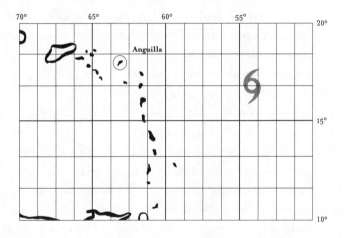

Bob, Pat, and I were glued to the Weather Channel, getting a quick lesson in tropical meteorology. John Hope, the channel's hurricane specialist, told us that the storm had been first detected nine days earlier as a tropical disturbance swirling off the coast of Africa. It was heading directly for the northeastern Leeward Islands. Four days later it strengthened to a tropical storm, and two days after that a well-defined eye formed, winds increased to 75 mph, and Luis turned into a category 1 hurricane. It took only three more days to turn into a category 4 storm, with sustained winds of 135 mph.

SAFFIR-SIMPSON DAMAGE POTENTIAL SCALE

CATEGORY	WIND	PREDICTED DAMAGE
1	74–95 MPH	MINIMAL
2	96–110 MPH	MODERATE
3	111–130 MPH	EXTENSIVE
4	131–155 MPH	EXTREME
5	155+ MPH	CATASTROPHIC

Flights to Anguilla were canceled because they were moving all the smaller American Eagle planes out of the region. Bob booked a flight to St. Martin for early the next morning and called Frankie Connor, who said he would meet him at the dock by the airport with his boat. Pat and I drove Bob to Boston that night and made him promise to keep in touch.

John Hope fast became our only link to the storm's progress. He had a new report every three hours, with updates on the projected path of the storm, changes in wind velocity, and the speed at which it was moving. We learned that a hurricane's forward motion could slow down, in which case it would strengthen even more.

I called Bob at his hotel in Boston and asked him not to go. John Hope was warning people in the islands to put together hurricane emergency kits with drinking water, canned foods, batteries, flashlights, and radios. "Bob, how can you fly down there knowing how dangerous it is? This is crazy. Let me come back to Boston and get you."

"I'll be fine. My flight gets in at one o'clock, Frankie will pick me up, and I'll be safe in our apartment. It's very well built, and we'll board up all the windows. Nothing can happen. I want to be there to help Lowell and Clinton get everything ready, and I think it's a good idea for me to be there afterward to help do whatever has to be done."

"But this is your life we're talking about. As Lowell said, this storm ain' makin' no joke."

"Mel, stop worrying. I'll be fine."

SEPTEMBER 4—5 A.M. TROPICAL UPDATE

LOCATION: 57.40 W   17.00 N

SUSTAINED WINDS 138 MPH

GUSTS UP TO 150 MPH

EYE IS CONTINUING TO DEVELOP

INTENSIFICATION EXPECTED

CATEGORY 4 HURRICANE

MOVING 12 MPH WNW

350 MILES FROM ANGUILLA/ST. MARTIN

PREDICTED LANDFALL: 30 HOURS

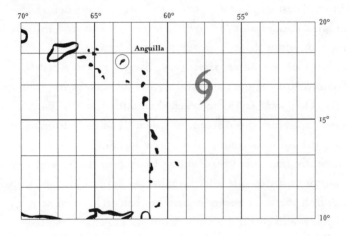

At six the following morning Bob was with a sleep-deprived crowd at an American Airlines gate at Logan Airport. People were becoming unruly, and his voice grew louder as his patience was running out. He had become the spokesman for the rest of the passengers, and they were waiting for a supervisor to announce whether or not the flight to St. Martin would be canceled.

"Look," he said to Mr. Whitfield, the ticket agent at the counter, "we are all confirmed on this flight and have to get down there. If that plane doesn't go, we could lose everything we have."

"Sir, we're trying to get an updated position on the hurricane," Mr. Whitfield said as he frantically punched keys on his computer.

Bob was convinced he was staring at the computer screen to avoid making eye contact with the customers. Another gate agent had already announced that the tower was calculating how bad the weather would be when the plane landed in four hours.

Bob pressed on. "With only about forty people on that jumbo jet, this is obviously not a profitable trip for American Airlines. But this is our livelihood. We have to get down there to protect our property. The hurricane is still two hundred and fifty miles east of St. Martin and moving at twelve miles an hour. It's easy math. The storm won't hit the island until tomorrow," Bob said. He had just seen the latest tropical update on a TV in his hotel before checking out, and wondered if Mr. Whitfield expected to find information in his computer that was somehow more current.

Most of the other passengers, like Bob, had interests in St. Martin or one of the surrounding islands such as Anguilla or St. Barts. They were trying to reach their little piece of paradise and secure it against the oncoming storm. The only tourists were a group of four Germans who spoke absolutely no English and apparently had not heard about Hurricane Luis, and a young honeymooning couple who thought they were in for a great adventure. Bob paced the room for another half an hour wondering how much it would cost if everyone chipped in to charter a plane.

"May I have your attention, please?" Mr. Whitfield had stopped punching his keyboard and spoke into the microphone. "American Airlines announces the boarding of flight five-sixty-one to St. Martin. Passengers in first class and those needing assistance or traveling with small children may now board through gate seventeen."

"Does he see anyone here taking small children on vacation into a hurricane?" Bob said to a man standing next to him. "We're probably crazy enough going down ourselves."

The flight was uneventful and quiet. Passengers were lost in their own thoughts about what they would encounter in the hours to come.

As the huge, empty plane began its approach into St. Martin, the captain's voice came over the intercom. "Well, folks, it looks like the landing could be a little rough today." He didn't sound as confident as Bob would have liked. "The storm is still a ways away, but we've got some pretty stiff gusts of wind, so please make sure your seat belts are fastened. I'll try to make it as smooth as possible."

When the plane touched down, it somehow seemed to be moving sideways. It bounced a couple of times, the engines roared, and the big bird careened down the runway, coming to a stop not fifty feet from the end of the tarmac. The pilot turned the plane around, and as it lumbered back toward the Princess Juliana Airport terminal, Bob stared out the window, trying to imagine what the scene would be like in twenty-four hours. Pummeled by the wind, the palm trees already looked like inside-out umbrellas, and the storm hadn't even arrived yet.

Inside, the terminal was complete mayhem. The hot breeze brought no relief as more than a thousand people desperately tried to get a ticket for the last departing plane out—which held only three hundred passengers. The airport was about to be shut down. Tickets and boarding passes were being sold auction style by a large local woman standing on a chair surrounded by a jostling, clamoring crowd, and the bidding was up to $2,000 per ticket. As Bob pushed his way through the mob, dragging his bag behind him, he wished he had stayed up north.

Outside the terminal, the wind was unrelenting. He leaned into the gale and headed across the road, where he had arranged to meet Frankie's boat to take him over to Anguilla. Rays of sun streaked down between the dark clouds and sparkled on the water. *This is so strange,* Bob thought. *The worst hurricane in thirty-five years is about to hit us head-on, and the water is the most incredible shade of green I have ever seen. How can it be so beautiful in the middle of such a disaster?*

The small wooden dock where Frankie's boat tied up belonged to a grocery store and restaurant that serviced the sailing crowd.

The owners of the little complex were busy boarding up their windows. Bob heard hammers pounding from all directions and remembered how peaceful it had been in that same spot so many times before. Rounding the corner, he saw two teenage boys wrestling with a piece of plywood. They were trying to nail it over a window in the store, and the wind kept wrenching it away from them.

Bob's heart sank as he looked up and down the dock and realized Frankie's boat was not there.

"You guys seen Frankie Connor?" he asked, hoping they would say he'd be right back.

"Frankie gone," one of them replied. "Ports all close."

"Does that mean the regular ferries aren't running either?"

"No, man. Everything close. See ferries out there." The young man stopped fighting with the plywood for a minute and pointed toward the harbor, where a group of Anguilla ferryboats was anchored, preparing to ride out the storm. *Okay,* Bob thought, *I'll just go back to the airport and call Frankie. He'll come get me.*

The line for the two telephones in the terminal was at least fifty people long, so Bob quickly returned to the store, hoping to use the phone there. He went inside to ask for the phone and waited patiently in the checkout line behind an angry man who was cursing at the owner. The customer was stocking up on supplies, and prices had doubled with the impending hurricane.

"You a wicked son of a bitch, Mitchell. These prices ain' right," the customer protested.

"James, you gonna buy this stuff or not?" the storekeeper asked with his arms crossed.

James reluctantly threw some money on the counter, muttering, "Greedy son of a bitch."

Mitchell didn't seem to mind being called names, and as he turned to Bob it was obvious he would not let him use the phone without some form of remuneration.

"I have a little problem," Bob began as Mitchell turned and headed for the door to check on the progress of his two young assistants.

"Yeah. Wha'?" he said over his shoulder.

"I have a restaurant in Anguilla, and Frankie Connor was supposed to pick me up, but he's not here. I was hoping to use your phone to see if he—"

"Phone ain' work," he interrupted.

Bob was not so easily put off. "Would twenty dollars make the phone work?" he asked.

"Fifty dollars the phone could work." He glanced at Bob. *Truly a greedy son of a bitch,* Bob thought.

He gave the storekeeper a $50 bill and was shown into a grimy cubicle. The phone sat on a desk on a pile of papers with an overflowing ashtray and assorted candy wrappers alongside it. Empty beer cans covered whatever surface of the desk was left. Bob pulled out his address book for Frankie's number.

"Hi, Sylvanie, it's Bob Blanchard."

"Hi. Where are you?" Sylvanie was Frankie's wife, and she sounded surprised.

"I'm here in St. Martin. The plane came in an hour late. Where's Frankie?"

American Airlines was taking off across the street, and the sound was thunderous. Bob was miserably hot, could hardly hear what Sylvanie was saying, and really wished now that he hadn't come down.

"He tie the boat up in the harbor. He waited for you but you ain' reach."

"Well, I've reached now. Do you think he could come back and get me?" Bob asked hopefully.

"No, man. Sea already runnin' fifteen feet. He lucky he reach home. All the boats tie up."

"Do you know anybody who would come get me?" Bob asked desperately.

"No. Sorry, Bob. This a bad storm, you know. Everybody home barrin' up."

Bob sat alone in the grubby office. Suddenly the seven-mile passage to Anguilla could have been the width of the Atlantic Ocean. Picturing himself lashed to a post in the airport by his luggage straps, Bob searched through the debris on the desk for a St. Martin phone book. He spotted one under the ashtray, which he then accidentally knocked over, and the smell of old cigarettes made him feel sick. Beginning with *A,* he held his breath and called the hotels listed in the yellow pages.

The few that answered said, "We're closed. Don't you know there's a hurricane coming?" Most of the numbers just rang and rang. Finally someone at Port de Plaisance answered in a surprisingly civilized manner. "May I help you?" the man said calmly with a British accent.

"Please don't hang up," Bob began. "I have a restaurant in Anguilla, I've just landed here in St. Martin, and I can't get across. I really need a room for the night."

"Which restaurant?" the man asked.

Bob wondered why it would matter but answered, "Blanchard's."

"And are you Mr. Blanchard?" the British gentleman on the phone asked.

"Yes, I am," said Bob, happy to have at last struck up a normal conversation with someone.

Hesitantly the man said, "Come on over. We've spent the whole day trying to empty the hotel, but we'll find a place for you. We still have about forty guests who couldn't get a flight. Just ask for me, Mr. Spittle. I'm the manager here." Bob wondered what would have happened had he owned the wrong restaurant.

The hotel was a few miles away, and Bob was thrilled to find an available taxi at the airport. After check-in, Mr. Spittle drove Bob on a golf cart to his room, a job usually reserved for a bellman, but all the employees at Port de Plaisance had gone home to board up their houses. He was given a suite on the third and top floor, with a living room and a separate bedroom, both with sliding glass doors opening onto a patio facing the marina. Bob dropped his luggage, thanked Mr. Spittle, and went back outside to survey the construction of the building he was about to entrust his life to. Hurricane Luis was inching closer.

The buildings at Port de Plaisance Hotel were arranged in a circle on a small peninsula protruding into the Pond, as the locals called it. The Pond is actually an inland harbor accessible from the sea by two drawbridges—one on the French side in Marigot, and the other on the Dutch side near the airport. Bob had never seen so many boats there before, and Mr. Spittle had explained they'd come from surrounding islands to ride out the storm in a safe harbor. There were small sailboats, giant yachts, steel barges, work boats, ferryboats, and dredging equipment, all battening down and anchoring in preparation for Hurricane Luis. Mr. Spittle had heard on the radio that the coast guard estimated there were 2,500 boats in the Pond.

Bob walked around the manicured grounds, assessing the building and its stormworthiness. He spotted a man barking orders into a two-way radio and hoped he might be someone who could shed light on the soundness of the structure—specifically, whether being on the top floor with two unprotected glass doors in a hurricane was a good idea.

The man turned out to be the hotel's engineer. Jimso, as his name tag indicated, weighed about three hundred pounds and was not in the mood to speak with a hotel guest. He continued yelling into his radio. "No, man, I toll you, move the things from the lobby into the storeroom. I tellin' you, that side gonna get hit hard. Move it all now.

"Wut chu wan'?" he asked Bob as he headed off toward the main building.

"Do you know how this building is constructed?" Bob asked, running to keep up with Jimso's quickening pace.

"You from the insurance company?" Jimso responded with disdain.

"No, I'm just a guest here. I live in Anguilla and I can't get home, so I'll be here for the storm. Is there anything I can do to help?"

"Jus' stay in your room when the storm hits." And with that, he disappeared into a maintenance shed, slamming the door behind him.

Bob decided to try to find Mr. Spittle again. Perhaps he would be more helpful. His main concern was how the roof of the building was attached to the rest of the structure. If it was simply wooden rafters sitting on top of concrete walls, the chances of its being blown off were pretty good. Bob had seen pictures of Hurricane Andrew in Florida and how it had ripped entire wooden roofs right off the buildings.

Mr. Spittle, in his golf cart, was going across the little bridge that connected the main part of the resort, where the rooms were, to the front desk and dining room area. Bob flagged him down and waited while he finished his conversation with someone on the other end of his radio.

"Mr. Spittle, do you happen to know how the roof is attached to the main building? Is it poured concrete or wooden rafters?"

Mr. Spittle stared at Bob. Clearly he did not know the answer and had probably never before been asked that particular question. "Jimso will know," he said. "Jimso, come in, Jimso," he repeated into the radio.

"Jimso here," crackled the reply.

"Jimso, do you know how the roof is attached?"

"Roof hook down good. Glass doors gonna be the problem," Jimso warned. "All the floors and ceilings be concrete. Rafters poured into the ring beam."

That was music to Bob's ears. It apparently meant nothing to Mr. Spittle, since he started to ask what a ring beam was, but Jimso had to go, and shut off his radio.

"That's very good news," Bob said to Mr. Spittle. "It means that the ceiling in my room is poured concrete and the rafters were set right into it. The roof should be okay; even if the wind were to rip off the metal roofing and plywood, the concrete slab over our heads wouldn't get damaged. He's right, though—the sliding glass doors are going to be the problem."

"Well, I'm glad that answered your question," said Mr. Spittle, and away he went on his golf cart.

Bob felt much more confident about the building. Even if the sliding doors broke, he could always hide in the bathroom. He went back upstairs to call home and let us know where he was.

Pat answered the phone on the first ring. "It's him," she said, and handed me the phone.

"Hi. Are you in Anguilla?"

"No. I'm stuck in St. Martin. The sea is too rough and Frankie couldn't wait for me, so I was lucky to get a room at Port de Plaisance."

For a second I relaxed. Bob and I had been to Port de Plaisance for lunch several times, and I could picture him surrounded by the acres of lush gardens, rows of palm trees, and winding brick paths along the sea. It was an elaborately landscaped new hotel and didn't seem like such a bad place to be stranded.

"Did they board up your windows?" I asked.

"They have about half the place boarded, but they haven't gotten to my section yet. Don't worry, though. I've checked out the construction and I'll be fine. The whole building is concrete. It's eerie outside now. The air is perfectly still. It's the calm before the storm—even the birds have stopped flying. There were three yellow bananaquits on my balcony, but they're gone now. They know what's coming."

I chimed in with helpful words of advice. "I heard on the Weather Channel that the safest place to be is in the bathtub with a mattress over you. I know that doesn't sound like something you would do, but keep it in mind if things get scary."

"Okay," Bob answered compliantly.

I continued with my Weather Channel report. "The winds are steady now at a hundred and forty miles per hour, and it's headed right for you. I mean *exactly* where you are. They keep drawing a big white line showing the hurricane's projected path, and it couldn't be a more direct hit. It should be there tomorrow around noon. I wish you hadn't gone down there. I don't like this at all."

"I'll be fine." Bob was trying to calm me down, but I could tell he might be regretting his decision to be there. "I was really lucky to find a room," he said again. "I have the Weather Channel on too. The hotel is setting up a buffet for us tonight. Wouldn't you love to be here for that?" Bob knew how much I loathed hotel buffets.

"The electricity is being shut off on the whole island at midnight," he went on, "so the phones won't work after that. We'll be out of touch for a little while. Oh, also, while I was wandering around the hotel, I found an ice cream freezer loaded with three-gallon tubs of Häagen-Dazs. Since they'll melt once the power is off anyway, I don't think anyone would mind if I brought a chocolate one up to my room. It would be a shame to waste it."

Suddenly the absurdity of the situation hit me, and I started to laugh. I pictured Bob sitting in the bathtub with no lights, eating a giant tub of chocolate Häagen-Dazs ice cream, with a category 4 hurricane raging outside his door.

"They brought me bottles of water and candles a little while ago too. Oh, and cheese curls," Bob said. "So you don't have to worry. I won't go hungry. Hold on, somebody is at my door." He put down the phone, and I could hear the conversation in the background. "Oh, great," I heard him say. "My favorite. Thanks a lot."

He picked up the phone again. "I'm *really* okay now. They brought me a case of warm diet Coke." We both laughed hard, knowing full well he wouldn't drink a sip.

"Listen, I'm going to get off the phone now, because I think they're starting the buffet and I don't want to miss that. I have the camera and the zoom lens, and I'm going to take pictures of everything for you. I'll call you later before the power gets shut off."

"Okay, but Pat and I are too restless just sitting here, so we're going over to Maine to keep ourselves occupied. We'll be at the Anchorage Hotel in Ogunquit. They've already assured me they get the Weather Channel, so we'll be following everything that happens. We should be there in two hours."

"I love you," Bob said.

"Take care of yourself. I know you think you're invincible, but try to take this seriously."

"I'll be fine. Don't worry. Talk to you later."

"Let's go," I said to Pat.

We quickly packed our bags and headed for the coast of Maine. It had always been a favorite refuge for Bob and me. The Anchorage Hotel lobby was filled with tourists reading brochures about area attractions and local restaurants. They had no idea we were in the middle of a crisis. Pat and I wanted to confirm again that we could get the Weather Channel, but the young girl at the desk couldn't have cared less about a hurricane in the Caribbean. She handed us the key to our room.

We left the happy tourists downstairs and went to our room to turn on the TV. John Hope was our lifeline to Bob. His authoritative voice spoke right to us: "In about three minutes we will have new coordinates and updated information on Hurricane Luis." Pat and I sat side by side on the edge of the bed waiting for the latest report. It was eight o'clock, and the last data we had was already three hours old.

SEPTEMBER 4—8 P.M. TROPICAL UPDATE

LOCATION: 60.20 W   17.10 N

SUSTAINED WINDS 140 MPH

GUSTS UP TO 170 MPH

CATEGORY 4 HURRICANE

MOVING 10 MPH W

200 MILES FROM ANGUILLA/ST. MARTIN

PREDICTED LANDFALL: 20 HOURS

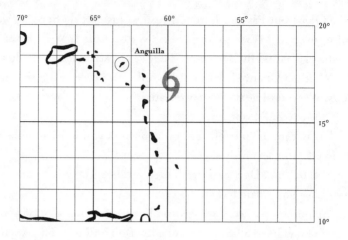

The familiar map of the Caribbean appeared on the screen—a sea of blue with a giant mass of swirling orange and red representing the storm. With every new report the mass had moved closer and closer to the islands, and John would take his marker and draw a bold arrow showing its predicted track. His arrow went right from the eye of the storm to Anguilla and St. Martin, around which he would draw a circle.

The meteorologist's words were serious. "This is a dangerous hurricane with sustained winds that are now a hundred and forty miles per hour, with gusts up to one-seventy. It is moving westward and has slowed to ten miles per hour. This could cause further intensification. Luis is currently two hundred miles from Anguilla and St. Martin, and we expect severe damage on those islands. If you are in the warning area, you should be doing your final preparation right now. All windows and doors should be boarded shut, and you should have a good supply of flashlights, extra batteries, a battery-operated radio, bottled water, and nonperishable food. Those of you in low-lying areas should seek shelter on higher ground, as this storm is almost certain to cause serious flooding as well. The storm surge is expected to be as high as twenty feet."

Pat and I listened intently and wondered what Bob was doing. Luis sounded more serious with each update. It was still three hours before he was scheduled to call us again, so we took a break from the TV and went out for lobster rolls and chowder at Barnacle Billy's, our favorite Maine hangout. We sat outside looking at the quiet harbor filled with boats and tried to imagine what it would be like in a hurricane. There wasn't even a breeze and the water was as calm as a lake.

We stopped at a candy store on the way back to the hotel and filled little bags with old-fashioned penny candy. Watching John Hope repeat the last tropical update information, we ate our bags of caramels and red licorice, waiting for Bob's call. We listened endlessly to statistics about how many storms pass through the Caribbean each year, and predictions that Luis could be the worst in decades. We were becoming hurricane experts.

The phone rang at eleven o'clock, as promised, and Bob gave us a full report. The buffet at Port de Plaisance was comical, he said. All the kitchen help had gone home, so Mr. Spittle and his assistant were in charge. They put out whatever food they could find, and the guests could do what they wanted with it. Bob had made a peanut-butter-and-jelly sandwich, grabbed some potato chips, and sat down on the steps to eat. All the furniture had been moved out of sight.

I felt guilty admitting to Bob that we had enjoyed our dinner and even gone to the candy store. He laughed and said he wished he were with us. We dragged out the phone call as long as possible, trying to ignore the fact that we were both frightened of what was about to happen. Finally, at about ten minutes before twelve, we said our goodbyes. I hung up the phone, glanced at Pat, and realized I was crying.

The electricity went off promptly at midnight, plunging all of St. Martin into darkness. Bob picked up the phone to see if by chance it worked, but it was dead. He lit the two candles on the nightstand next to the bed and tried to read Pat Conroy's *Beach Music*, which I had given to him at the airport. The flickering light made it difficult to concentrate, but the book was gripping enough to keep his attention for a while. He dozed off for about an hour and woke up trying to remember exactly what was going on. With no radio or TV, he had no idea what the storm was doing—only that it wasn't supposed to hit until the next day around noon. He felt completely alone and stranded.

He got up and went out onto the balcony to see if he could detect any signs of Luis yet, grateful that the heat of the day had finally given way to cooler breezes. He wondered if Mr. Spittle was going to get his sliding door boarded in the morning. It was still relatively calm outside and eerie to see St. Martin so dark. From Anguilla the lights on St. Martin had always reminded us of Las Vegas, and the darkness seemed very strange. The Pond was actually much brighter than the island itself, as the boats stayed lit from their own generators. The lights atop their masts rocked gently back and forth, and several large motor yachts were lit up like floating cities. People were out on their decks laughing and enjoying themselves, and Bob wondered if they were planning to stay on board during the storm. It was two o'clock in the morning, and he decided to call it a night and try to get some rest.

Pat and I slept restlessly with the Weather Channel on the whole night. Every time there was a new update, we'd wake up and watch in disbelief as the storm continued its direct path for Bob.

Chapter 15

SEPTEMBER 5—5 A.M.

TROPICAL UPDATE

LOCATION: 61.40 W   17.40 N

SUSTAINED WINDS 150 MPH

GUSTS UP TO 180 MPH

CATEGORY 4 HURRICANE

MOVING 10 MPH WNW

100 MILES FROM ANGUILLA/ST. MARTIN

PREDICTED LANDFALL: 9 HOURS

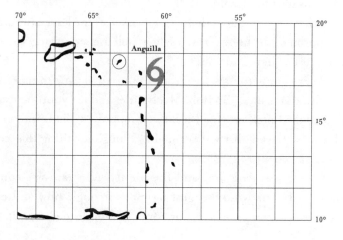

Predictions for landfall remained the same. Anguilla and St. Martin would be experiencing hurricane-force winds by around noon. The temperature there was eighty-one degrees and it was raining hard already. I called Jesse early in Washington so that I'd catch him before he went to classes. We had spoken on and off during the past few days, but now that Bob and I were completely out of touch, I thought Jesse and I had better keep in close contact. He said he'd check in with me throughout the day.

Under darkening skies, the pace had picked up around Port de Plaisance and in the harbor. People were still anchoring their boats, securing them in four directions, and shuttling back and forth to land on dinghies. Some were removing valuables from on board, while other die-hard sailors stocked up with supplies, apparently planning to ride out the storm on their boats.

Mr. Spittle and several young boys were throwing all the patio furniture, including tables, lounge chairs, and umbrellas, into the swimming pool. Putting things under water was safer than just leaving them loose around the pool. Bob went over and helped fill the pool with furniture.

"Thanks for your help," said Mr. Spittle. "We only have a few hours until the storm hits, so I want all guests in their rooms when the winds start to pick up."

"What else can I do to help?" Bob asked as the last chair sank to the bottom of the pool. "You might as well use me any way you can. I can't just sit here and wait."

"We're going to walk the grounds one final time to make sure everything is inside." So Bob, Mr. Spittle, and the young assistants combed the hotel, moving trash cans and potted plants into empty rooms. By eleven-thirty it seemed as though anything that could become airborne was inside.

The sky was dark gray and the wind-driven rain was coming down hard. The wind was gusting more strongly now and came in bursts, carrying the rain horizontally. Bob leaned into it, and when it stopped, he'd have to catch his balance again. Mr. Spittle instructed the guests to go to their rooms and stay there until the storm ended, and Bob went inside to change out of his wet clothes. It was clear by now that his glass doors were not going to be boarded up.

By noon the gusts had turned to fury, and the steady howl of the wind grew louder and more ominous. Bob locked himself in his room and watched in awe from his balcony as the sheets of rain blew across the harbor. The wind was whipping past the front of the railing. Bob felt as though he were sitting in the front row of a movie theater, but he knew that if he got too close to the edge, he might get sucked right out into the storm. He watched, staying three or four feet back from the railing, as Hurricane Luis intensified. The snarl of the wind sounded like Niagara Falls.

SEPTEMBER 5—2 P.M. TROPICAL UPDATE
LOCATION: 62.80 W   18.00 N
SUSTAINED WINDS 152 MPH
GUSTS UP TO 200 MPH
STRONG CATEGORY 4 HURRICANE
MOVING 10 MPH WNW
DIRECTLY OVER ANGUILLA/ST. MARTIN

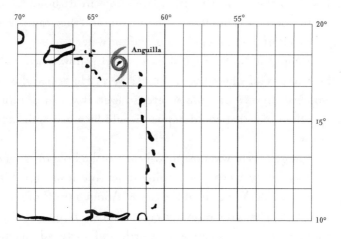

The trees bent with the wind, and palm fronds were blown straight out to one side. Branches snapped off and flew across the harbor, bouncing off the boats and disappearing into the storm. By three o'clock visibility was almost nonexistent, and it was very hard to tell what time of day it was. The light was grayish black, and thick walls of horizontal rain blocked any view in front of the balcony.

In between the sheets of rain, boats occasionally appeared and disappeared from sight. Each time Bob caught a glimpse of one of the boats, it would be in a different position. The mast on the closest sailboat looked as though it was almost touching the water, first on one side and then on the other.

One of the smaller motor yachts broke away from its mooring and smashed into a fifty-footer next to it, chewing a hole in its bow, until the gash got so big, the boat began to take on water. Wedged against the dock, the smaller yacht pounded against the larger, over and over. Finally it snapped its remaining line and broke free, moving down to the next boat and crashing into it with such force that a corner of the third boat was ripped off completely.

The rogue boat, having destroyed two others, was now loose in the harbor and heading straight toward the Shell fuel station at the end of the pier. At the last instant it veered off to the left and crashed into the dock, ripping a large hole in its bow. As water started to flood the cabin it listed to one side and then sank, leaving only the roof of the cabin poking out of the water.

Bob stared at the big Shell sign, wondering how much fuel was in the pumps and where the fuel tanks were. He hoped the tanks were buried up onshore somewhere, so even if a boat did hit the pumps, the worst that could happen would be a bad spill, not an explosion.

The largest yacht was now sinking too as the hole in its side let in more water. Its stern was dipping lower and lower until water swept over the deck and filled the cabin. About a third of the roof remained in sight as the rest was dragged under. Bob tried to guess how much these two boats were worth and pictured insurance adjusters arguing with the owners over million-dollar claims. He shuddered as he envisioned the damage Blanchard's might be sustaining on Anguilla.

A sailboat came into view to the right of the fuel dock, having apparently broken its anchor lines; the sleek blue-and-white craft was being blown toward shore. It ran aground just beyond the fuel dock and tipped over on its side, snapping the mast in half. As soon as the broken half of the mast hit the ground, the wind picked it up like a toothpick, and it was gone. Bob wondered what damage that mast might cause and pictured it flying through the air like a spear. The water level had risen at least six feet and now covered the dock and parts of the path that wound around the resort.

As the wind increased, it began to snap palm trees like twigs, sending the tops careening through the air as if they were weightless. A piece of red galvanized roofing flew right by Bob's balcony and disappeared out into the harbor. Bob had heard earlier warnings on the news about galvanized roofing coming off and turning into flying razor blades, slicing through anything in their path. Several more pieces blew by, this time skipping across the water. Each time a piece touched down, a spray of salt water would shoot up into the air and mix with the rain, becoming horizontal like everything else.

As the pieces of roofing danced their way across the water and disappeared into the storm, Bob peeked around the corner of his balcony to see where they were coming from. One of the hotel's restaurants was a West Indian–style building built right on the pier, and Bob watched as Hurricane Luis dismantled it. The sheets of metal roofing were being peeled off like paper. Pieces of plywood came off next, leaving a skeleton of rafters exposed. The wind rushed into the building. In one swift, sharp move, the roof was ripped apart, rafters and all, and exploded into the air, disappearing into the storm. With the inside of the kitchen now completely exposed, Bob watched as glasses, dishes, pots, and pans joined the rest of the building's debris. Now airborne missiles, they smashed into the boats, breaking windows and shattering wood. Pieces of wood sheared off lampposts and snapped palm trees like giant power saws. The sound of the wind masked the racket of crashing boats and breaking glass. Bob's mind filled with images of Blanchard's being destroyed the same way.

Within minutes, the only thing left of what was once a charming little building was a cement block wall that had been the back of the kitchen, and a few pieces of heavy equipment, including the range and grill. A stainless-steel refrigerator had tipped over on its back, and both doors had been ripped off; bottles of wine were being sucked out and were flying through the air and into the harbor. The refrigerator skidded along the pier like an empty cardboard box, finally tipping over the edge and sinking from sight.

Bob thought of the wine cellar in Blanchard's. He pictured his bottles of 1982 Château Margaux getting sucked out to sea.

SEPTEMBER 5—8 P.M. TROPICAL UPDATE
LOCATION: 63.01 W   18.00 N
SUSTAINED WINDS 150 MPH
GUSTS UP TO 200 MPH
STRONG CATEGORY 4 HURRICANE
MOVING 4 MPH W
DIRECTLY OVER ANGUILLA/ST. MARTIN

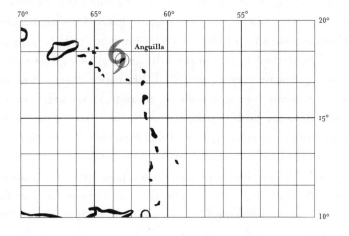

The Weather Channel update at eight o'clock that night reported at least twelve deaths on St. Martin, and I was going out of my mind not being able to talk to Bob. I called the Red Cross, hoping they knew something. I always thought they were on top of all emergency situations, but the woman I spoke with didn't even know there was a hurricane. *Doesn't she watch the Weather Channel?* I fumed.

Frustrated, I called the Vermont state police, thinking it was their civic duty to help me get accurate information on damage, injuries, and maybe the names of any Americans reported dead or missing. The officer was sympathetic and suggested finding someone with a ham radio. He said that was the only way of communicating in a situation like this. After a dozen or so phone calls, I found myself talking to the president of a ham radio club, who listened to my story and then politely said, "I'm sorry, ma'am. Our radios don't reach the Caribbean."

It was hopeless. We just had to wait for Bob to call. Pat tried to keep me smiling, but as the hours went by, I imagined the worst. I was sure Bob was too stubborn to lie in a bathtub with a mattress over him. In fact, knowing him, I wouldn't have been surprised if he was outside taking pictures.

Pat and I slept again with the TV on all night. We set our alarm and woke up every three hours for the latest coordinates on the storm. It was hardly moving. John Hope made it clear that Luis was pounding Anguilla and St. Martin with sustained winds of 150 mph and gusts up to 200. The forward motion had slowed to a painful 4 mph, and it would be another twenty-four hours before Luis moved on to its next target. Extreme damage was predicted.

The noise from the wind was deafening, and as it began to get darker outside, Bob knew it was going to be a long night. *The storm*

must be half over, he thought. He had no radio and no way of judging where the eye of the hurricane was. He knew that once the eye passed over, it would be halfway through. He also knew that the winds on the front side of the eye travel in one direction and on the back side they go the other way. So far nothing was coming into the balcony, only flying past it, so the sliding doors were not yet threatened. But if the wind shifted around, the thought of broken boat masts, palm trees, or sheets of metal roofing crashing into his room began to scare Bob.

He decided to drag the mattress into the bathroom and cover the tub with it as a precaution. If the doors blew in, he would run for cover. In the meantime, he lay on the couch.

The full force of the storm was pounding against the back door to Bob's room, which opened onto a long, narrow walkway. He hadn't even thought about that door before, because it was made of steel and set into a concrete wall. The pressure against it, however, was incredibly strong, and around the edge of the door a spray of water forced its way into the room and shot in three feet toward the bed. It looked as if the wall had sprung a leak. There was also a stream of water entering through the tiny hole in the wall that carried the phone line. This stream was about an eighth of an inch in diameter, and it too shot out three feet into the room. Bob put his finger over it for a second, feeling like the little Dutch boy plugging the hole in the dike.

He tried to think of what he could use for a plug. A box of toothpicks might work, but there were none. He decided to use some of his wooden matches but broke them in half first, saving the good ends just in case the candles went out. Using the flat end of a knife to push with, Bob jammed several of the match ends into the hole, trying not to damage the phone line in the event phone service was restored the next day. He succeeded in reducing the stream of water to a fine spray, then turned his attention to the door.

Using the knife to force a sheet from the bed into the crack around the door, Bob was able to stop most of the water from spewing into the room. He jammed a towel under the door and used another to mop up the water, wringing it out in the bathroom sink.

Debris pummeled the back door as the storm howled outside. The door was made of steel, but what would happen if some heavy flying object hit it hard enough? Bob doubted it could withstand a boat mast traveling at 150 mph.

He decided to open a can of cheese curls. Sitting down on the couch in the candlelight, he listened to the roar of the wind and wished he were with me watching it all on television.

The night seemed to last forever. After a second can of cheese curls, Bob started to doze, but every five or ten minutes something would hit the steel door and wake him up. Each time he would jump to see if the wind was shifting to the sliding glass doors, but it seemed to be staying the same. *Where is the eye?* he wondered. Maybe St. Martin wasn't in the center of the storm after all and there wouldn't be an eye. If that was true, then it could be almost over. It had been eighteen hours since it started, and it was getting light outside.

The sky in Maine the next morning was clear and blue, and Pat and I felt disoriented by the beautiful sunshine. It was surreal to talk about nothing but the storm and see nothing but blue sky above. We walked across the street and had blueberry pancakes and talked about how long it would be before we heard from Bob.

SEPTEMBER 6—8 A.M. TROPICAL UPDATE

LOCATION: 64.00 W   19.20 N

SUSTAINED WINDS 145 MPH

GUSTS UP TO 185 MPH

CATEGORY 4 HURRICANE

MOVING 7 MPH WNW

LOCATION 90 MILES NW OF ANGUILLA

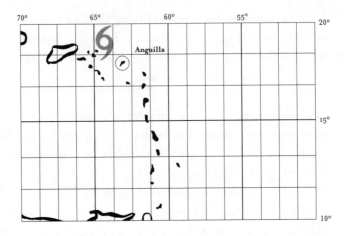

Bob got up and pressed his hand against the sliding door. He could feel the glass flex in and out as the pressure outside changed with the wind. He cracked it open, and it was as if the wind was fighting to yank the door from its frame. He stepped hesitantly onto the balcony. The walls outside were covered with sand; leaves and palm fronds were plastered against them, as if with glue. The wind showed no signs of letting up, and it was still too dark to see much through the rain.

Not having any idea how much longer the storm would continue, Bob went back to reading by candlelight, which in a matter of minutes lulled him to sleep. He woke up around ten and cracked open the door again. The wind seemed to be letting up a little, and the rain was lighter. Bob noticed that all but one of the seven boats tied to the pier in front of his room had sunk during the night—the sailboat masts and cabins of the motor yachts protruded from the water. It was doubtful they could be salvaged. He spotted a group of teenagers across the harbor walking along a chain-link fence that separated Port de Plaisance from the vacant lot next door. They clung to the fence in the wind and made their way slowly toward the main building. *What are they doing out in this storm?* Bob wondered. Either they were seeking shelter because their house had been destroyed, or they were up to no good. It became clear that they were not seeking shelter as one of them climbed the fence, jumped to the other side, and made his way to the Port de Plaisance storeroom. A second boy followed over the fence and boosted the first one up to a hole in the concrete wall where there had been a window the day before. After some scrambling, the first kid disappeared inside and soon began passing bottles of liquor through the hole, where they were carefully packed into backpacks. Once the packs were full, the group continued to empty the storeroom, making a pile of loot on the other side of the fence. There was enough contraband to warrant a second and possibly even a third trip to remove it all.

One of the boys climbed back out of the window and dropped to the ground, but rather than scale the fence again, he decided to go down to the pier and see what else he could find. He lunged from one piling to another, hanging on to the posts during the gusts of wind. He climbed into the cabin window of one of the half-sunken yachts and thirty seconds later emerged with what appeared to be a radio. He made his way back to the others, climbed the fence, and ran.

Documenting the entire event through his zoom lens, Bob found it amazing that the storm wasn't even over yet and looting had already begun.

John Hope reported that after a day and a half of hammering the islands of Anguilla and St. Martin, Hurricane Luis was finally moving on. He had no word of specific damage, but the worst was definitely over. I had told Bob we'd be back in Vermont waiting for news after the storm was over, so Pat and I drove home that afternoon. We sat in the living room, still glued to CNN and the Weather Channel, hoping to hear some bit of news about Anguilla or St. Martin. As initial reports trickled in, I imagined the worst.

By two o'clock, the wind had calmed even more, and Bob desperately needed to get out of the room. He unlocked the back door, removed the waterlogged sheet from around the jamb, and opened the door for the first time in nearly thirty hours. He stared in disbelief at the devastation. Lush landscaping had been reduced to rubble, with not a green leaf or a palm frond in sight. All of the trees had either been snapped off near the top, leaving what looked like a telephone pole, or had been uprooted. The poolside bar was simply gone. The furniture in the pool appeared still to be there, but it was hard to tell because the crystal clear water from the day before was black and filled with leaves, branches, and awning material from the bar.

Bob climbed over tree limbs and broken boards that had been blown against the back of the building. As he made his way down to the main level, his first thought was to get to a phone and let me know he was okay. He went around the corner of the building and saw two men turning toward the shore. He followed them and watched in shock as they pulled a man out from under some debris. Before he knew it, Bob was helping to carry this battered man back over to the hotel, where they stretched him out on a couch in the room where the buffet had been.

The man's head had a terrible gash, and he was babbling in French. He looked like Robinson Crusoe, with a long furry beard, leathery skin, long silver hair, and only a pair of boxer shorts on. A small crowd had now gathered around as more and more guests ventured out of their rooms. A short fat man came around the corner announcing he was a doctor, and everyone moved out of his way.

"Mr. Spittle," the rotund doctor said, "I will need a needle and thread to sew up this cut." The Frenchman was wailing as Mr. Spittle returned with a sewing kit from the laundry. One of the other guests was interpreting, and trying to explain to the injured man that a doctor was going to stitch up his head. Mr. Spittle had produced a first-aid kit, and after the doctor sterilized the needle and thread with some brown liquid, he sewed up the gash in front of the crowd. The old man screamed; Mr. Spittle held his head, and Bob and several other guests held his arms and feet. His head was then bandaged, and he sat up and stared at everyone in disbelief.

The interpreter translated his story, and Bob and everyone else listened as the man described the events of the previous night. He had been living on his catamaran, sailing around the islands for years, and had come to St. Martin to weather the storm in a safe harbor. During the night he felt his boat being lifted out of the water and found himself flying through the air and thrown against the shore. His catamaran was completely demolished, and he was pinned under a section of the hull with water up to his neck.

He spent the night trapped under the debris, hoping the hull wouldn't shift and drown him. When the storm finally died down, he started to yell, and the two guests had heard him and dragged him out from under the remains of his boat. He was lucky to be alive. He also said that his radio was going all night and he listened to people pleading for help as their boats sank.

Bob was beginning to realize the magnitude of the disaster. Sunken boats were everywhere. An unimaginable number of masts stuck up out of the water. Down in the far corner toward the airport, a pile of boats lay tangled and destroyed beyond belief. Hundreds of motor yachts, sailboats, and barges were heaped on top of each other in a tangle of ropes, masts, broken glass, hulls, sterns, and keels.

He had to call home. He imagined pictures of the devastation on CNN and knew I would be frantic with worry. All the lines were down at the hotel, and Bob thought maybe he should start walking to Marigot to look for a phone. As he headed out the long, winding entrance to Port de Plaisance, stepping over branches and other debris, a car pulled up behind him. "Need a lift?" a man asked.

"Where are you going?"

"I know where there's a phone," the man said. "I'm going to call my wife and tell her I'm alive." It was as if he had read Bob's mind.

"Great," Bob said as he climbed into the backseat.

There was a man in the front passenger seat talking on a two-way radio. Bob couldn't help but notice they were wearing dark suits, unusual attire for the islands.

"Are you policemen?" Bob asked after listening to a little of the radio conversation. It was clear that the storm had disrupted something they had been working on and that the chances of resuming their project were not good.

"We work for the DEA," the driver said. "We've been coordinating a drug bust here for two months with Scotland Yard, the French police, and the Dutch police out of Curaçao. This damned storm screwed everything up."

"So how do you know about a phone?"

"Some of our men are staying at another hotel, and they told us by radio this morning that there's a USA Direct phone in the lobby that still works for some reason. Here it is now." The car pulled into a parking lot in front of the Atrium Hotel near the airport.

Inside the lobby there was a tremendous crowd waiting to use the phone. Bob stood behind the driver of the car and waited patiently for his turn; the line was long but moving quickly. The woman behind the front desk was collecting a dollar a minute for the use of the phone in addition to the charges put on everyone's calling card. She had a thriving business going.

John Hope, by now my arbiter of all matters of importance, said phones and power would be out for an extended period of time, so I knew we wouldn't be hearing from Bob right away. Pat and I went out for pizza, and when we returned home, we were surprised that Bob had left a message on the answering machine.

"Hi, it's me. I'm alive and well in St. Martin. I'm fine, but there's mass destruction everywhere. Don't worry about me; just worry about the restaurant. I'm going to try to get to Anguilla now. Bye."

I called Jesse right away and we talked for an hour about how relieved we were. Jesse was anxious to speak with Bob directly and made me promise to let him know when I received more information.

As Bob hung up the phone he looked around for his newfound friends, the DEA agents. They were nowhere in sight. Bob walked back outside and spotted the car. Knowing the men were in the hotel somewhere, he sat on the railing of the parking lot and waited. After almost half an hour he went back inside and walked up to the counter, where the girl was continuing to collect her dollar per call. The line was still about twenty people long as each person reported in to their loved ones. Bob asked if the girl had seen two men in dark suits with a two-way radio. She said, "A whole bunch a them on three."

Bob made his way up to the third floor and walked down the dark hall toward the end where he could hear voices. He was standing outside an open door, trying to decide if he should knock, when out came the two men who had given him the ride.

"Ready to go?" asked one without surprise, and Bob followed as they walked downstairs. The three climbed into the car and drove back toward Port de Plaisance.

"I guess that's it, then," the driver said to the other man who simply stared out the window.

Bob sat in the backseat, sympathizing in silence with the men and their failed sting operation. He looked out the windows at the damage. The shacks on the hillside were demolished, and he wondered if people had gotten out in time. Store windows had completely vanished, and cars lay upside-down in yards. He was grateful to have gotten a ride to a phone.

Back at the hotel, the guests were now out walking around the grounds, inspecting the damage. Suddenly famished, Bob went to the room that had held the ice cream freezer. There he found Mr. Spittle and his assistant putting out food for the guests. They were dragging a large barbecue grill outside but had no charcoal. Bob offered to build a fire using some of the branches strewn on the ground. As he gathered bits of boards, broken chair legs, and branches, other guests joined in, and soon they had the grill heaped with wood and palm fronds. Hungry guests lined up while Mr. Spittle cooked steaks and chicken salvaged from the hotel's freezer.

It began to get dark, and Bob decided to get some sleep. He would have to wait until the next day to get back to Anguilla.

Up at five-thirty the next morning, Bob noticed that the boats that had survived the storm moored in the Pond were finally beginning to move around again. He ran down to the pier and saw that one of the Anguilla ferryboats was cruising in circles around two others. Just then a little rubber dinghy with an outboard motor came shooting out into the harbor. Bob waved his arms frantically to get its owner's attention. The man in the dinghy turned toward the dock and, pulling alongside, asked Bob what he needed. Bob said, "Can you take me out to those boats?"

The man shrugged and said, "Get in." Abandoning his luggage in his hotel room, Bob climbed into the dinghy. It was only about five feet long and barely held the two men.

The man said he had been living on his sailboat, which had sunk during the night; he was lucky to be alive. He had managed to get off his boat into the dinghy and had cut the rope between the two just before the sailboat sank. He told Bob the only thing he had left in this world was the rubber dinghy. Even his wallet had gone down with the sailboat. Bob pulled out a twenty-dollar bill and gave it to the man as they approached the Anguilla boats.

Hubert, the captain of one of the ferries, spotted Bob coming and shouted, "Blanchard! Blanchard!" as if Bob were bringing a rescue crew. When Bob climbed from the dinghy up onto the big steel ferryboat, he realized there were about ten guys on board. Inside, the floor was covered with empty soda cans, beer bottles, and potato chip bags.

Hubert said, "We been here for two days. Only three of us still floating. Look there." He pointed to a small island about a hundred yards away, where a ferryboat had run aground.

"Look there," he said again, pointing toward the airport. Another ferry was out of the water and sitting up on the road by the runway.

"Some a these guys come off the other boats. We goin' home now, soon as *Lady Maria* get her engines goin'."

They continued cruising in circles around *Lady Maria*. Finally her engines fired up in a cloud of black diesel smoke, and the three big ferries motored toward the channel that leads out of the Pond.

"How do we get under the drawbridge?" Bob asked Hubert.

"Oh, they lifts it up for us," said Hubert.

"But there's no electricity," said Bob.

"I think they gots a generator," Hubert said, clearly hoping this was true.

The boats cruised over to the drawbridge that spans the little channel, which leads out into the open sea. They stopped and drifted while Hubert tried to raise someone in the small building by the drawbridge, first by radio and then by yelling from out on the deck.

There was nobody in the little booth, and after about half an hour Hubert announced, "We drop anchor an' wait."

"But they're talking about the power being off for weeks," Bob said. "There must be another way out of the Pond."

"This the onliest way," said Hubert, and he threw the anchor over the side.

"Okay, I have to get back to Anguilla," Bob said. "You guys can stay here and wait if you want, but there must be a smaller boat that can fit under the drawbridge."

Hubert shut off the engines and sat down on a bench to think. One of the other guys aboard said, "Grandfather." He was pointing to a small, stubby boat chugging slowly across the harbor.

Hubert jumped up and yelled, "Grandfather, Grandfather."

"Whose grandfather is he?" Bob asked.

"He jus' call Grandfather," Hubert replied. "Yo, Grandfather," he yelled again, and the boat turned toward Hubert.

As Grandfather pulled alongside, Hubert said, "You wanna take the man to Anguilla?"

"Gonna cost ya," Grandfather said, grinning at Bob.

"How much?"

"How much you got?"

"How about a hundred dollars?" Bob offered, knowing this might be his only chance of getting home for days.

"I ain' goin' Anguilla for no hundred dollar," Grandfather replied, and crossed his arms. "Seas still pretty high."

"Look," Bob said, "I only have three hundred dollars, and I'm going to need some money when I get there. Don't rip me off."

Hubert jumped in and said, "He okay, ya know, Grandfather. He a friend a we."

"Okay, since he a friend, I take two hundred."

"Let's go," Bob said, and after he climbed down onto Grandfather's boat, the rest of the men followed. Bob was apparently paying for the trip, and the others were coming along for the ride.

The seven-mile voyage, which usually took twenty minutes, took two hours. The boat chugged along slowly; its engine stopped twice, and each time Grandfather would tinker for a while and get it going again.

Bob had never seen waves like this before. They were easily fifteen feet high, but without any crest or whitecaps. They were just huge swells that rolled along, and Grandfather's boat would work its way up one side, over the top, and down the other side, only to head up another one again. At the bottom of each roll Anguilla would disappear from sight, and then it would reappear as the old boat made its way to the top again.

Approaching Anguilla, Bob could begin to make out a huge crowd standing on the dock and up onshore, waiting for the boat to arrive. As they got closer, voices from the crowd started shouting, "Look, it Hubert." Several other names were called out as more faces were recognized. "I see Blanchard. Blanchard comin'.'" It was Clinton. Bob realized they were probably Anguilla's first contact with the outside world since Luis had attacked, and everyone was at the dock to hear the news from St. Martin.

The sea was rolling so hard that Grandfather could not tie up. He motored up as close as he dared, and as each man jumped off the bow onto the dock, Grandfather would reverse and back up again to prevent his boat from being smashed against the cement pier.

Bob leapt off and the crowd caught him, pulling him onto the pier. As he made his way toward Clinton, he felt a bit like a celebrity as everyone pressed around him, eagerly asking about the condition of St. Martin.

"What 'bout Marigot?" someone shouted. "You see my brother?"

"How the Pond? Any boats sink?" another called out.

Bob and the men from the ferries were deluged with questions and did their best to answer. Most people wanted to know about relatives who lived in St. Martin, but there was little information to give. Bob was afraid to mention the shacks that had been blown away on the hillside near town.

Clinton patted Bob on the back several times, happy to have him home. "Lowell tell me you couldn't make it to Anguilla. Where you sleep during the storm?"

"It took a while, but I found a hotel room at Port de Plaisance. It was scary, though. They didn't board my windows, and I was right on the water. What about your family? How is everyone?"

"Everyone cool at home," Clinton said. "We get a lotta water in the house, but everything cool."

"What about the rest of the staff? Have you seen them?" Bob asked.

"I see most a them," Clinton said. "They okay. An' the radio say nobody hurt here in Anguilla. But lotta boats sink. A big cargo ship mash up Sandy Ground. She sittin' right up on the beach. An' there an empty container up by the airport. The wind blew that thing right on top a Harrigan's rental cars. They all mash up."

"Have you been to the restaurant?" Bob finally asked.

"The restaurant ain' so good," Clinton said quietly.

"What happened to it?"

"Dining room gone," Clinton answered as they got into his white minibus.

"What do you mean, gone?" Bob asked.

"She blow away. Whole roof came off. All them shutters gone. Just the floor leff. An' the plants mash up real bad. Mel gonna cry long tears when she see it. The sea come right through the restaurant an' into the salt pond. Meads Bay flood out."

The drive to the restaurant took twice as long as usual. Clinton had to drive off the road to avoid broken telephone poles and uprooted trees; electric wires were strewn in tangles everywhere. As they pulled into the parking lot at Blanchard's, Bob felt numb. There had been four large, stately palm trees right in front of the restaurant, and all but one were lying on the ground.

He stepped over one of the downed trees and onto the walkway that led through the picket fence and up to the bar door. Several sections of the fence were broken off, although tangled bougainvillea vines held the pieces in place. There were tiny scraps of the teal shutters scattered about. The side of the building facing the road looked amazingly intact, but all the paint had been sandblasted off, in some places right down to raw wood. Whatever paint was left was no longer clean and white but yellow and dirty.

Bob wanted to cry as he inspected the gardens. The lush greens and vibrant flowers were gone. Not one palm frond. Not one leaf. Not one petal. Only broken stems, roots, and bare tree limbs remained. As he made his way around the side of the building, the big sea grape tree came into view. It was on its side, split down the middle. More full-sized palm trees that we had brought in from Florida lay tipped over, roots in the air. All the path lights were missing, and the fountains were black with leaves and murky water. There was nothing living in sight.

Picturing me up to my elbows in potting soil, surrounded by flowers, Bob was overwhelmed by the devastation, but the worst was yet to come. When he continued down the path, he saw that the entire dining room was indeed missing.

Bob stared at the tile floor where the building had been, and his teary eyes slowly scanned the destruction. No roof. No walls. No tall teal shutters. He remembered pushing open the shutters that first night of business, opening the dining room to the lush gardens with beach and sea beyond. The only part of the room still standing was a plywood-covered structure where the glass windows of the wine cellar had been. He realized that the plywood was actually covering the glass doors and saw that there was no roof over them.

"Me, Shabby, an' Lowell board that up before the storm," Clinton said. "Jus' in case."

"Clinton," Bob said, "you saved the wine cellar! That was brilliant. Is the wine still in there?"

"Yeah, man. She all there. So, wha' we gonna do?" Clinton asked.

"You must have more cleaning up to do at home," Bob said. "Why don't you go do that today, and tomorrow be here first thing in the morning with your tools and as many of your brothers as you can round up? I'll see if I can find the rest of the staff, and we'll start to clean this mess. We've got to get rebuilt so we can open for the season."

"So we ain' closin'?" Clinton asked.

"Closing?" Bob asked. "No, we're not closing. We've got a lot of work to do. Drop me off at home so that I can get the truck and see what damage I have there. What about the phones?"

"Cable an' Wireless got one line goin', but you gotta go into town an' use it in their office," Clinton replied. "They gonna have some more soon."

As they drove away Bob looked back at the beach and tried to picture what everything had looked like only three days before. The sky was blue now, and a gentle trade wind had returned from the east. A goat stood on the side of the road, munching a bare branch and watching the minibus drive by. Finding food was going to be a challenge for the animals until some greenery returned. Earning a living was going to be a challenge until the tourists returned.

Chapter 16

DURING THE TWO WEEKS that followed the storm, I was back in Florida at Home Depot. Bob and Clinton made a list of the materials we needed to rebuild, and we kept in touch through Bob's nightly calls from the Cable & Wireless office. I rushed around, repeating what I had done only a year before—the same fabric for the chairs, the same printer for the menus, the same glasses and dishes and silver. It felt odd to be doing it again so soon.

After arranging to have our containers shipped to Anguilla, I filled three suitcases with batteries and flashlights and called American Airlines to get on the next flight back. But getting home was not to be as easy as that.

American Eagle was not flying any passengers into Anguilla. They were only bringing in emergency supplies for an undetermined period of time and told me I'd have to go through St. Martin. Looting on St. Martin, however, had forced the Dutch and French military to put the island under martial law. A six o'clock curfew was in effect, and airlines were told they could bring in only residents of the island. They didn't want journalists or tourists seeing the island in such a state. What they hadn't addressed was how residents from the surrounding islands were to get home; Anguilla, St. Barts, Saba, and St. Eustatius were now cut off from air service. After two days of negotiating with the governor of

St. Martin, several phone calls to the chief minister in Anguilla, and dozens of conversations with supervisors at American Airlines, I finally boarded a flight from Miami to St. Martin. It was made very clear, though, that I could not remain there for any time at all. I would not even be permitted to go inside the terminal without an escort from immigration. The ferries were still not running, and I needed a private pilot to meet me on the runway, escort me through immigration, and fly me directly to Anguilla.

My flight down was eerie. The giant Airbus had only a few scattered passengers and I kept to myself. It was my first chance since the storm to prepare myself for what I might see when I arrived. Bob had described the damage in detail, but I knew seeing it with my own eyes would still be a shock.

I wasn't looking forward to the estimated two months without electricity, and not knowing when Cap Juluca would reopen was scary as well. If the hotel didn't finish its repairs before the season, there wouldn't *be* much of a season. But Malliouhana was working around the clock and had set an opening date of November 17, and two new hotels were also opening—Sonesta was planning to open by Christmas, and Cuisinart Resort and Spa was under construction. They were bound to help the economy, I hoped.

Bob arranged to fly over from Anguilla with Ben Franklin, the pilot who brought in our restaurant food from St. Martin. My plane was scheduled to land at three, and at two-thirty Ben and Bob were on the tarmac in Anguilla, ready to go. They taxied onto the runway, prepared to take off, and stopped. Ben was arguing with someone through his headset, but Bob couldn't figure out what the problem was. Exasperated, Ben turned the plane around and taxied back to the terminal.

"What's going on?" Bob asked, as Ben shut off the engine.

"They got too mucha style over there," Ben muttered. He climbed out of the plane and instructed Bob to stay put. "I'm going up to the tower to talk to St. Martin," he said.

Bob was sweltering as he sat in the copilot's seat of the little plane. When he couldn't stand it anymore, he unfastened his shoulder harness, and stepped out onto the tarmac to wait for Ben. It was two-forty-five, and he was getting nervous. If they weren't there to pick me up, the St. Martin officials would send me right back to Miami. He scanned the sky anxiously, looking for my flight.

Ten minutes later Ben came out of the tower and sauntered back to his plane. "Leff we go," he said as he started up the engine.

"What happened?" Bob asked.

"The phones aren't working yet in St. Martin," Ben explained. "One of the guys in the tower over there has a brother in Tortola, and he hasn't heard from him since the storm. He wouldn't give clearance to land until I called his brother from the tower here to say that he's okay. Too mucha style."

The flight took five minutes, and then Ben filled out paperwork in the St. Martin immigration office. As I stepped off my plane an immigration officer greeted the small group of passengers and escorted us inside. Just then Ben and Bob rounded the corner. I was so happy to see Bob that I didn't want to let go of him, but Ben said immigration couldn't wait for hugs. He rushed me over to find my luggage and have my passport stamped, and then the three of us ran back out to Ben's plane.

I pressed my head against the scratched window, and from the air, Anguilla looked pretty much the same: flat and scrubby, but browner than usual, since there wasn't a single leaf left on any tree. It looked like the aftermath of a forest fire. The water, however, was still a magnificent blue-green, and I could see the coral reefs as we got closer to shore. The outrageous beauty of Anguilla's coastline hadn't changed. The immigration officer in Anguilla smiled as I entered the terminal. "Good afternoon," she said. "Welcome home."

On the way to our apartment, I could hear the sporadic hum of engines as we passed those lucky enough to have generators. We drove by a group of shirtless men gathered around an Anglec truck, and several backhoes nearby were erecting new telephone poles.

"That's the British navy," Bob explained. "They've sent in two hundred troops to help restore the power. It's still going to take about six more weeks."

Rugs were draped over porch railings to dry in the sun. An old man was getting a haircut on his front steps, and a herd of goats meandered into the road in front of us, forcing us to stop and wait until they had crossed. "Island time," I said out loud. "Things don't really change."

But one thing, sadly, had changed. From the top of South Hill I looked out at the tranquil bay where Sandy Island was supposed to be. It was gone. Its landmark tuft of palm trees was nowhere to be seen, and the little white island was completely under water.

"Everybody's saying that Sandy Island will come back," Bob reassured me.

"We're really lucky nobody got hurt here," he went on. "I've heard stories of several close calls. A lady in Sandy Ground retreated into a back room of her house when the storm chewed away at the front walls. She moved furniture against the doors and the wind just blew it across the room, pushing her back farther and farther. Another woman in Island Harbor was huddled in a closet for over twenty-four hours. All of her windows were blown out, and it was the only place she could find to hide."

I could see people everywhere putting their lives back together. Men were cleaning up fallen trees, some with chain saws, most with machetes. Others were still pulling off the plywood that had been nailed over windows before the storm. As we pulled into Christine's for a cold drink, there was a domino game in full swing under the big tamarind tree in her yard. The tree looked naked without its leaves.

Inside, Christine was her same jolly self. "Mrs. Blanchard, it is so good to see you, but I'm sorry to hear about your restaurant." She came out from behind the counter and we squeezed each other hard.

"At least nobody in Anguilla was hurt," I said. "Our restaurant can be replaced."

Lowell's mother was hanging laundry on the line as we drove past her house. "All right, all right," she said, waving and smiling.

"Okay, okay," we answered together.

We drove over the top of the hill, and Long Bay appeared below us. Overlooking the sea, our apartment was as spectacular as I remembered. Bob had cleaned it up pretty well, though it still smelled damp and all the furniture legs were discolored from sitting in water.

I opened the door to our balcony and stepped onto the shady terra-cotta floor. It was cool and smooth under my bare feet, and I stared at the waves on the beach below. Bob unloaded my luggage and came out to join me.

"Living here makes up for a lot of the bad stuff," he said. "Think how awful it would be if we still lived by the gas station."

"How have you been taking showers?" I asked, somewhat afraid of the answer.

"I have a surprise for you." He smiled. "Follow me."

We went back to the driveway and up the steps to the yard. Bob lifted a blue plastic tarp, and there was a brand-new Honda generator, just like the one at the restaurant. He turned the key, pulled the start rope, and it roared into life.

"It runs the whole apartment," Bob said proudly. "The hot-water heater, the pump, the lights—everything. I got it in St. Martin. The government issued a moratorium on duty for generators because of the storm. So we also saved twenty-five percent. The only problem is finding gas for it. There has been a shortage, but they say a tanker is on its way and should arrive any day now. And I have six full gas cans at the restaurant."

"This is great," I said. "I can't believe you didn't tell me about it! Now I have a surprise for you too," I said, pulling out the latest issue of *Wine Spectator*. Bob flipped open to the page I had marked with a yellow sticky note. The year's list of recipients of the coveted Award of Excellence included Blanchard's Restaurant.

"I can't believe it," Bob said. "Look, there are only five other awards for the whole Caribbean."

"I've known about it for a couple of weeks, but I wanted to surprise you."

"Thanks to Clinton, Shabby, and Lowell, we still *have* a wine cellar," Bob said.

"I can't wait any longer," I said. "Let's go see the restaurant."

"Are you sure you're ready? It looks pretty bad."

"Let's go," I answered.

We pulled into Blanchard's and walked around to where the front of the building had been. I had just bought all the materials we would need to rebuild it and had ordered an entire container of plants for the gardens, so I knew in my head what to expect. But the reality of the past two weeks finally hit me. It was just as Bob had described. The white fountains were black with muck, the landscaping was a disaster, and the dining room was simply gone.

Clinton and Lowell were shoveling wet sheetrock into a wheelbarrow. I ran over and hugged them both.

"How are you guys doing?" I asked.

"We jus' here in a cool, Mel," Clinton replied, grinning. "We gonna build this right back how she were. Don' you worry. Ain' no problem."

"Mr. Luis brought too mucha wind," Lowell said. "We gonna show him that he ain' gonna destroy Anguilla. He ain' gonna mash us up like St. Thomas and the rest a them islands. I hear they ain' even startin' to fix things up in those places. They waitin' for government to help. No, sir. Luis ain' gonna get the best a we."

As I looked away so the men wouldn't see my wet eyes, I noticed three green buds sprouting from what otherwise looked like a dead bougainvillea. *Clinton is right,* I thought. *There ain' no problem.*

I hugged Lowell and Clinton again, then went in to look at my kitchen. Everything was there, but nothing shone anymore.

The stainless-steel tables were coated with a dirty film, there was at least four inches of water on the floor, and the ceiling had been plastered with sand. Bob and I walked down the path to the beach, under what was left of the big sea grape tree. A lizard scampered toward the bushes, its tail swirling an intricate pattern in the sand, reminding me of the hot, sunny days on Meads Bay only a year before. We had watched the lizards dart in and out of the shade while we drew up plans for our restaurant under the blue beach umbrella.

We stood on the sand, the water washing away our footprints. A wave splashed over our ankles, and we stood perfectly still, mesmerized by the gentle rolling tide. The ocean was so calm—it was barely moving at all. A wisp of a breeze blew from the west. "How could this peaceful place have been such a disaster only a short time ago?" I asked Bob. "It just doesn't seem possible." But to our right, the wrath of Luis was evident at Carimar Beach Club, where the sand had completely eroded away and waves now splashed up onto the steps.

A pelican cruised past, missing the tops of the waves by only inches, its wings steady and unmoving in silent flight. A few flaps and it soared upward. A few more flaps and it circled once, flattened its wings against its body, and dove like a missile into the water. The bird bobbed up to the surface, gulped its catch, and floated contentedly in the bay.

Puffy white clouds drifted over the horizon, and a sailboat glided toward St. Martin. The shape of the beach had changed from the storm, as had our lives. I dreaded the impending insurance battle and prepared myself for another marathon of building and gardening before the season.

"Too mucha wind," I said to Bob, shaking my head as we walked back into the restaurant. "Too mucha wind."

"Hey, Lowell. You hear that? Mel sound like she from Anguilla," Clinton said with admiration. "She one a we, you know." He emptied his wheelbarrow and shoveled another load of debris. Lowell handed me some pruning shears, and I went to work.

Afterword

We lived for seven weeks without full electricity. Our two small generators gave us enough power to rebuild the restaurant and take showers at home. But life became even simpler than before: no television and no going out for lunch. Hotels and restaurants were closed and everyone was busy re-creating their own little world in hopes of reopening for the high season.

When the two containers of materials arrived from Florida, this time we knew to identify every single item purchased, and customs processed our entry in record time. The Davis brothers worked with Bob to rebuild the restaurant and neighbors from Long Bay came to help remove debris that Luis had dumped in our yard. A large tree had uprooted and crashed down over the front door, and it took six people to stake it back into its upright position. I nursed it with fertilizer and lots of water until it eventually took hold again in the ground.

Cap Juluca's beach had eroded badly, but they were spending a fortune to dredge the sand and get things back to normal. Malliouhana was moving ahead at full speed and the new Sonesta Hotel would open for the season. Cuisinart Resort and Spa still had a way to go, but we saw the plans and knew it would be a great addition to the economy.

We opened on November 17 and that night, Blanchard's kitchen was just as it had been before the storm. Bug was up to his elbows in soapsuds, Clinton hummed a little tune to himself, and

Ozzie danced as he chopped. Before the first guests arrived, Lowell and Miguel insisted that Bob and I celebrate with a relaxing dinner for two at our most romantic corner table. The newly painted teal shutters framed the garden, which was already starting to bloom in its many shades of pink and blue. Candles flickered, ceiling fans swirled overhead, and the sea breeze ruffled the new white tablecloths. Hughes grilled us two fresh lobsters and we were in heaven.

We listened to the waves break against the beach and raised our champagne glasses in toast. A little lizard wiggled in the sand, making rings around a newly planted palm tree. "Here's to dreamy Anguilla," I said.

The soft evening light made Bob's meltaway blue eyes even more entrancing than usual. He smiled and said, "Here's to living on island time."